IMAGES
of America

DUNCAN
AND STEPHENS COUNTY
OKLAHOMA

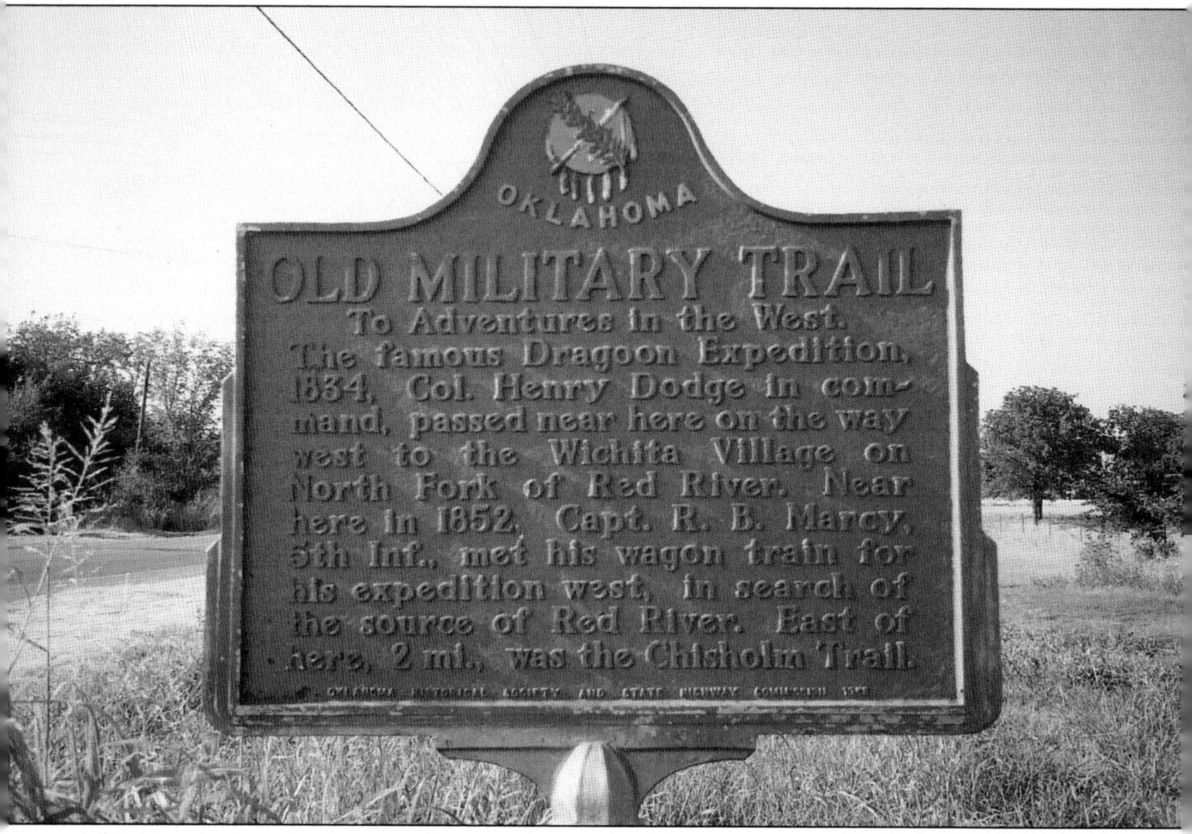

This historical marker, located about 6 miles south of Duncan on old U.S. Highway 81, provides a glimpse of the historical currents that flowed through the future Stephens County during the 1800s. The county was truly a frontier crossroads.

IMAGES
of America

DUNCAN AND STEPHENS COUNTY OKLAHOMA

Chris Jefferies, Ph.D. and "Pee Wee" Cary

ARCADIA PUBLISHING

ISBN 978-0-7385-0313-4

Published by Arcadia Publishing
Charleston, South Carolina

Printed in the United States of America

Library of Congress Catalog Card Number: 99066667

For all general information contact Arcadia Publishing at:
Telephone 843-853-2070
Fax 843-853-0044
E-mail sales@arcadiapublishing.com
For customer service and orders:
Toll-Free 1-888-313-2665

Visit us on the Internet at www.arcadiapublishing.com

CONTENTS

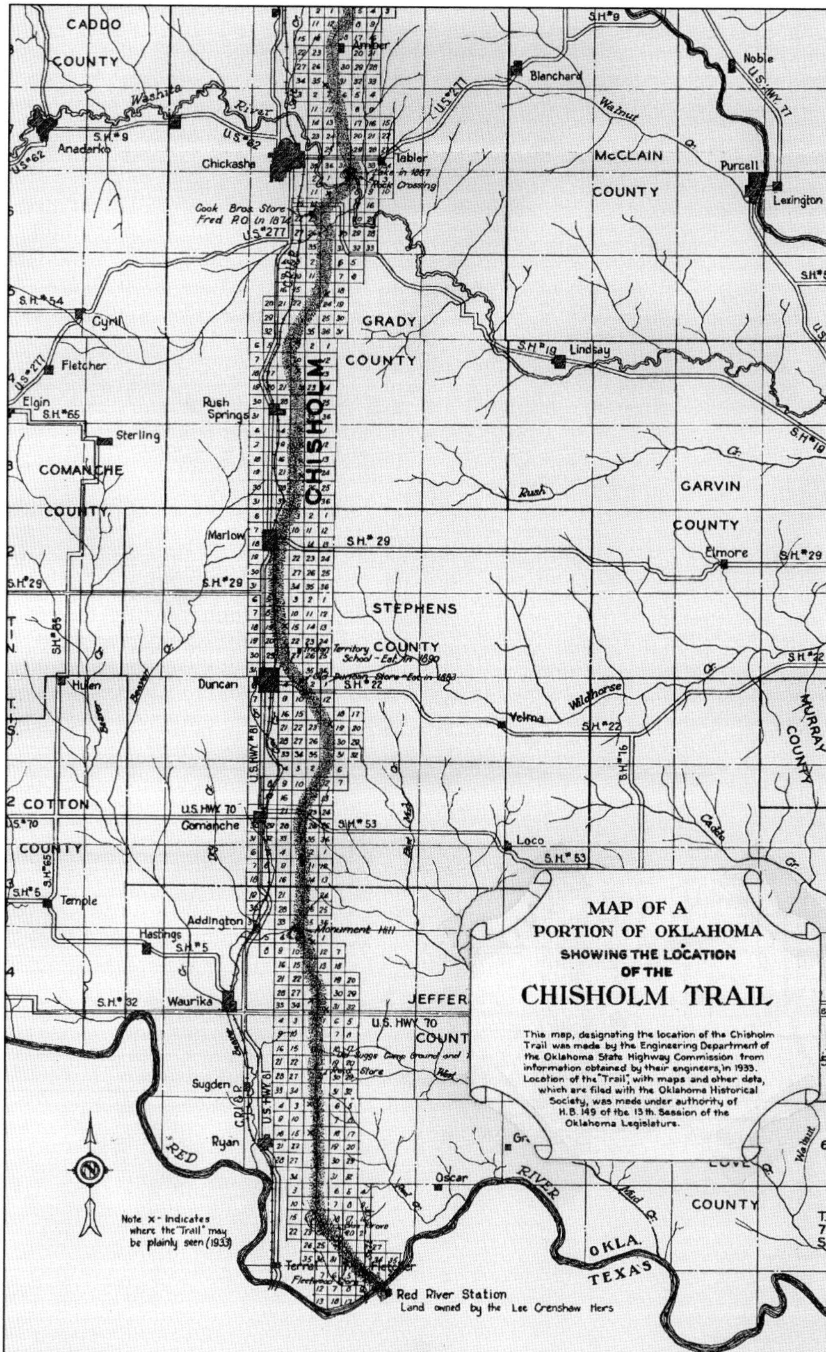

The old Chisholm Trail, the northern half of the Great Cattle Road that ran from southern Texas to the railroads in Kansas, passed directly through the future Stephens County and towns of Duncan and Marlow, overlapping the period of the area's first settlers. From 1867 to about 1885, over 4 million cattle traveled through the county, leaving traces of the Trail that can be seen to this day. This map dates from a 1933 survey conducted by the Oklahoma Highway Commission.

INTRODUCTION

Oklahoma's Great Plains country describes the grass-covered plains and rolling hills that cover Oklahoma's southwest corner. Long the preserve of the nomadic plains Indians, it is the site of myriad currents of history that swirled across its surface and whose impacts are still felt today. Early explorers, trappers, nomadic Indian tribes, the U.S. Army and Cavalry, cowboys, desperados, and outlaws have all left their tracks. Its earliest non-Indian explorers were the Spanish, who established an outpost just 25 miles due south of today's Stephens County on the Red River in the mid-1700s. They extended exploration and mining activities to the Wichita Mountains less than 30 miles due west of the county. The first eye-witness account of the region's exploration was by a member of the 1834 Dodge-Leavenworth expedition, guided, not coincidentally, by Jesse Chisholm, for whom the Great Cattle Road running through the county was later named. Their route passed just south of present Duncan. This early account portrayed a bleak and uninviting region, shunned by all but its Native American inhabitants, and trappers and traders. Stephens County lies on the far eastern edge of these plains, adjacent to the Cross Timbers.

The Cross Timbers is a geographic phenomenon that played a significant role in the development of the county. It describes a dense, almost impenetrable growth of Black Jack Oak and Post Oak timber that extends from north-central Texas northward to the center of Oklahoma. Only about 50 to 75 miles in width, it presented such an obstacle to early east-west travel that the trails and roads through the Cross Timbers converged in the few gaps that allowed passage. Thus, the Dodge-Leavenworth expedition, and the later Fort Arbuckle-Fort Belknap, and Fort Arbuckle-Fort Sill roads passed through the county. When the forceful removal of Native American tribes from the American southeast in 1837 led in 1855 to the creation of separate Indian nations in present-day Oklahoma, future Stephens County lay on the far western edge of the Chickasaw Nation's Pickens County. Almost isolated from the rest of the Chickasaw Nation, the region was largely ignored by the Tribal government. This neglect led, in turn, to early, if mostly illegal, settlement by a few non-Indians.

When Joseph McCoy sought to attract the large herds of cattle he hoped would be flowing north out of Texas after the Civil War to Abilene, Kansas, and his new stockyards, he sent posters and handbills south throughout Texas proclaiming a new, safer, and shorter route to the railheads. He hired surveyors to lay out a route, and they worked southward from Abilene to present-day Wichita, then south along Jesse Chisholm's trade route to his post on the North Canadian river near present-day Yukon, Oklahoma. From there, they went largely due south on a route that took them through future Stephens County to the Red River, and a crossing north of present-day Nocona, Texas. Their route through Stephens County resulted from the surveyor's efforts to stay close to the Cross Timbers and off the plains to the west, across which roamed the hostile Kiowas, Comanches, and Southern Cheyenne. McCoy's enticements worked, and thus was born the Great Cattle Road, more commonly known as the Chisholm Trail, over which about 4 million cattle traveled from 1867 to the mid-1880s. Another 6 million cattle went up the Western Trail in far west Indian Territory.

It was along the Chisholm Trail, near where it joined the Fort Sill-Fort Arbuckle military road for a few miles, that William Duncan purchased a trading post established several years before. He sold to the cattle drovers and travelers along the roads and became prominent in that part of Pickens County, serving as postmaster. Through his Masonic connections he learned that a railroad would be coming south. He and his Chickasaw wife claimed the land along the right-of-way, in which downtown Duncan is now located, as their allotments. He moved his business there in about 1890. Thus, the town of Duncan was born.

Marlow took its name from the Marlow family who moved into the area in the 1880s. First named Marlow Grove, the city grew rapidly, paralleling the growth in Duncan and Comanche, with the coming of the railroad in 1891–1892. Notices of settlement opportunities in all three communities were disseminated throughout the Territory and Texas, spurring immigration to the area. Even though the ownership of land in the Chickasaw Nation by non-Indians was illegal until Indian Territory was established in 1889, many came to the area, leasing land when they could, and just settling when they could not. All three communities competed for settlers. Until Stephens County was created with statehood in 1907, and Duncan designated as the county seat, the communities grew at about the same rates.

This book is not intended to be a comprehensive history of the county. Rather, it attempts through photographs available from the Stephens County Historical Society to illustrate the compelling, fascinating, and important legacy shared by all residents. In many ways, the history of the county and its three major communities parallels that of many other central plains counties, but still remains unique in its combination of events, influences, and outcomes, and, more important, its impact beyond the region's borders. In illustrating the history, we are necessarily limited by the availability of suitable photographs, and by the number we can include in this volume. There are many other wonderful photographs we just did not have the space to include. If by focusing on the three major towns in the county we have offended the smaller communities, we offer our sincere apologies. It was necessary to limit our scope to what we could handle in the allotted pages. Likewise, if we have offended families or individuals by our choice of photographs, using some and not others, we again offer our apologies. Unless indicated otherwise, all photographs are courtesy of the Stephens County Historical Society.

One

ON A FRONTIER CROSSROADS

PRE-1900s

Stephens County is situated on what was a major crossroads of the nineteenth-century southwest. Early exploration trails, military roads, the Great Cattle Road (or Chisholm Trail), and, finally, the railroads, all cross the county. Although most settlements along the railroad began with its arrival, Duncan has the distinction of being an earlier small settlement built around a trading post on the Chisholm Trail.

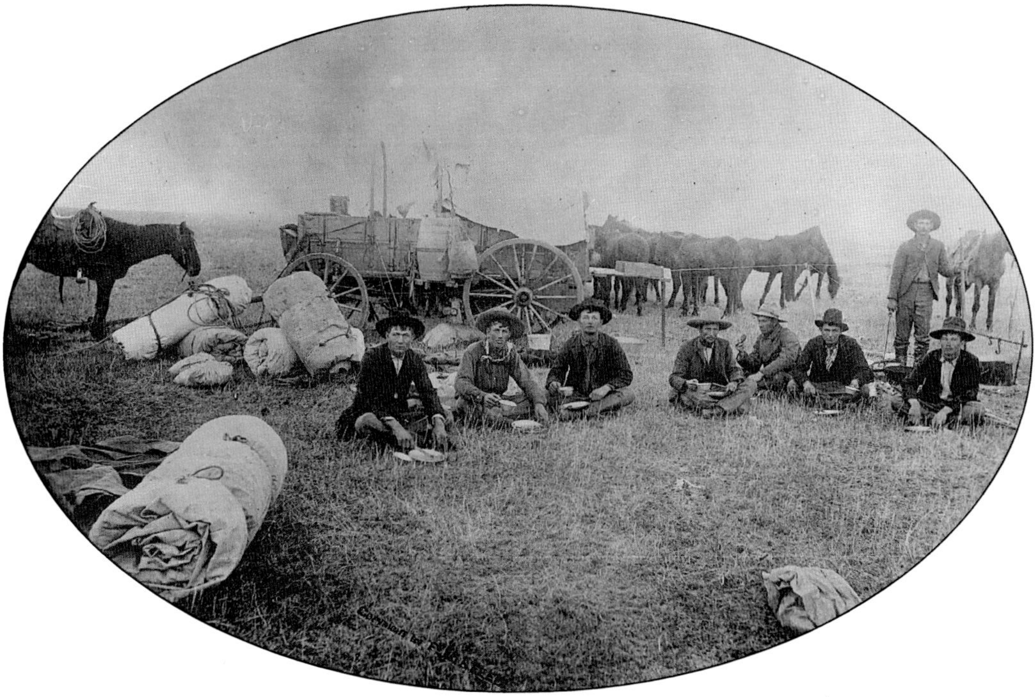

A cattle-drive cowboy camp appropriately introduces our first chapter. The streams running through Duncan offered inviting overnight camping areas for the many cattle herds traveling north, and the area's lush grasses made the future Duncan a popular location to rest the cattle for several days. (Courtesy Kansas State Historical Society.)

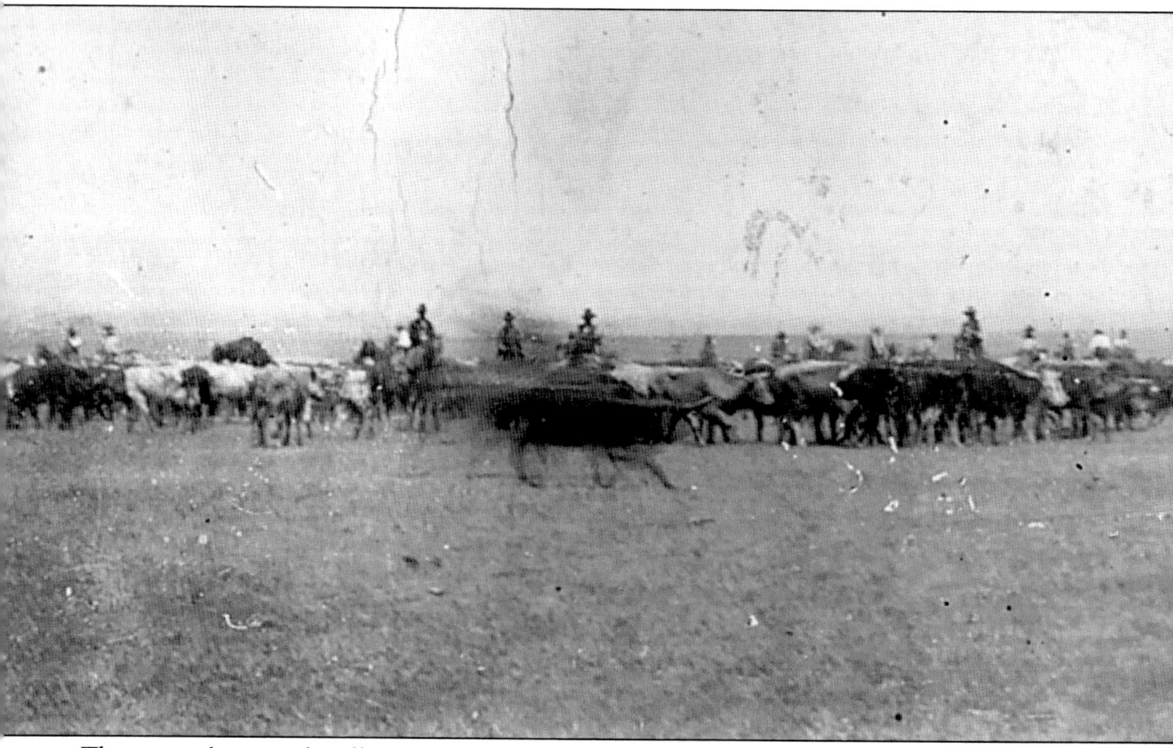

These two photographs offer rare glimpses of the old cattle drives. Above, cowboys are "throwing the cattle on the road," the phrase they used to describe getting the herd into its traveling

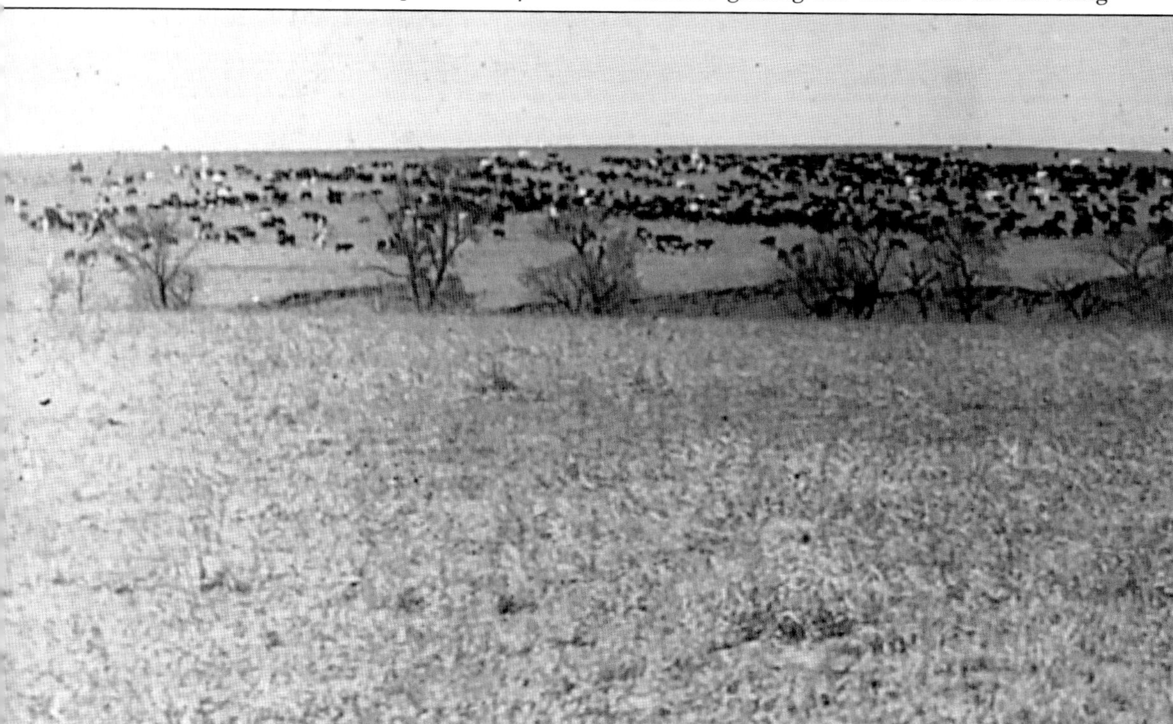

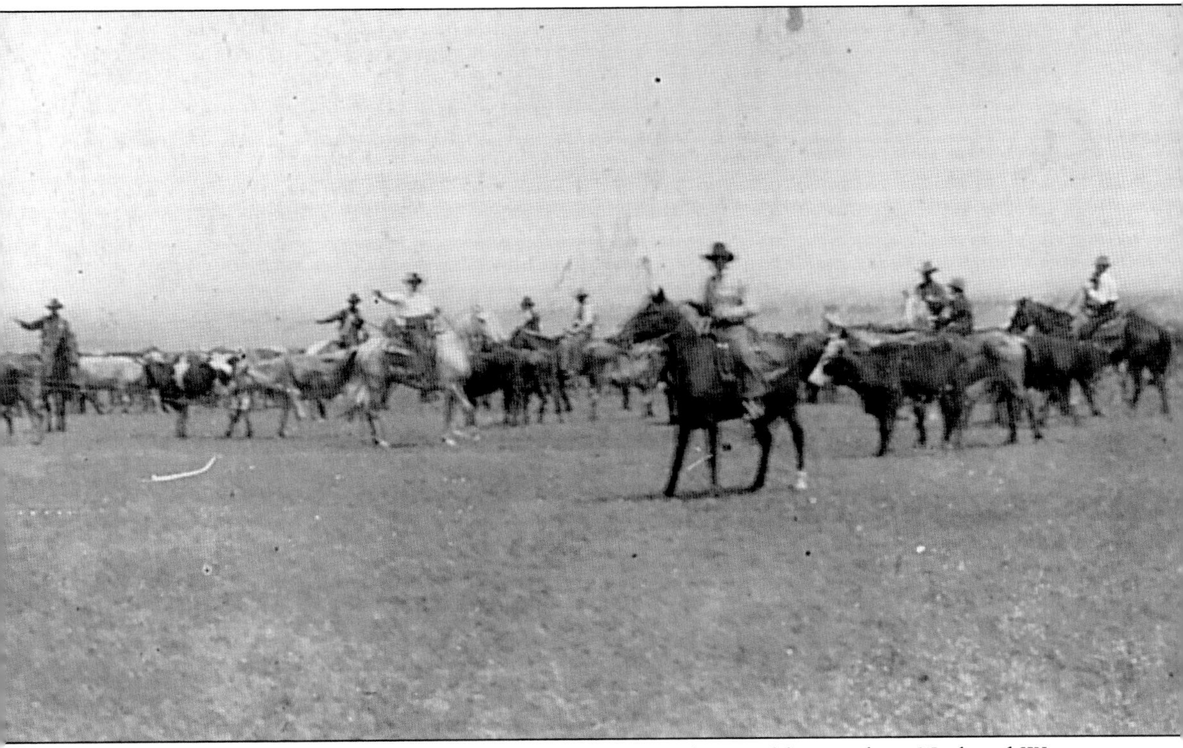

formation. Below, cattle driven from Albany, Texas, and owned by ranchers Nail and Weaver, arrive at their destination on Big Beaver Creek at the western edge of the county.

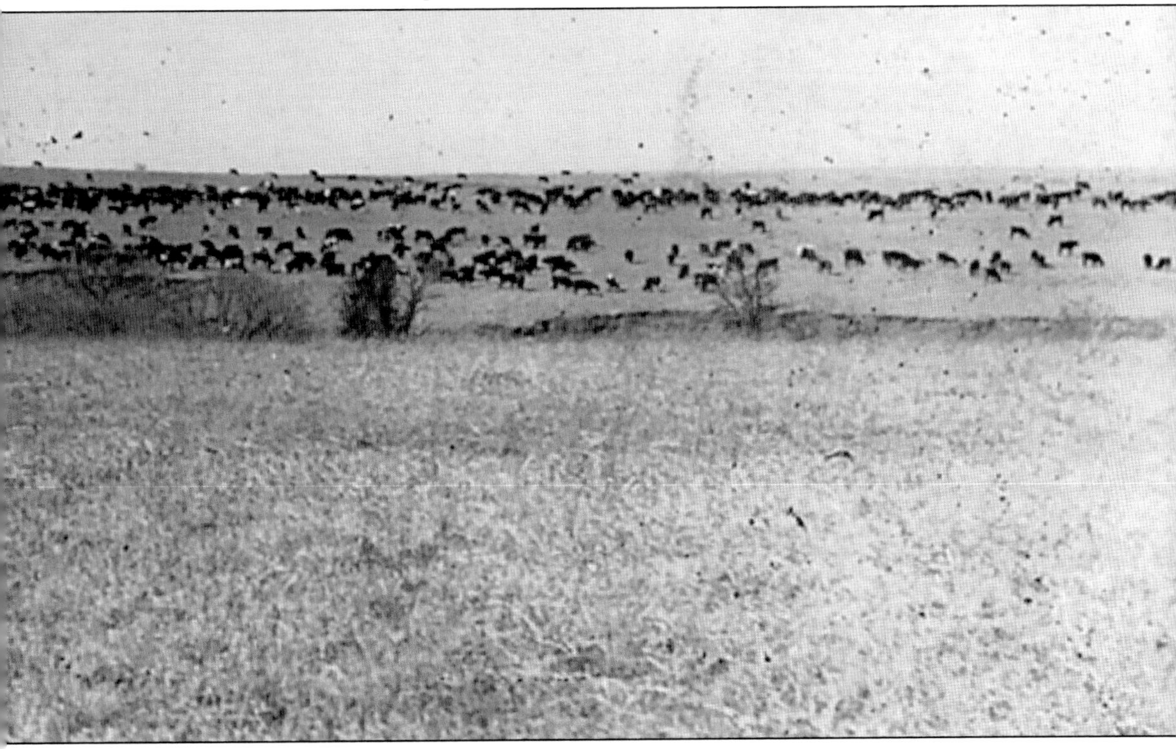

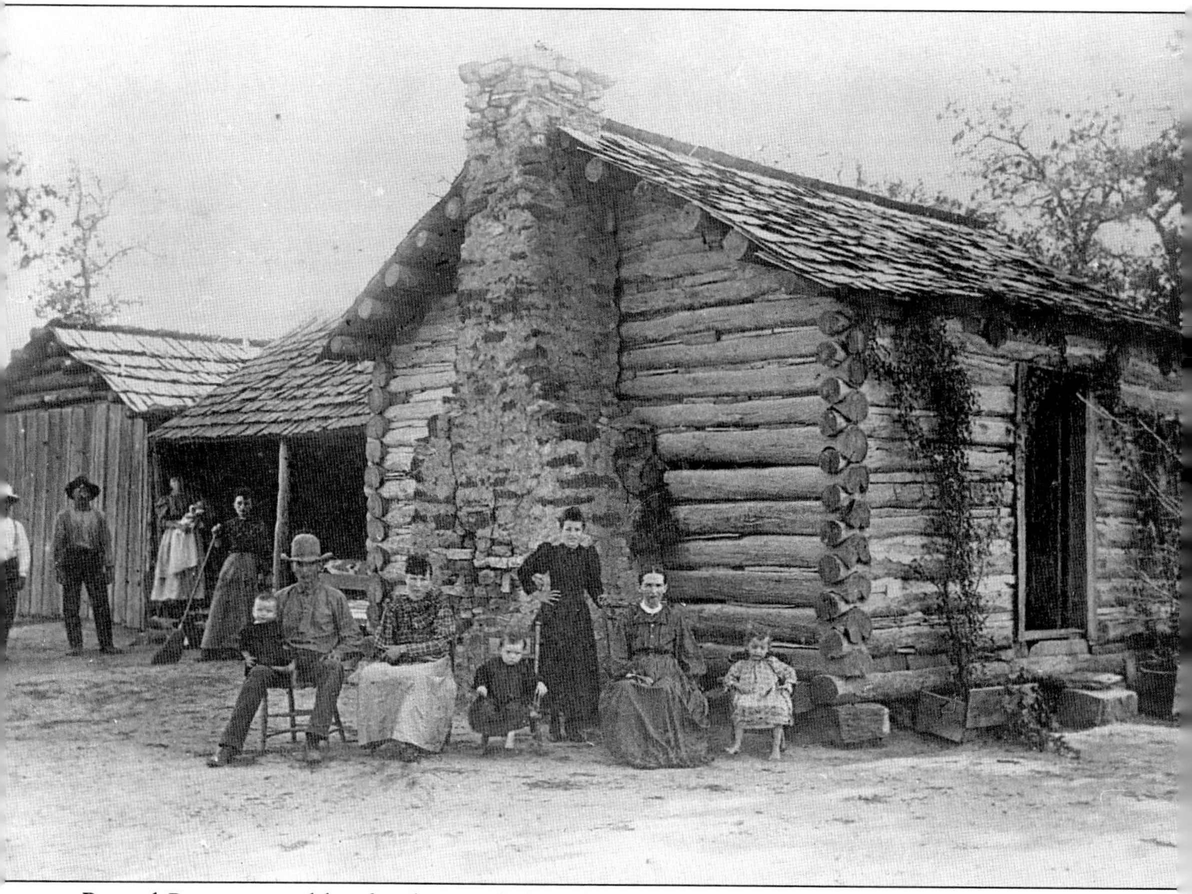

Bryand Passmore and his family pose before their homestead in the late 1880s, northwest of present Velma. Among the first white settlers in the area, they may have arrived as early as the early 1870s, and it is likely that they leased the land from the Chickasaw tribe in whose nation they settled. The apparent age and condition of the cabin suggests it had been standing for many years.

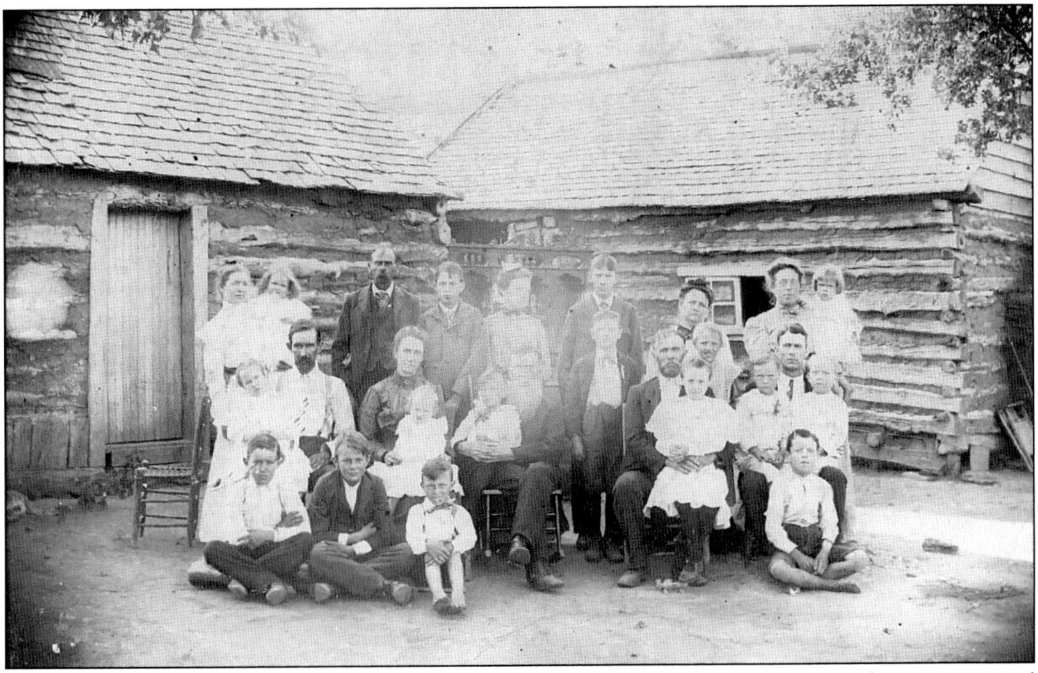

The John W. Jackson family, with John seated on the second chair from the right, are pictured before their Duncan homestead in the mid-1890s. John and his wife, Rebecca Elizabeth, came to Duncan in 1894 from Texas, and typify most of Duncan's early settlers.

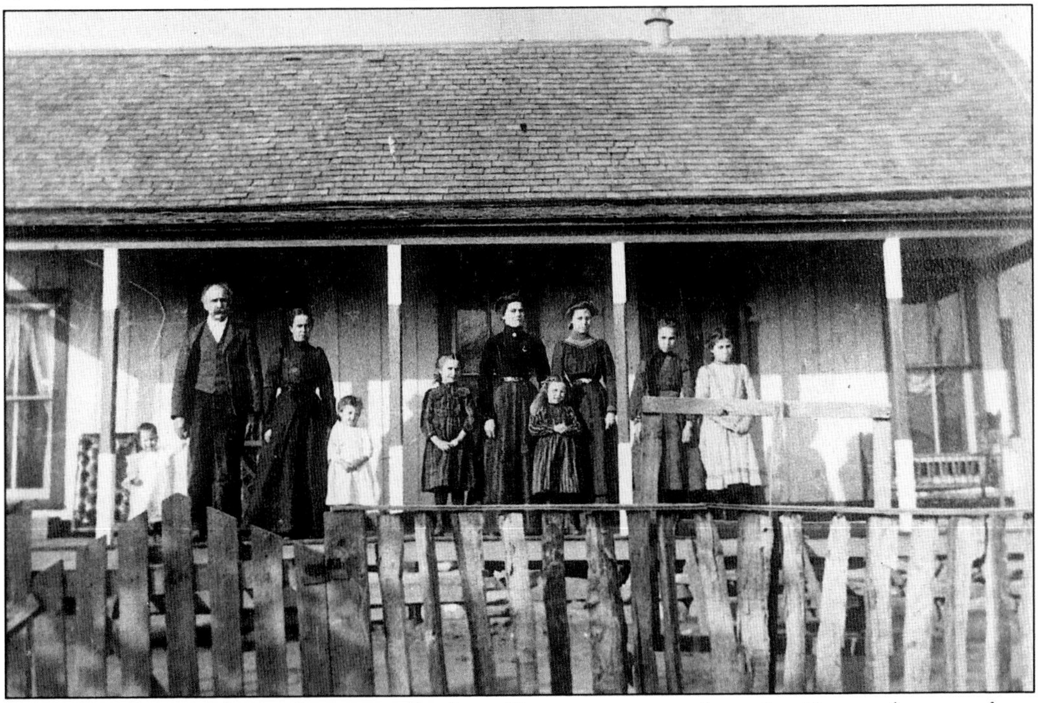

George Bailey and his wife, originally from Tennessee, moved to the Comanche area from Texas in about 1880. They settled east of the future Comanche, where most of the children were born, and share the distinction of being among the first settlers in the county.

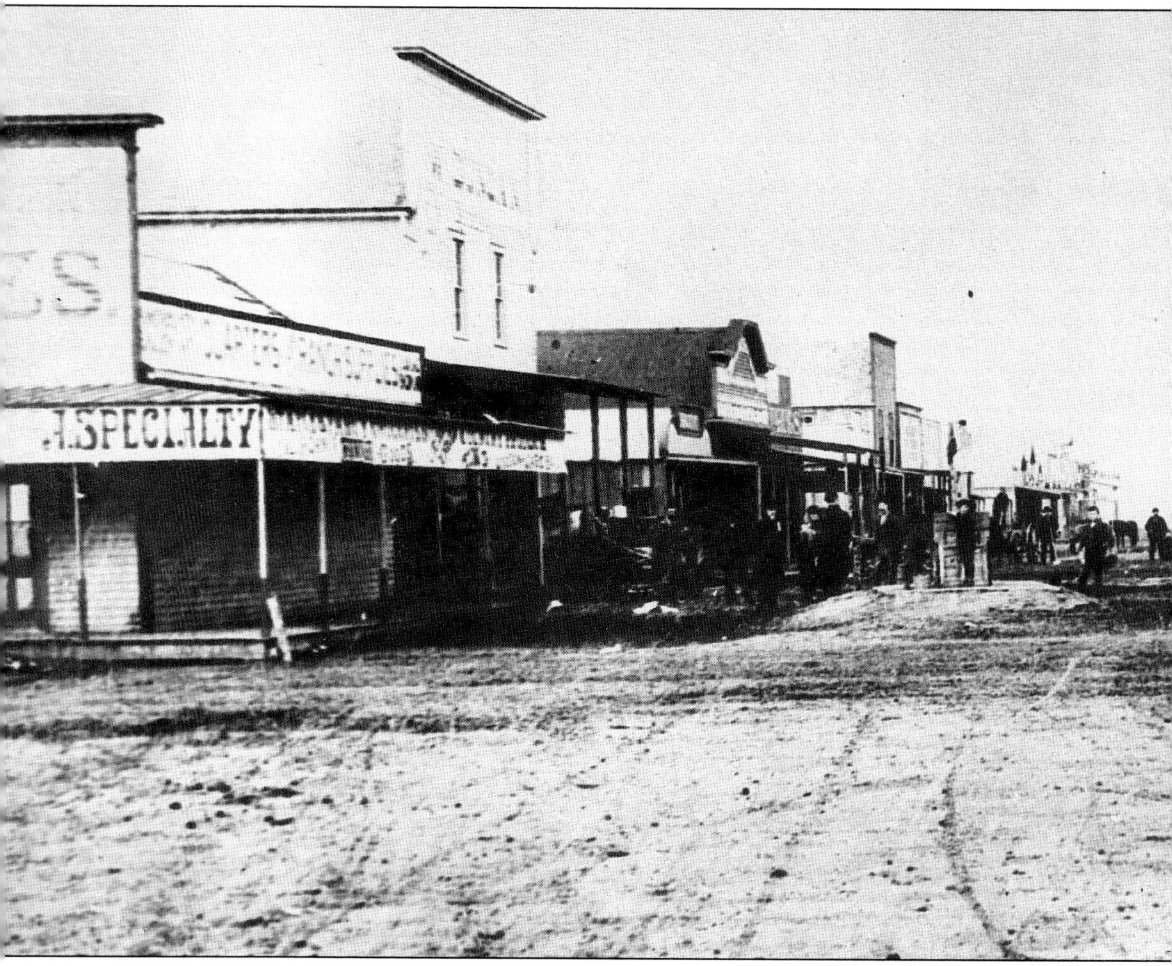
SPECIALTY

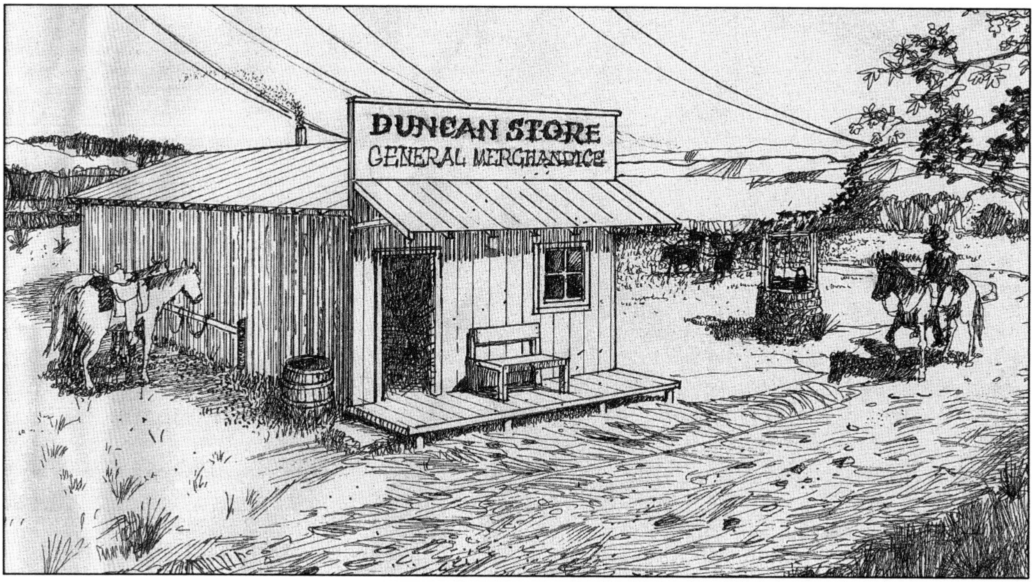
DUNCAN STORE
GENERAL MERCHANDICE

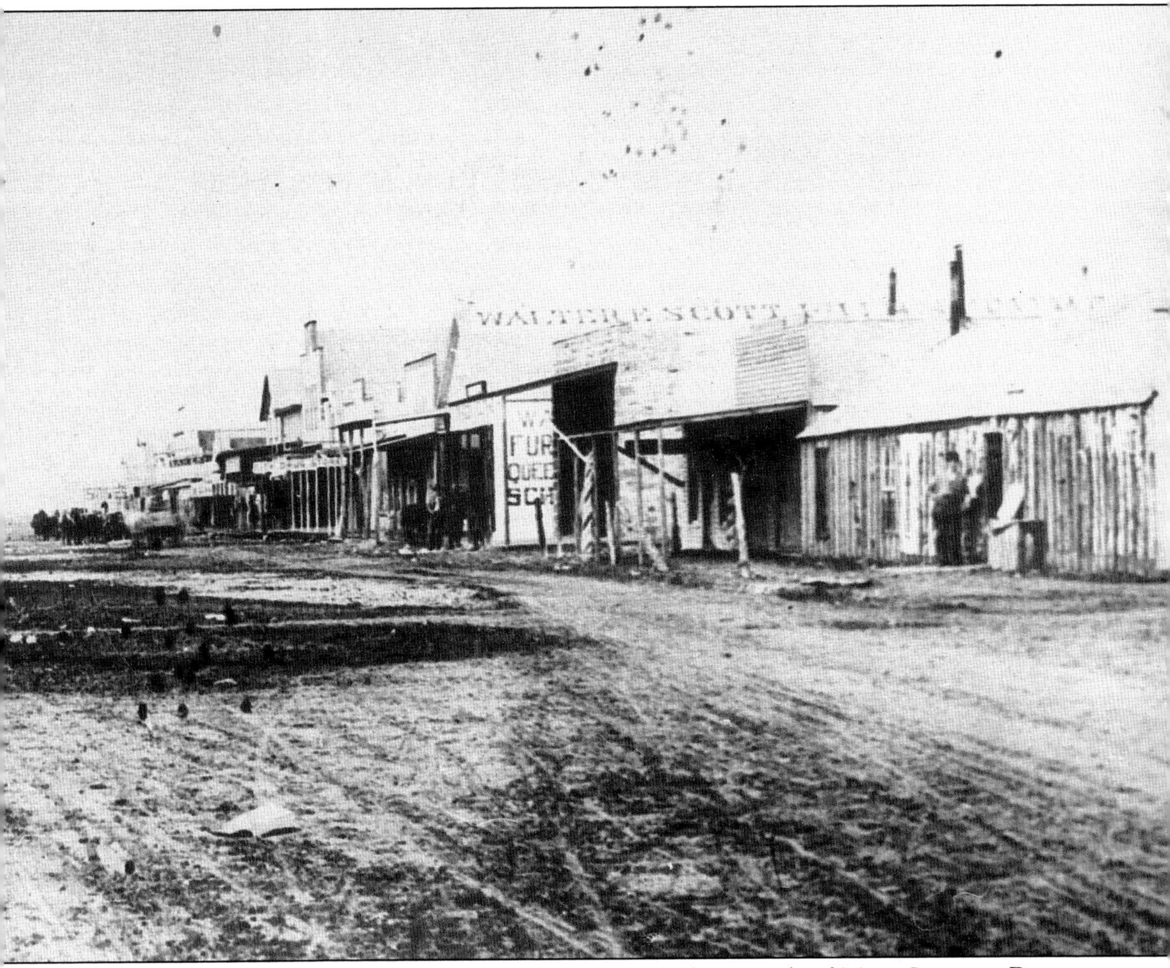

The image above is thought to be the earliest existing photograph of Main Street in Duncan. Dating from 1894, it was made two years after Duncan declared itself a town. Noteworthy is William Duncan's store, the first store on the left side of the photo facing the street. It was to this location that Duncan, the town's namesake, moved his business from a site on Cow Creek about 2 miles east by northeast.

On the preceding page (bottom) is a rendering of Duncan's original store, based on descriptions of those who were familiar with it. The original enterprise on Cow Creek, thought to have been established by Theodore Fitzpatrick in 1867 or 1868, was located on the Chisholm Cattle Road and the Ft. Arbuckle-Ft. Sill military road, just one-half mile west of their junction. Duncan, a co-worker of Fitzpatrick's in Ft. Sill's tailor shop, is believed to have purchased it from Fitzpatrick in the early 1870s.

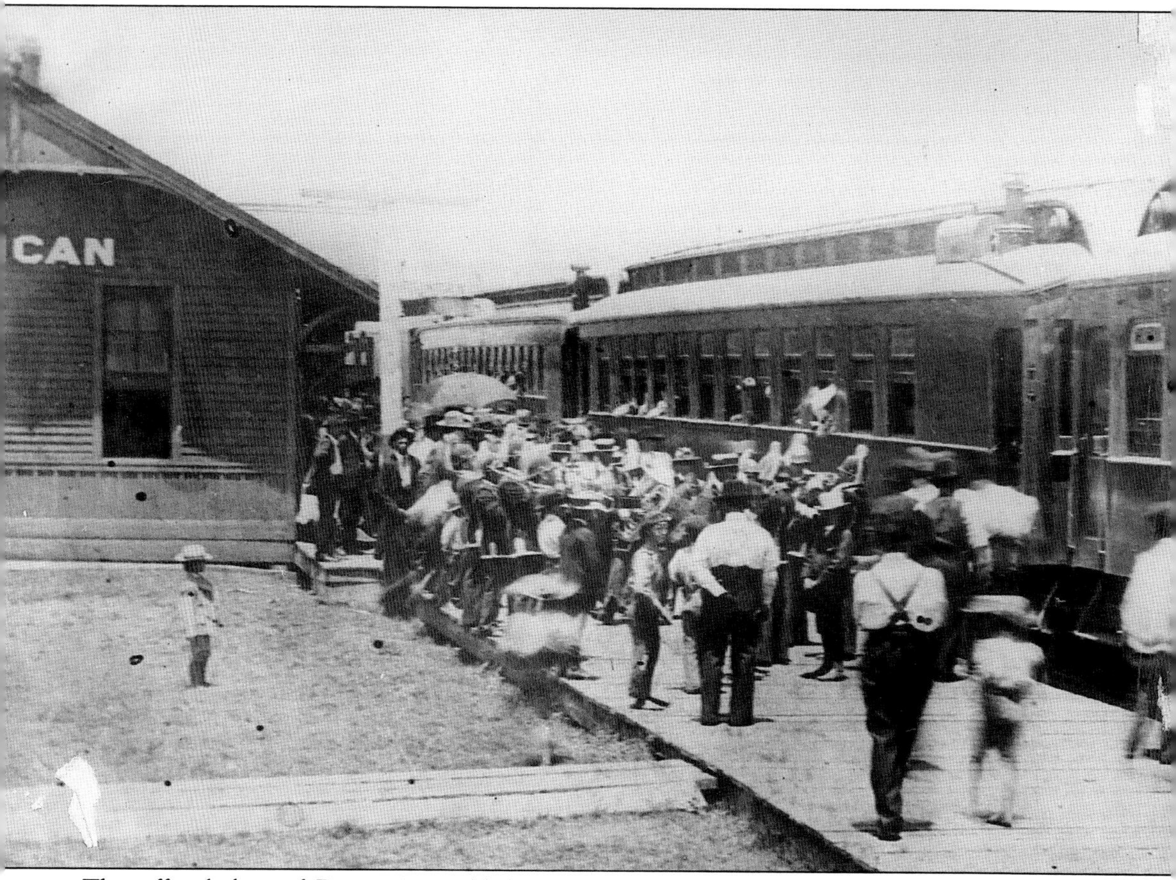

The official date of Duncan's establishment is June 27, 1892, the day the first scheduled passenger train arrived in Duncan on the new Rock Island Railroad recently completed through Duncan. The photograph above was taken on that occasion. Note the brass band adjacent to the train in the center of the photo, celebrating the momentous event.

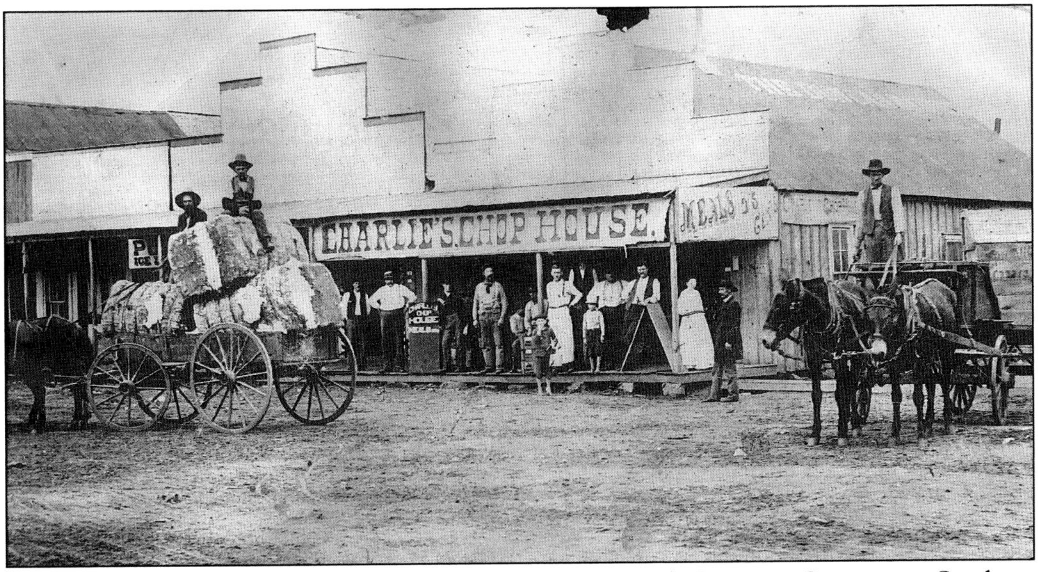

Charlie's Chop House was a popular gathering place in early Duncan. Cotton was Stephens County's first major cash crop, illustrated by the wagon to the left.

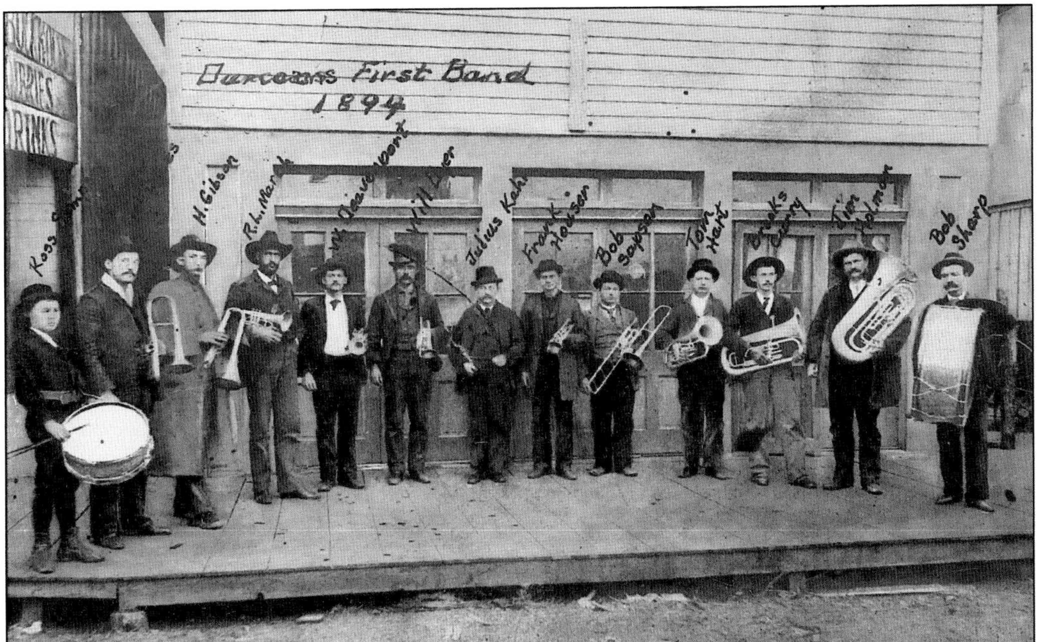

Brass bands were immensely popular in America of the 1890s, and in Duncan they were no exception. Bands performed on special occasions, such as the arrival of Duncan's first passenger train, for entertainment at social gatherings and dances, and at concerts. Duncan's first band is pictured on October 10, 1894.

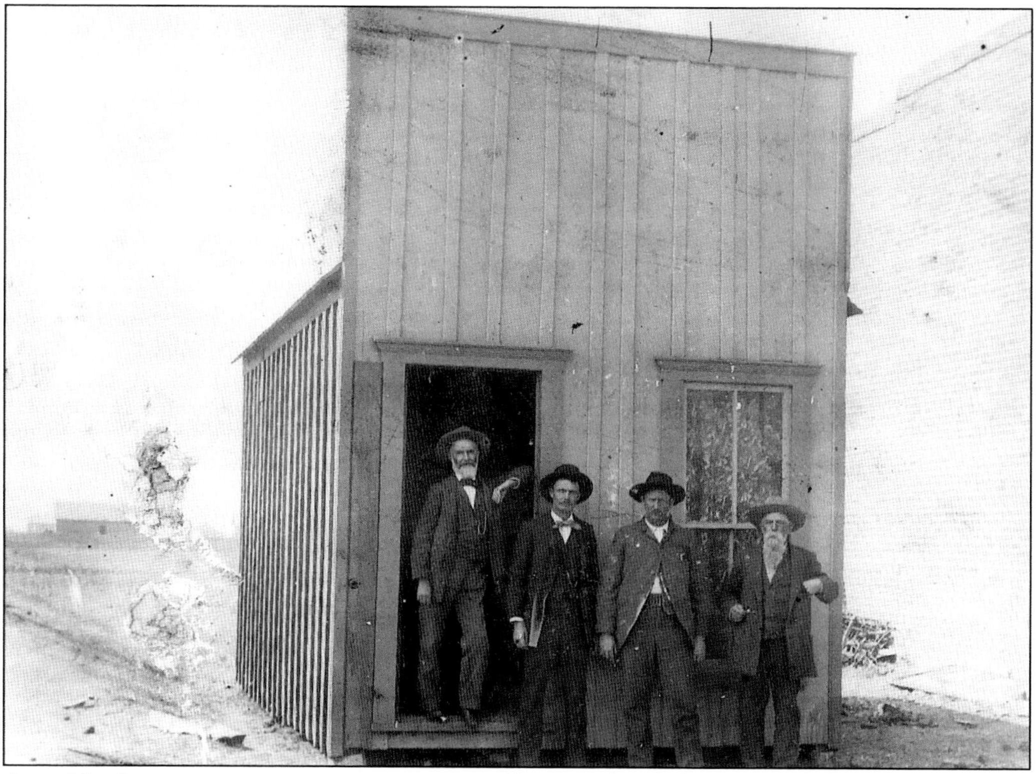

Arguably the most important enterprise anywhere in the early days of the Territory was the land office, where land claims could be filed and thus legalized. Duncan's land office is pictured here in 1893. Standing in front, from left to right, are the following: Colonel Ball, T.E. Lilly, Colonel Hoover, and Judge Rooks.

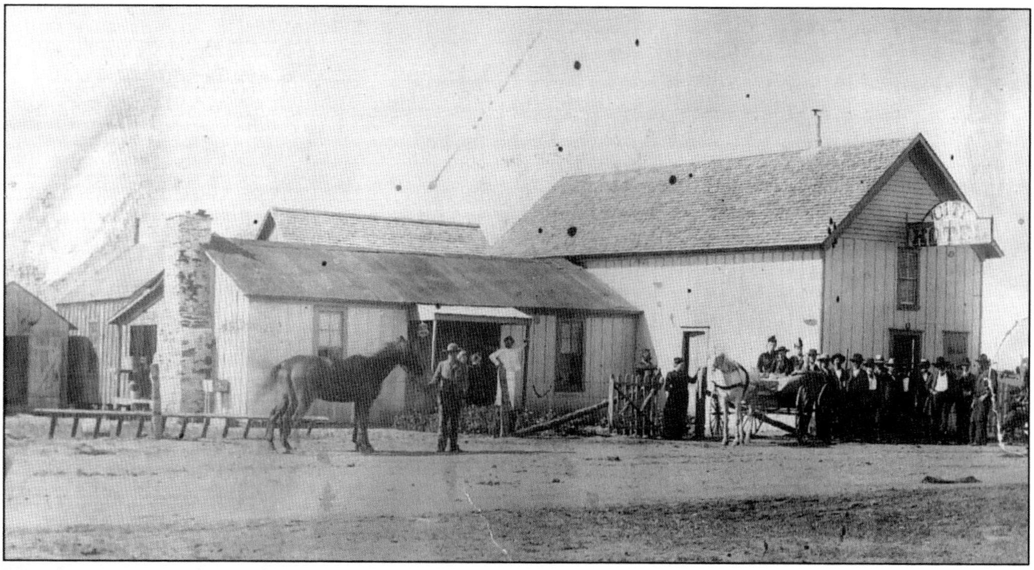

Hotels were popular gathering places in every community, where visitors were often the only source of news beyond the immediate area. Located near the railroad station on Seventh Street and Main, the City Hotel was one of Duncan's first.

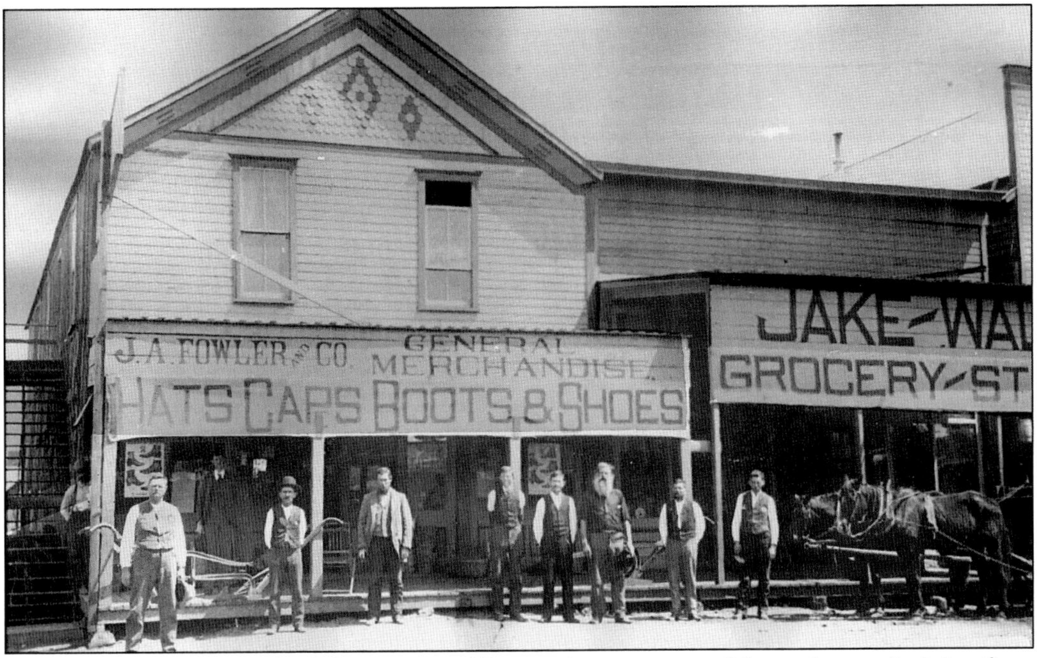

J.A. Fowler, standing at the left, was one of Duncan's most successful merchants. Arriving from Courtney Flats, Indian Territory, in 1892, where he owned a general merchandise store, he quickly established himself and, with Dr. J.W. Whisenant, later became a successful banker. The second floor of his store, pictured above in 1893, was occupied by a young lawyer, Bill Gilbert.

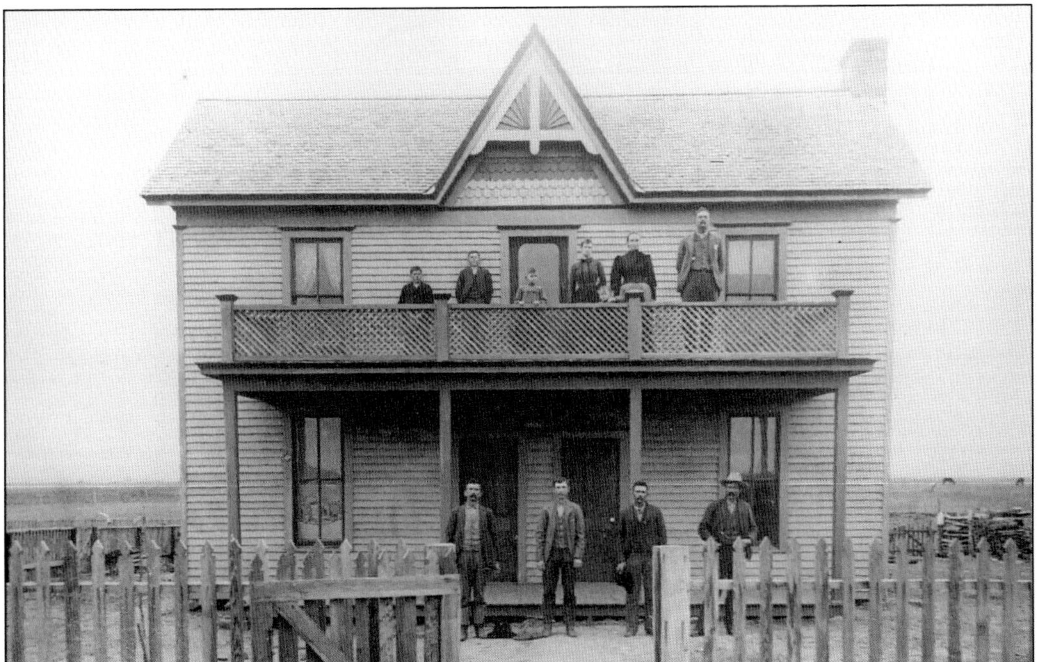

Reflecting his success, J.A. Fowler's home is pictured above at about the same time. He is standing on the balcony at the far right.

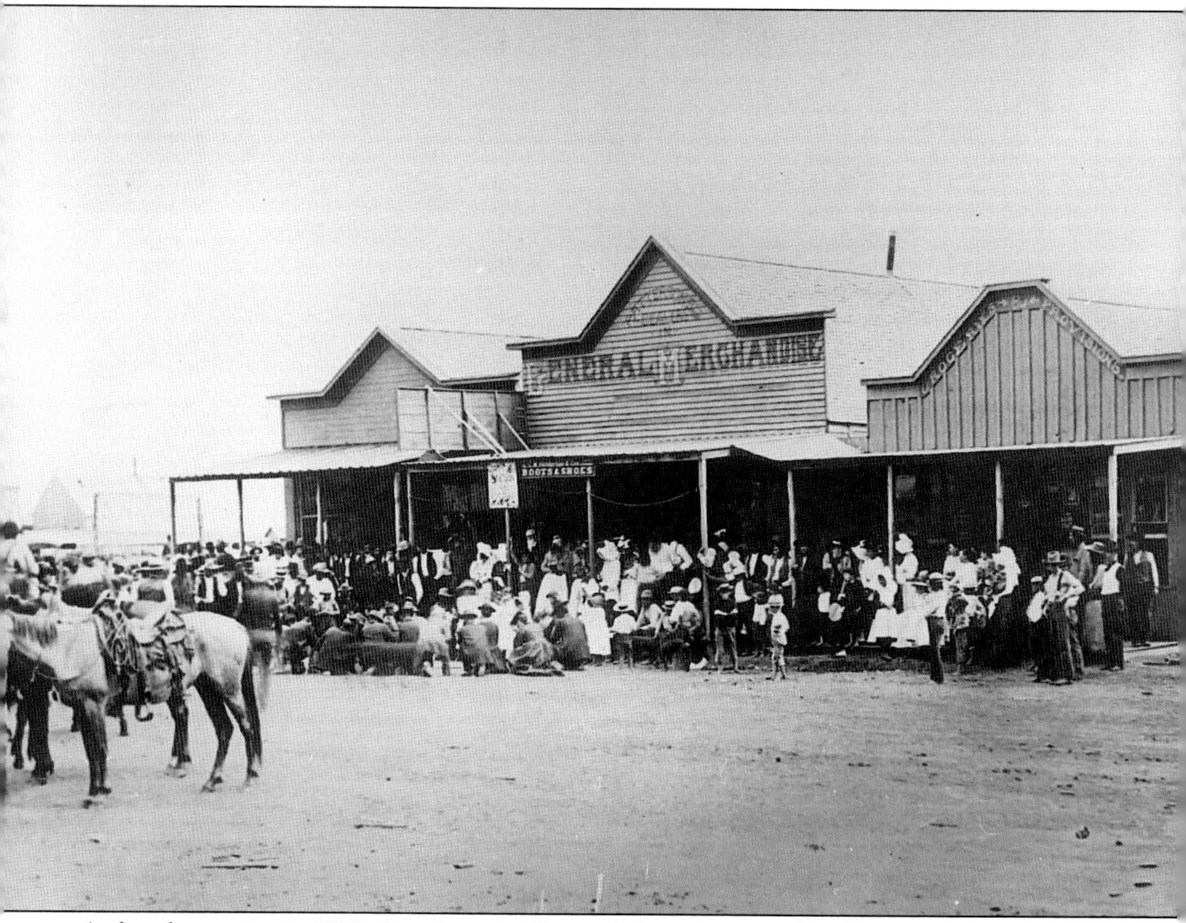

A church meeting in 1892, thought to be Duncan's first, is pictured in front of Patterson's store. Duncan would soon boast a dozen churches. Note the group in the center kneeling in prayer.

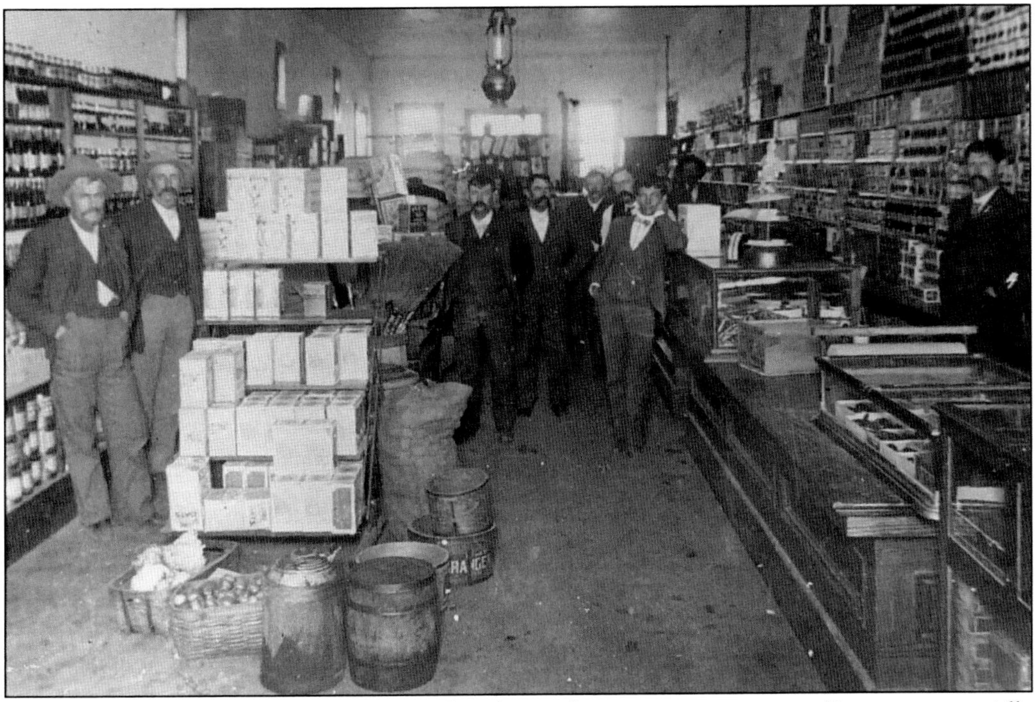

The number of early photographs of merchandise and grocery stores suggests Duncan was rapidly becoming a prosperous community. Above is the interior of the Allen and Fuqua grocery store, pictured at the turn of the century. Below is the Frensley and Brother store.

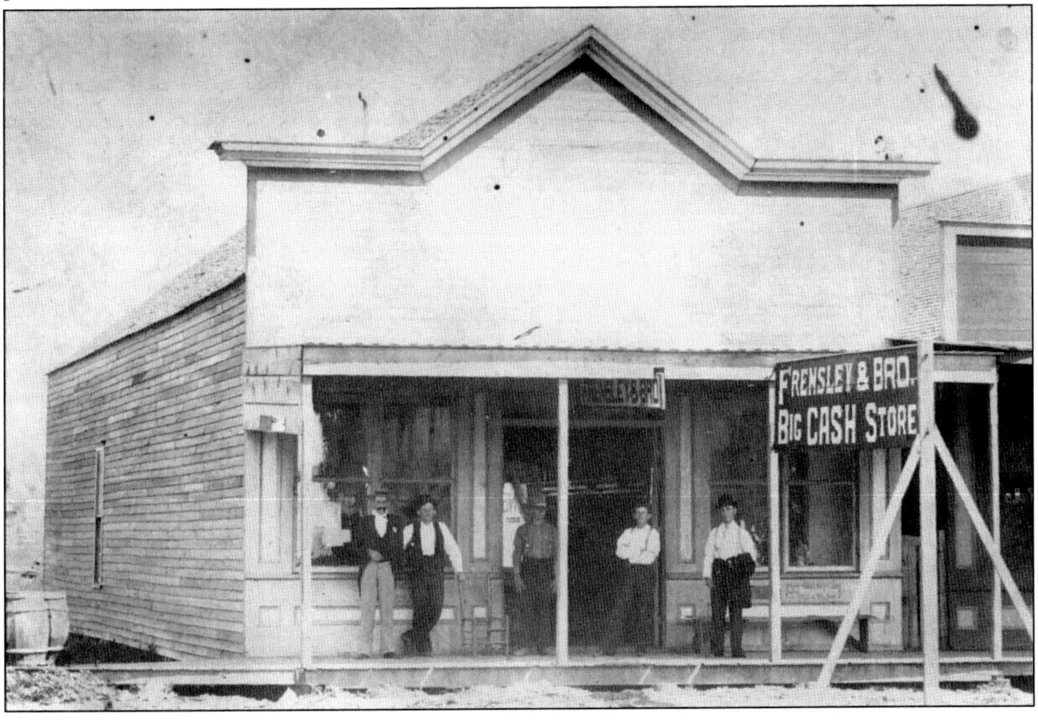

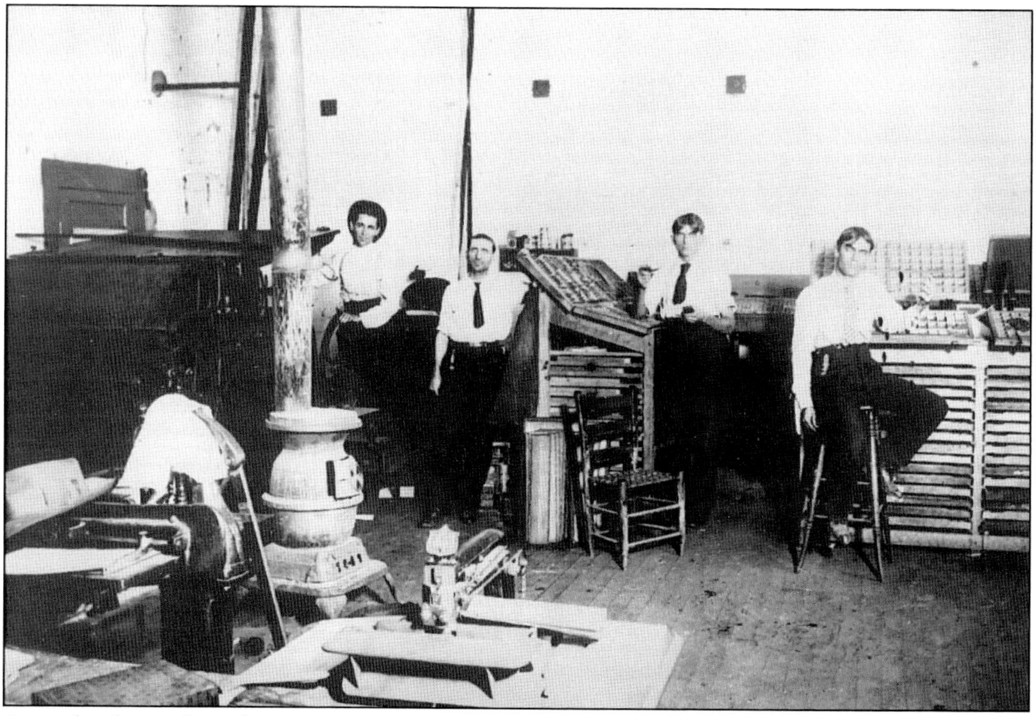

A mark of growth and prosperity in any community is a newspaper. Colonel J.P. Sampson, a Confederate war veteran pictured with his press below at left, established the first newspaper, *The Duncan Banner*, in 1892. Shown above is the copy room.

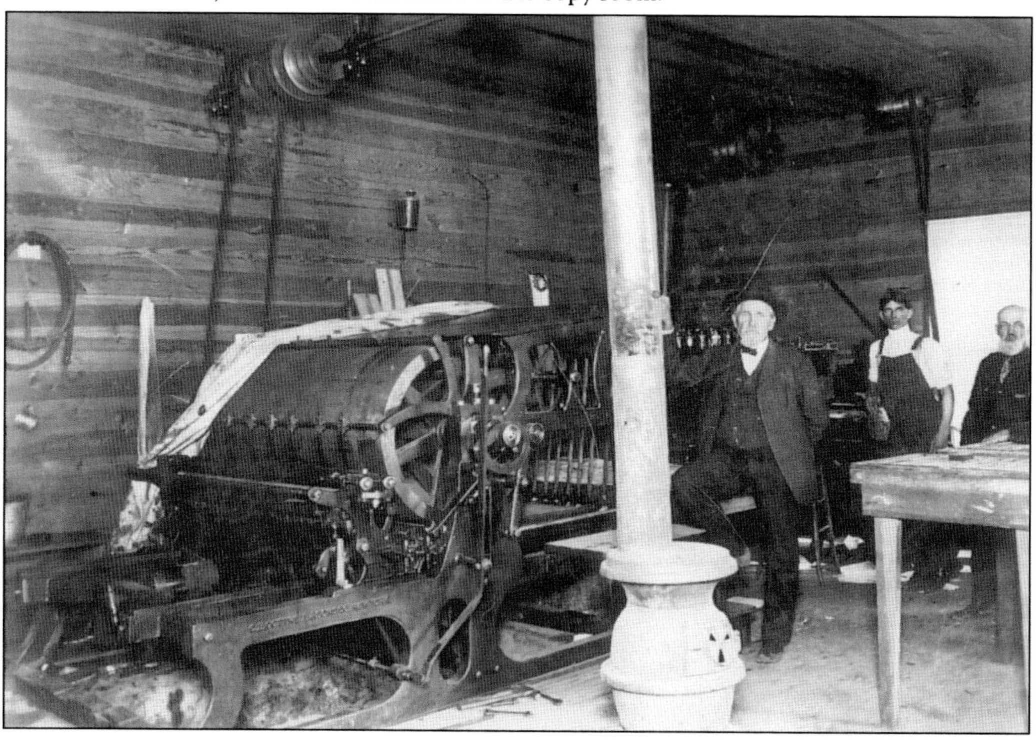

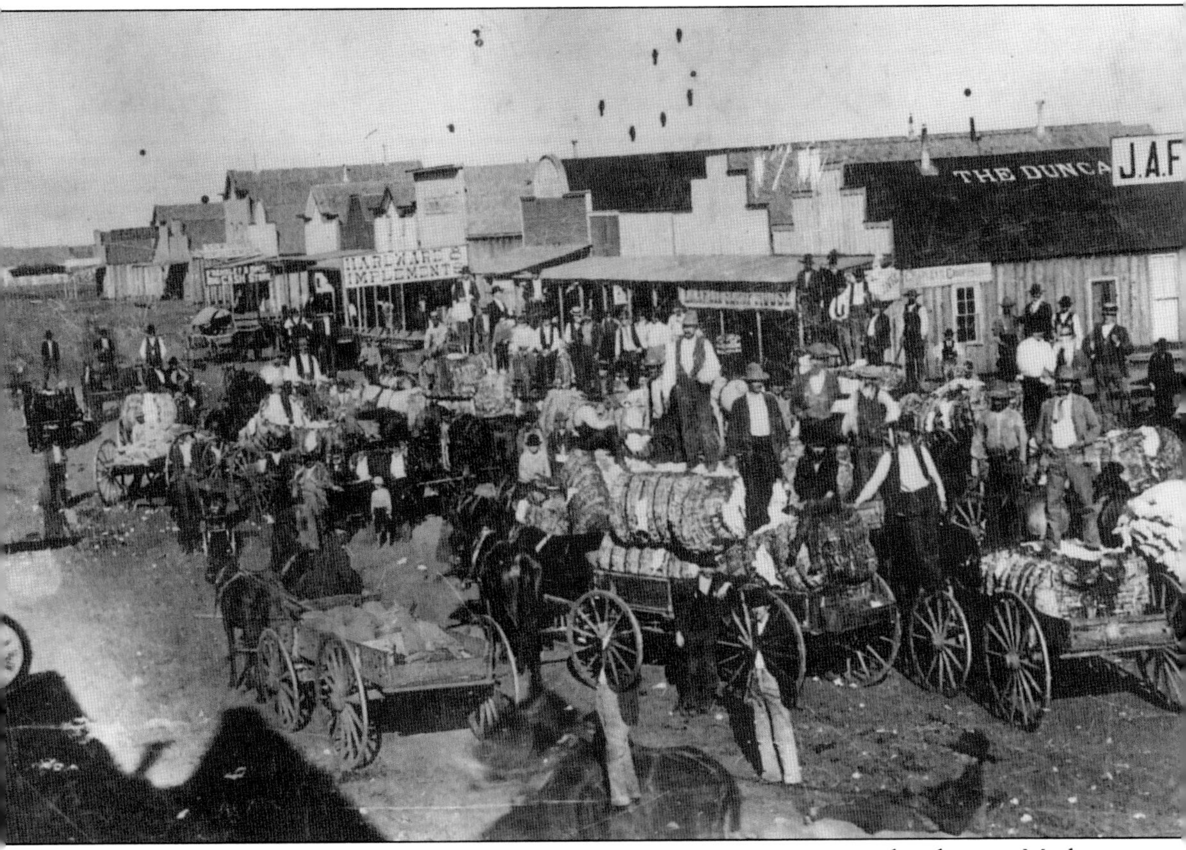

Cotton was the source of much of the area's early prosperity, a guaranteed cash crop. Marlow, Duncan, and Comanche all prospered from the crop. The market was so good that cotton was referred to as "white gold." In Duncan, farmers parked their loads on Main Street, and the buyers made their offers while inspecting the bales. This photo was taken on October 10, 1894, looking west.

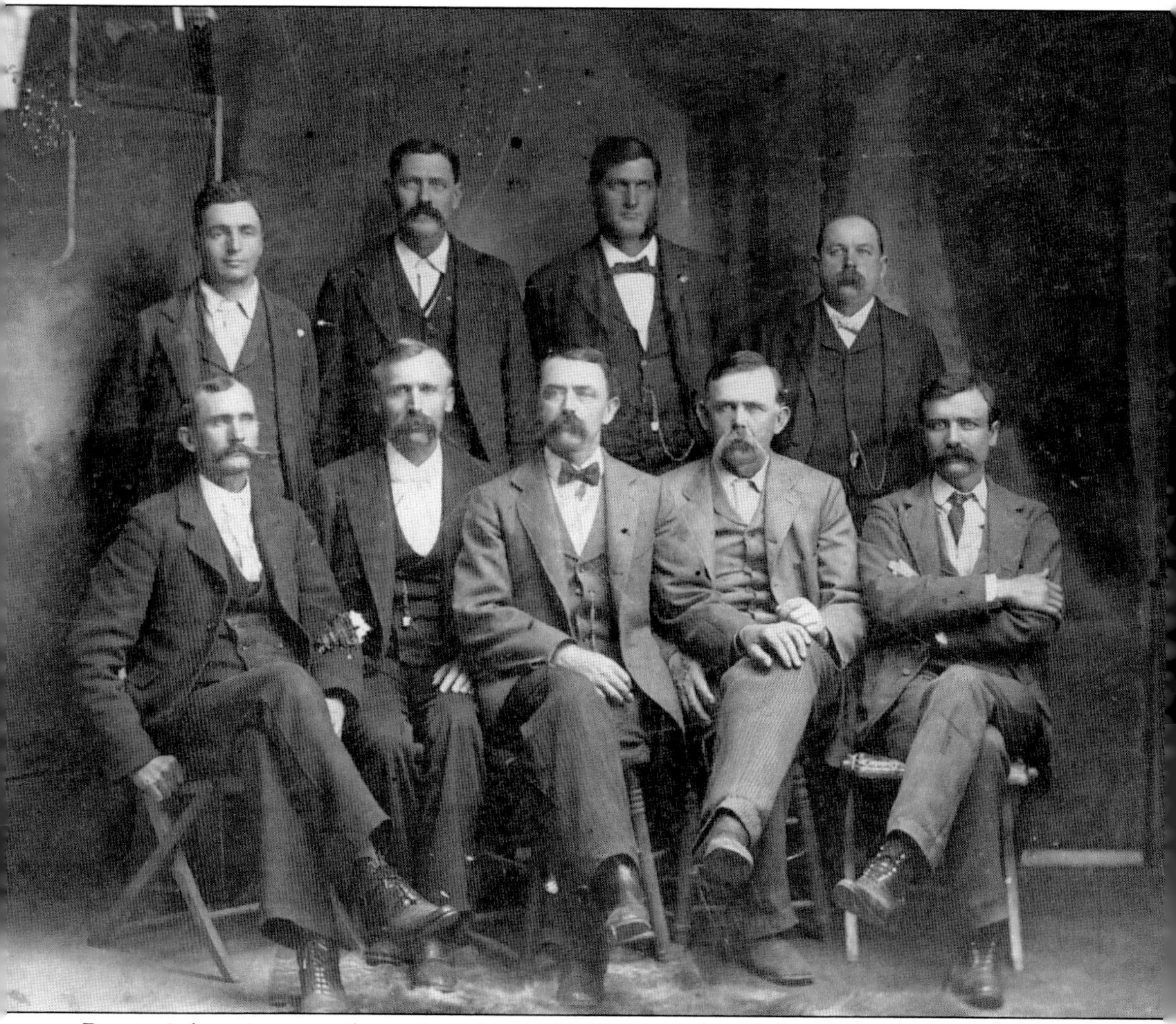

Duncan's first city council was elected in 1898. They are, from left to right, as follows: (seated) J.N. Duncan, alderman; Dr. J.F. Roberson, alderman; Frank Fuqua, mayor; A.R. Biggs, alderman; and R.E. Sharp, city clerk and treasurer; (standing) Jas. Leftwich, alderman; Mr. Groff, city marshal; Robert March, city attorney; and Robert Frensley, alderman. All were stalwarts of the new community

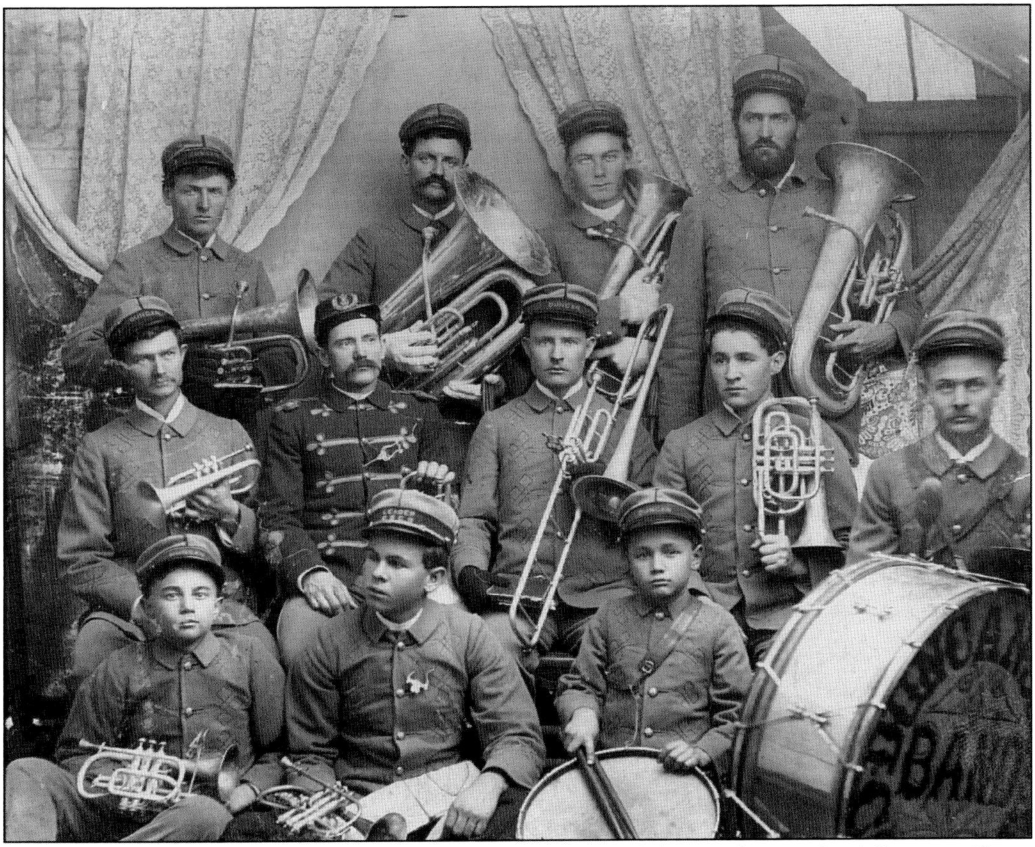

By 1898, Duncan's band sported uniforms. Pictured from left to right are the following: (front row) Frank Houser, a Butterbaugh brother, and Ross Sampson; (second row) H. Gibson, R.L. March, Bob Sampson, a Butterbaugh brother, and Bob Sharp; (top row) Rom Hart, Jim Holman, Charles Albright, and Will Dyer.

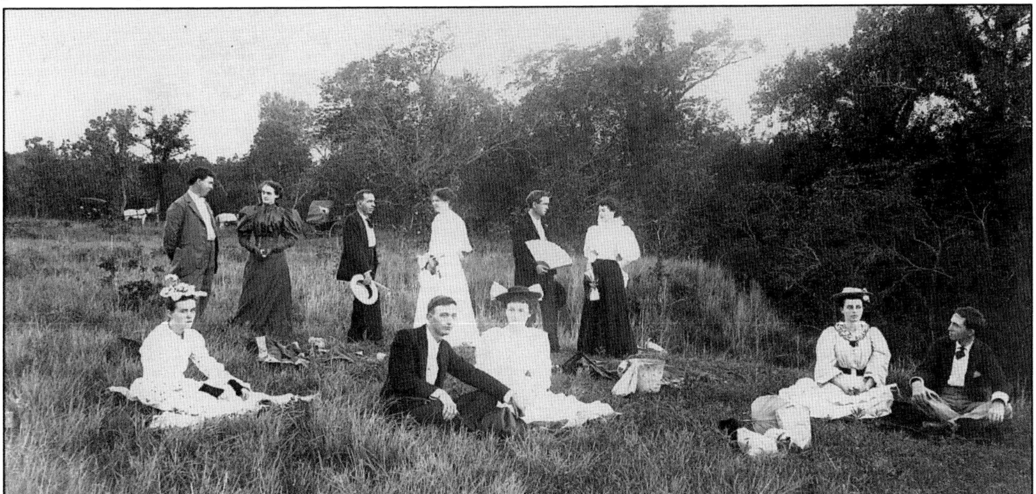

The new community did not neglect social occasions. Here, "Duncan's 400," an early social group, picnics in the mid-1890s on Little Beaver Creek, 8 miles west of Duncan.

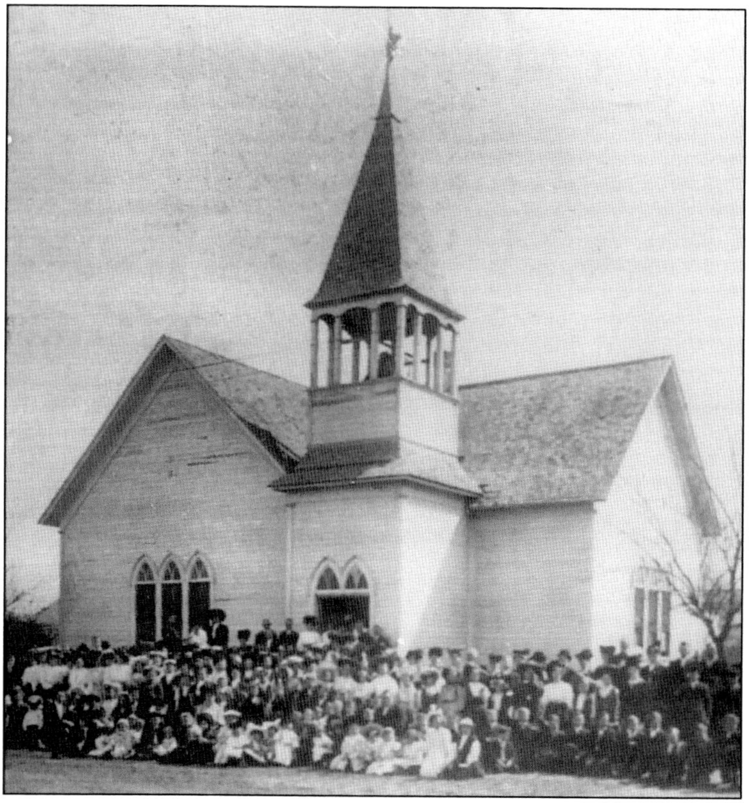

Duncan's first church building was the First Baptist Church, constructed in 1895. It is pictured here at the turn of the century.

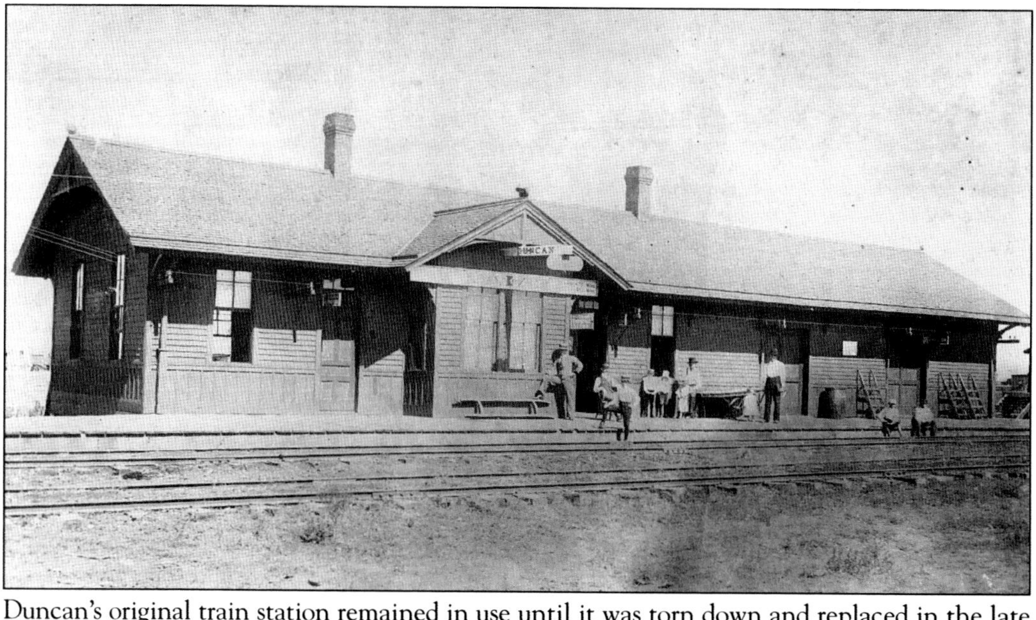

Duncan's original train station remained in use until it was torn down and replaced in the late 1940s. Pictured above is the station in 1898.

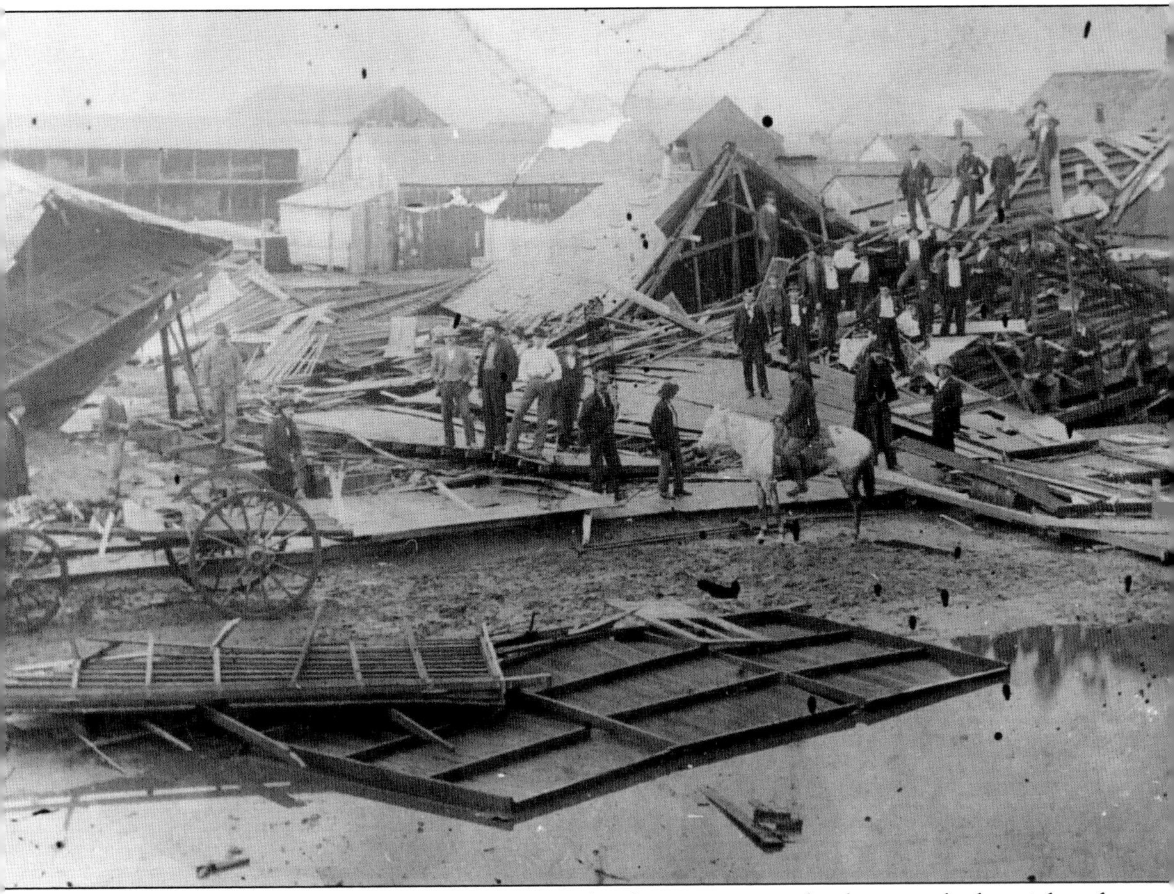

A watershed event of Duncan's growth was the disastrous tornado that struck the night of April 30, 1898. Many homes and businesses of the new community were destroyed. At the time, most of the business section lay east of the railroad tracks. Rebuilding, however, took place largely on the western edge of town, several blocks west of the tracks.

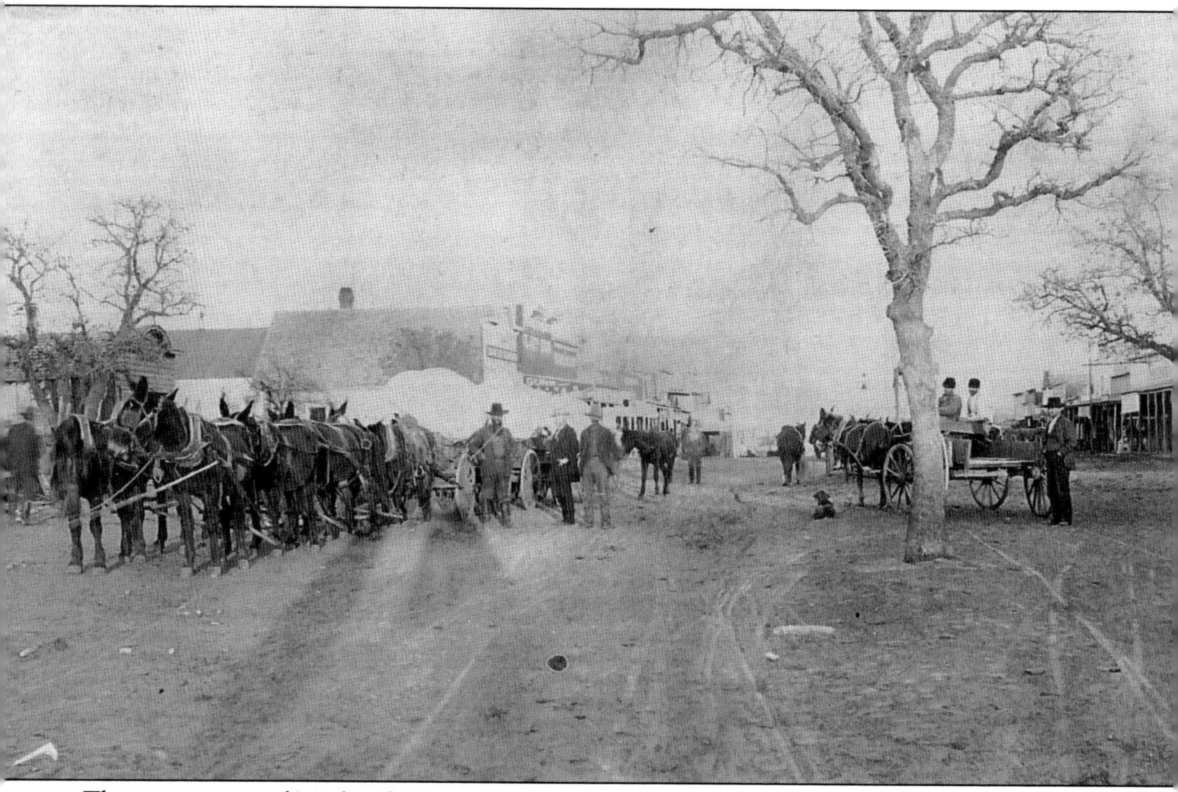

The community of Marlow began life as Marlow Grove, named after Dr. Williamson Marlow and his family, who came to the area in 1880. With the coming of the railroad in 1892, the community renamed itself Marlow. As photographed in 1898, the earliest known photo of the town, the community appears well established and prosperous.

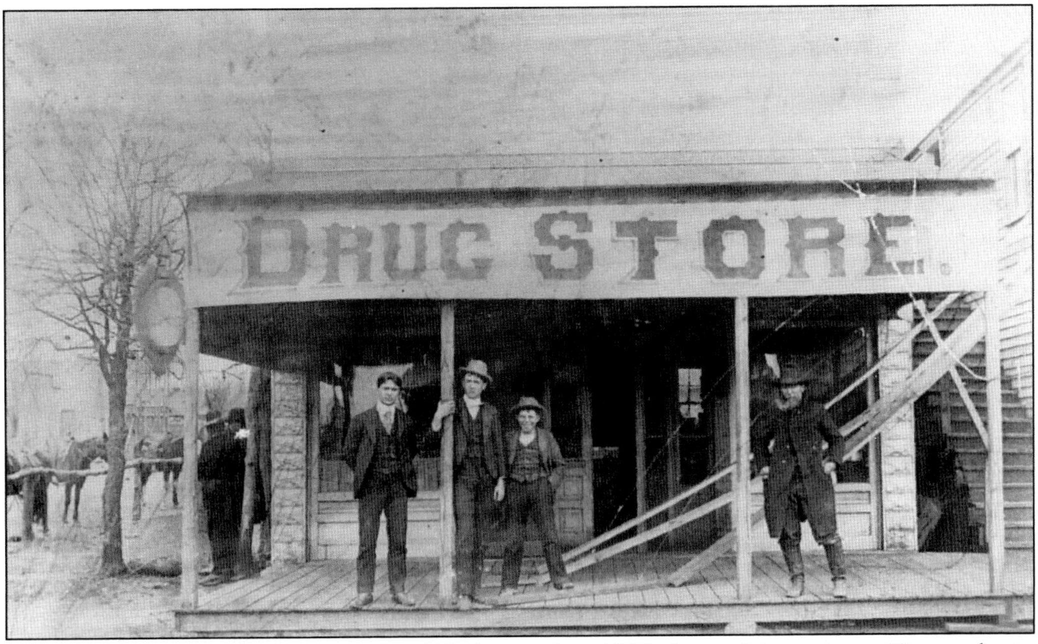

Comanche began as the community of Tucker, and in 1893 changed its name to Comanche in honor of the Indian tribe. Beyond the Weakley Drug Store, on the left of the photo above, we can faintly make out Comanche as it appeared in 1898. The three figures in the center are, from left to right, Herb Howard, Flem Vance, and Walter Witt. A major cotton-producing area, one of Comanche's many cotton gins is pictured beyond the train station. Though pictured after the turn of the century, both were constructed in the late 1890s.

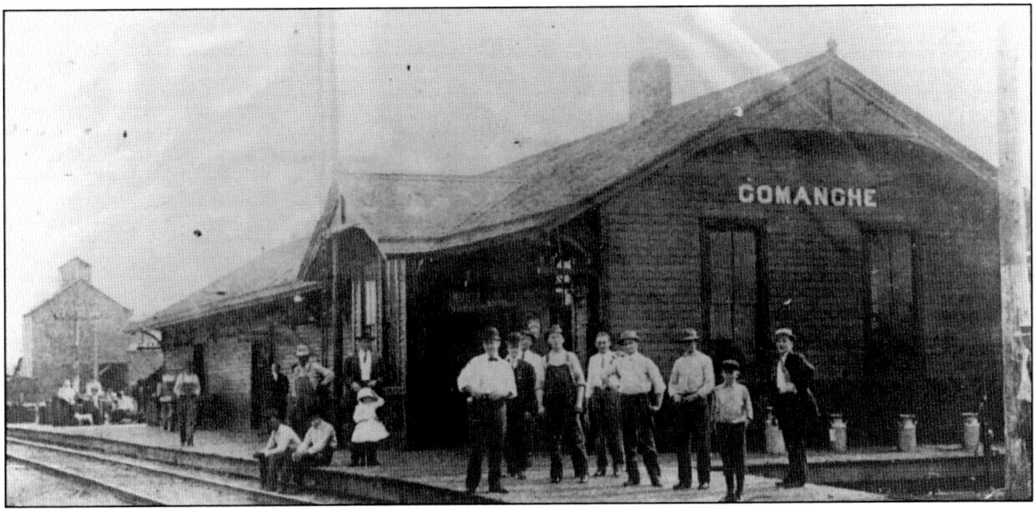

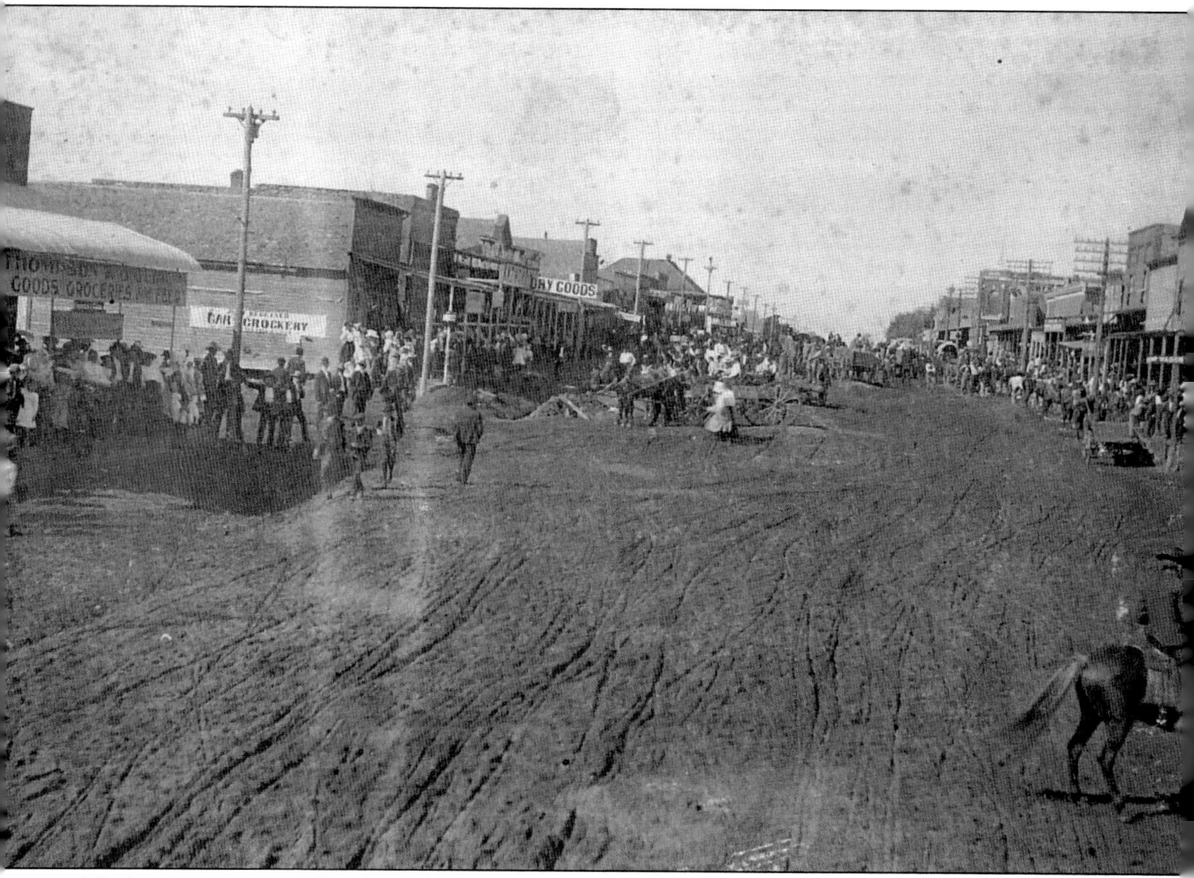

Marlow appears as a bustling, busy town around 1905. Indeed, the three towns of Marlow, Duncan, and Comanche were all well established by the first decade after the turn of the century, and each vied to become the largest.

Two

The Development of Community

Early 1900s

The three major communities of Stephens County—Duncan, Marlow, and Comanche—initially grew at about the same rates. Little served to differentiate them in size until statehood in 1907 created Stephens County, with Duncan as its seat.

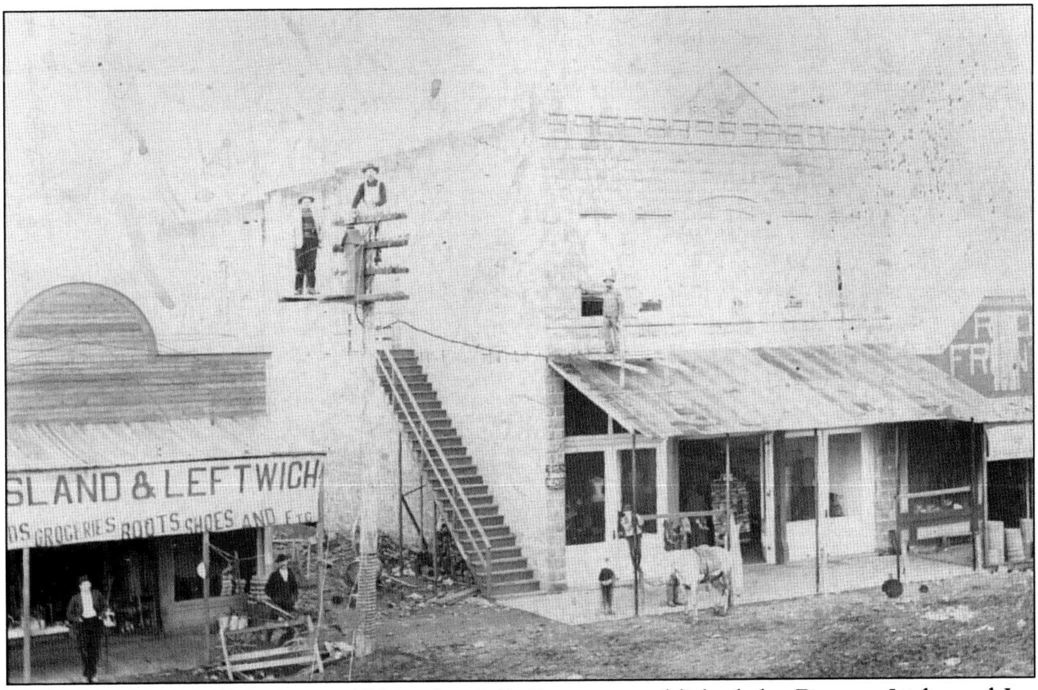

Electricity came to Duncan in 1904, after L.E. Bumpas established the Duncan Light and Ice Company and built the first power plant.

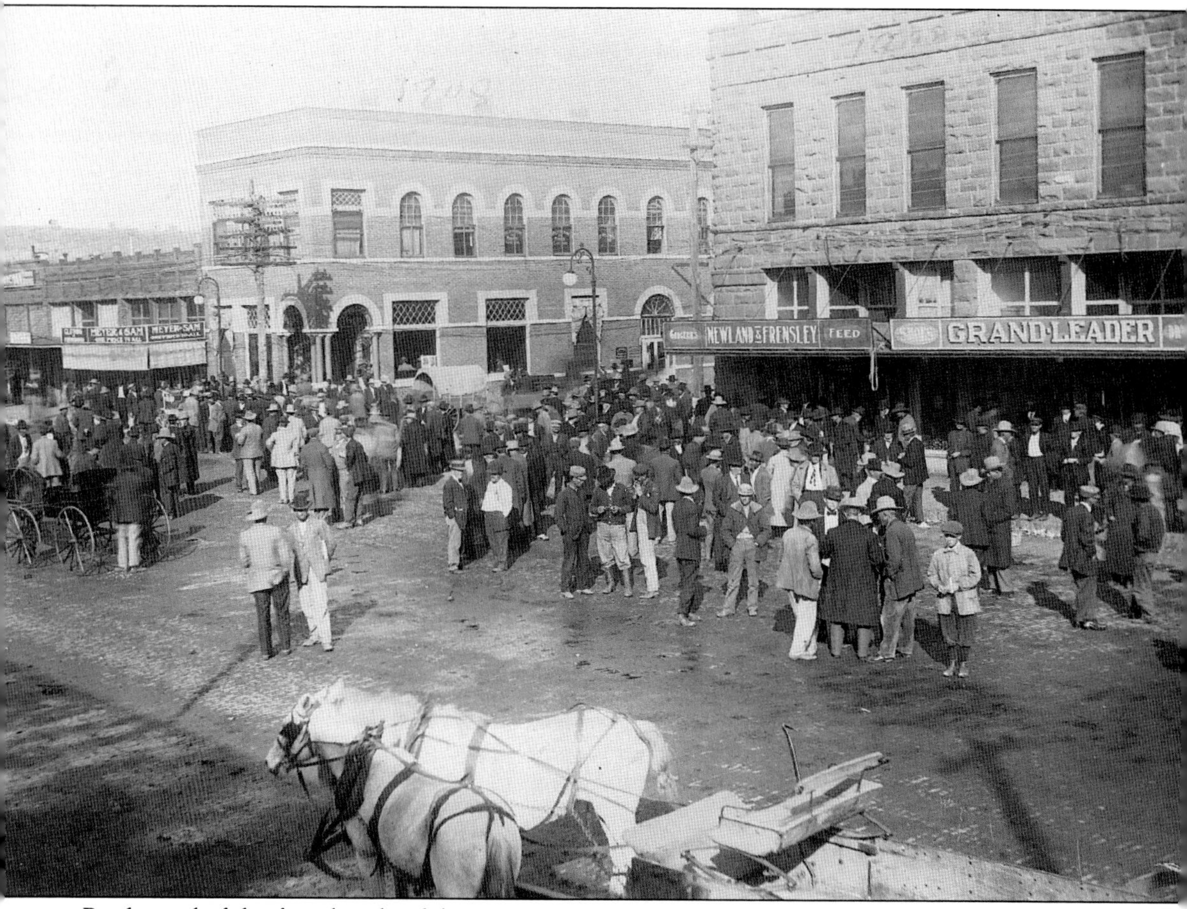

By the end of the first decade of the century, Duncan's Main Street had been paved with brick. This busy street scene suggests that Duncan was becoming the center of the county's economic structure. The photograph is looking northwest, at the corner of Eighth and Main Streets.

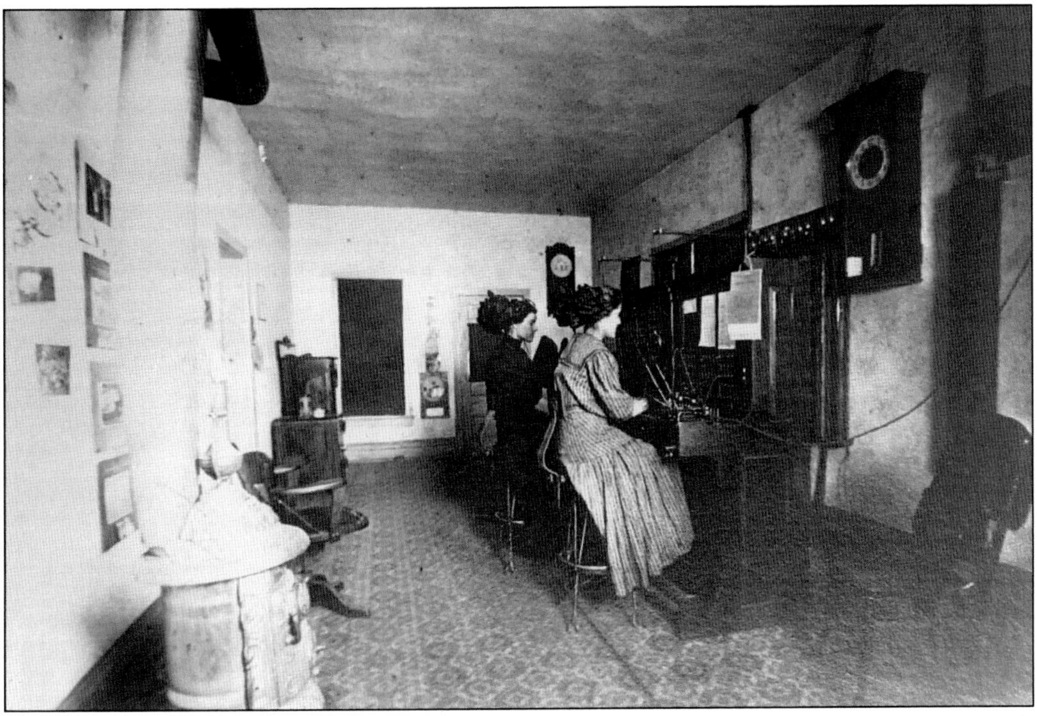

As early as 1903, Comanche's telephone system was in place. Pictured in this 1903 photograph are the town's first telephone switchboard operators: Kate Bailey (at left) and Susie Diehl.

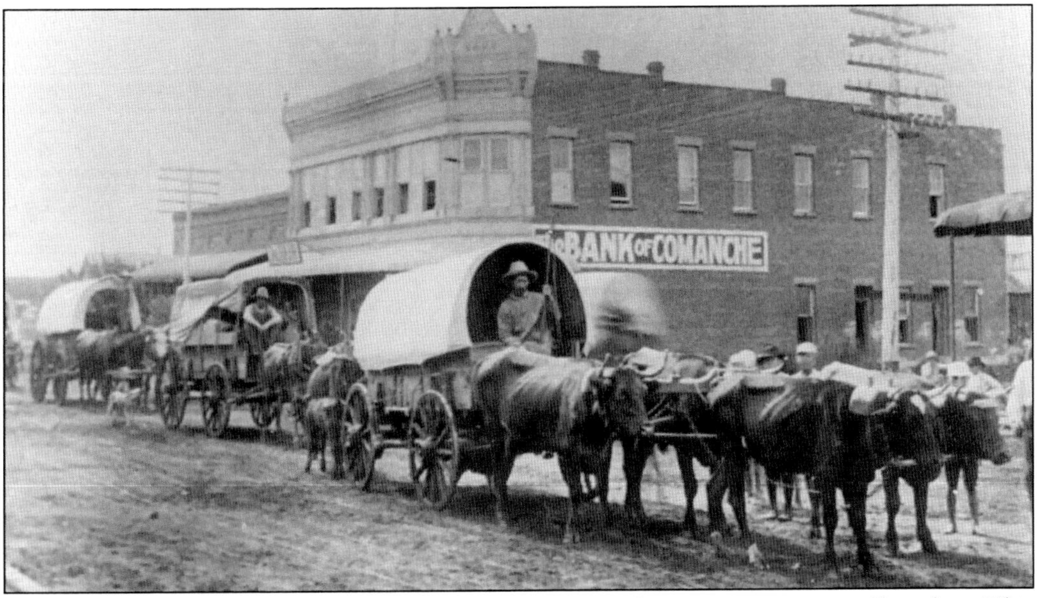

Though an anachronism by 1905, cattle-pulled wagons and wagon trains were still evident. This wagon train, identified as the last one westward through Comanche, is probably heading into the recently opened Oklahoma Territory lands west of the Indian Meridian, the former Kiowa-Comanche-Apache reservation lands. Unlike the famous land runs of the previous century, these homesteads were given out by lottery. Note the well-developed center of Comanche in 1905.

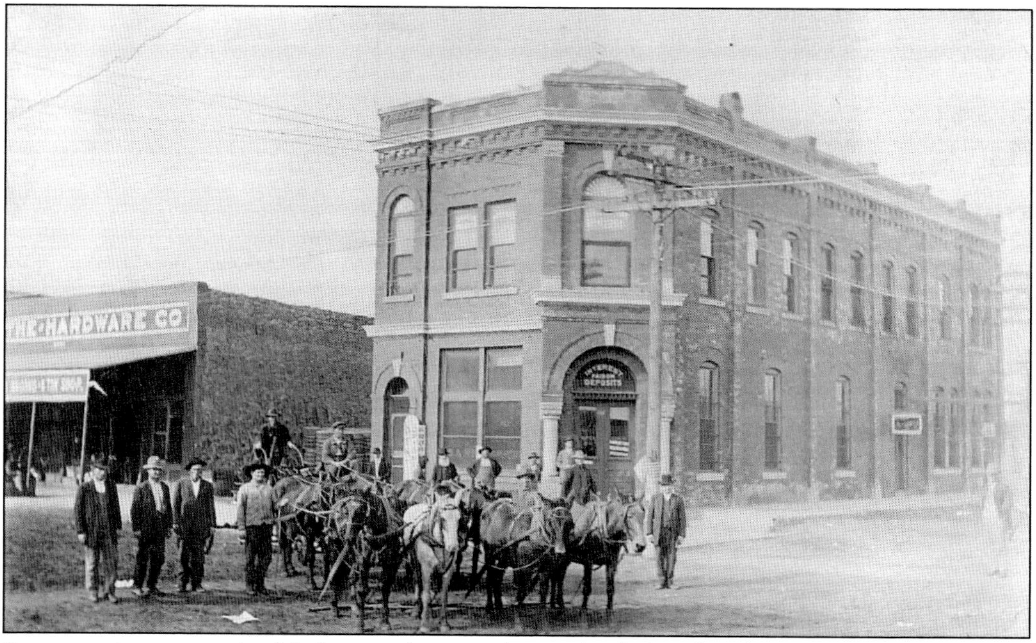

Street maintenance in Marlow as late as the end of the decade was simple by today's standards. Shown in front of the First National Bank building is a large team of mules used for periodic street grading.

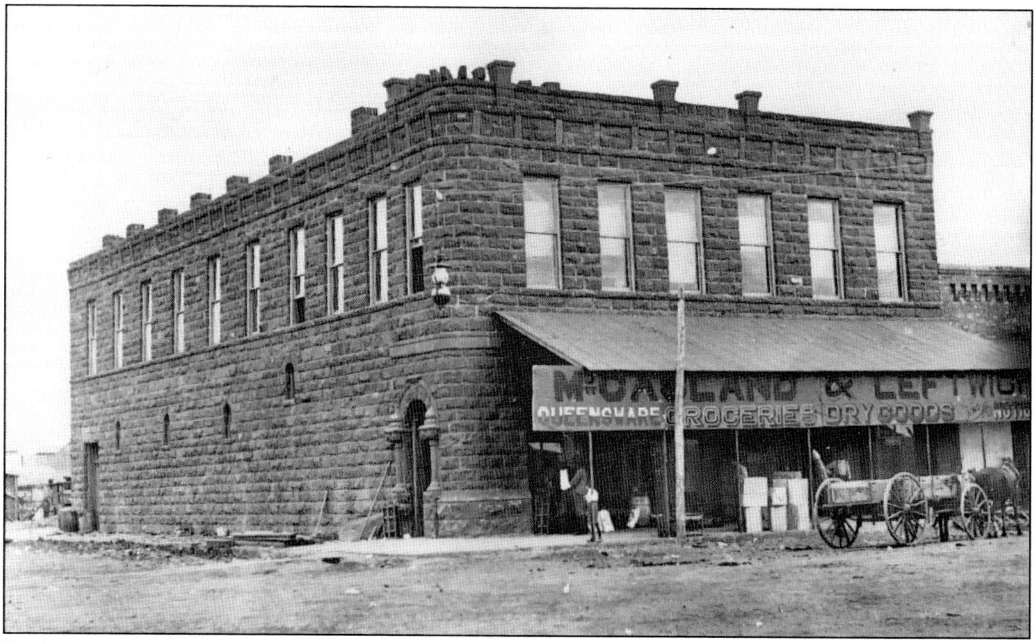

Built in 1901–1902 after fire destroyed an earlier store on the site, the O'Neill Building housed the McCasland and Leftwich Dry Goods store on the corner of Eighth and Main Streets. J.C. "Bud" McCasland was a successful merchant who, together with W.L. Brittain, later constructed the McCasland-Brittain Building still standing on Main Street. McCasland was the father of T.H. McCasland, founder of Mack Oil.

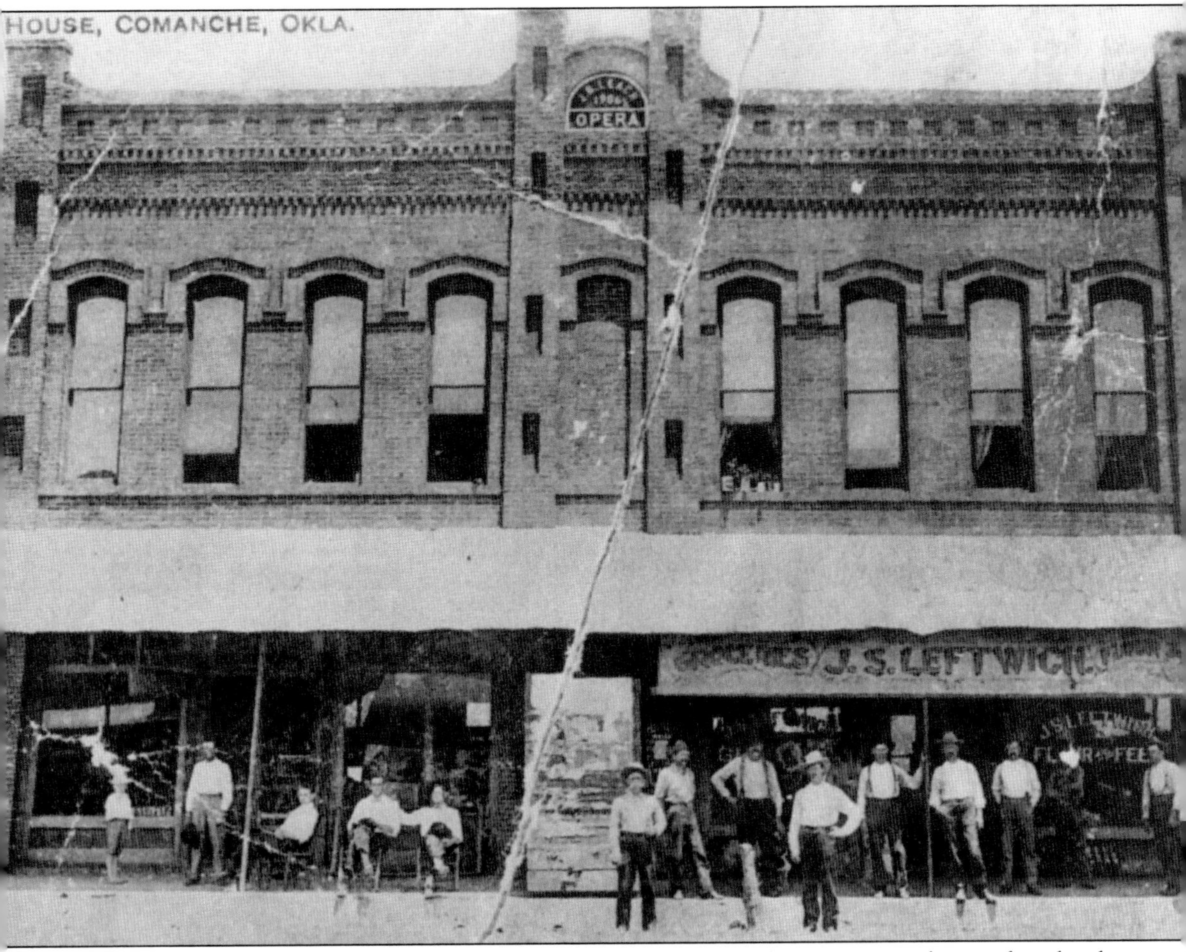

By the middle of the decade, Comanche boasted an opera house, situated in a fine brick structure. On the ground floor, at left, is the Leach store, and next to it, the Leftwich Grocery and Feed store.

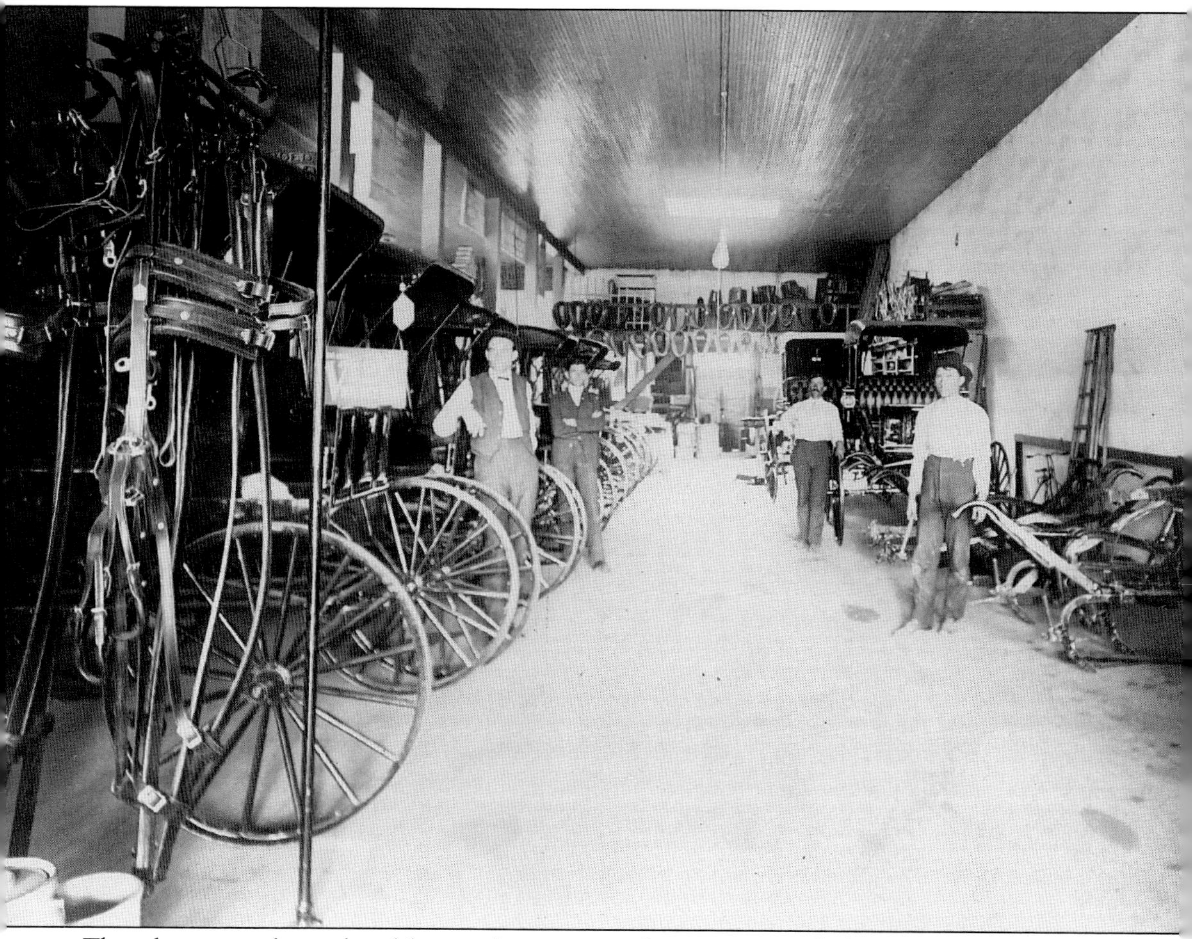

Though soon to be replaced by gasoline engines, horses were still the indispensable means of transportation in the middle of the decade. This Duncan store shows a complete array of tack and equipment.

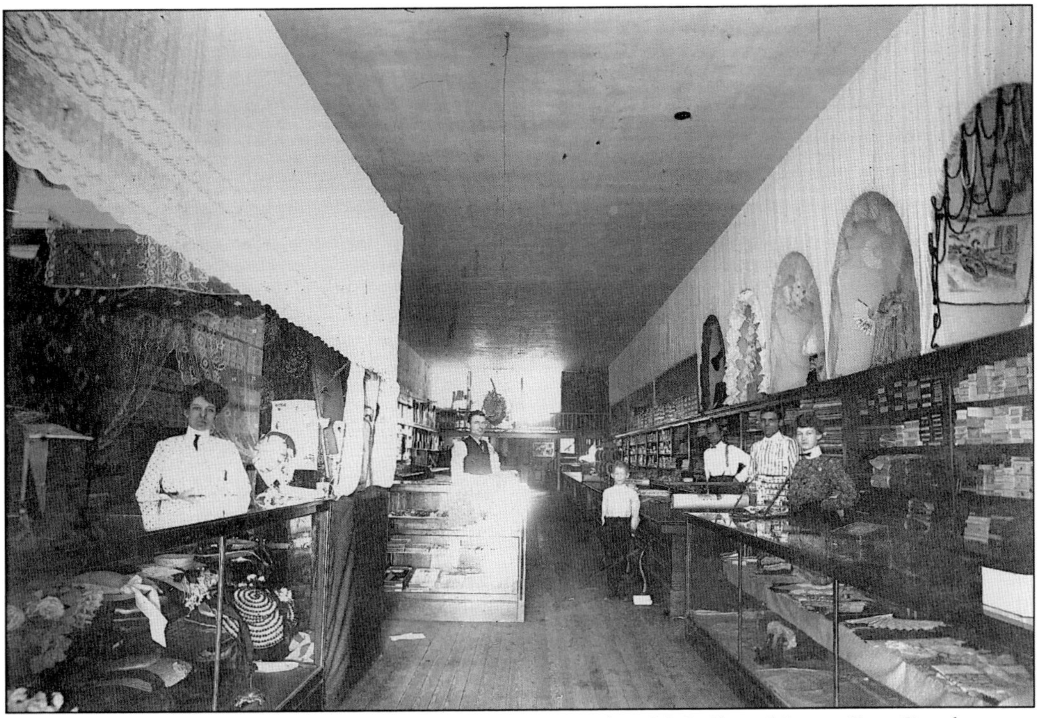

Among Duncan's successful merchandise stores were the O'Neill and Long Dry Goods store, pictured above in 1904, and the Sanitary Cash Grocery store, below. Both stores display a complete line of merchandise typical of the period.

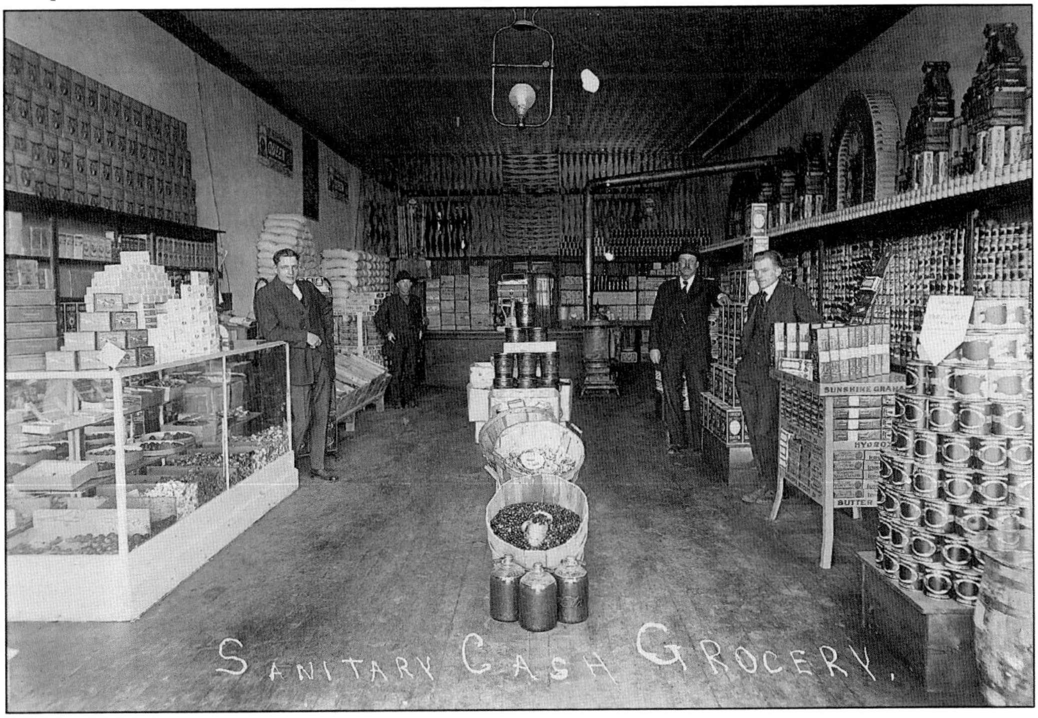

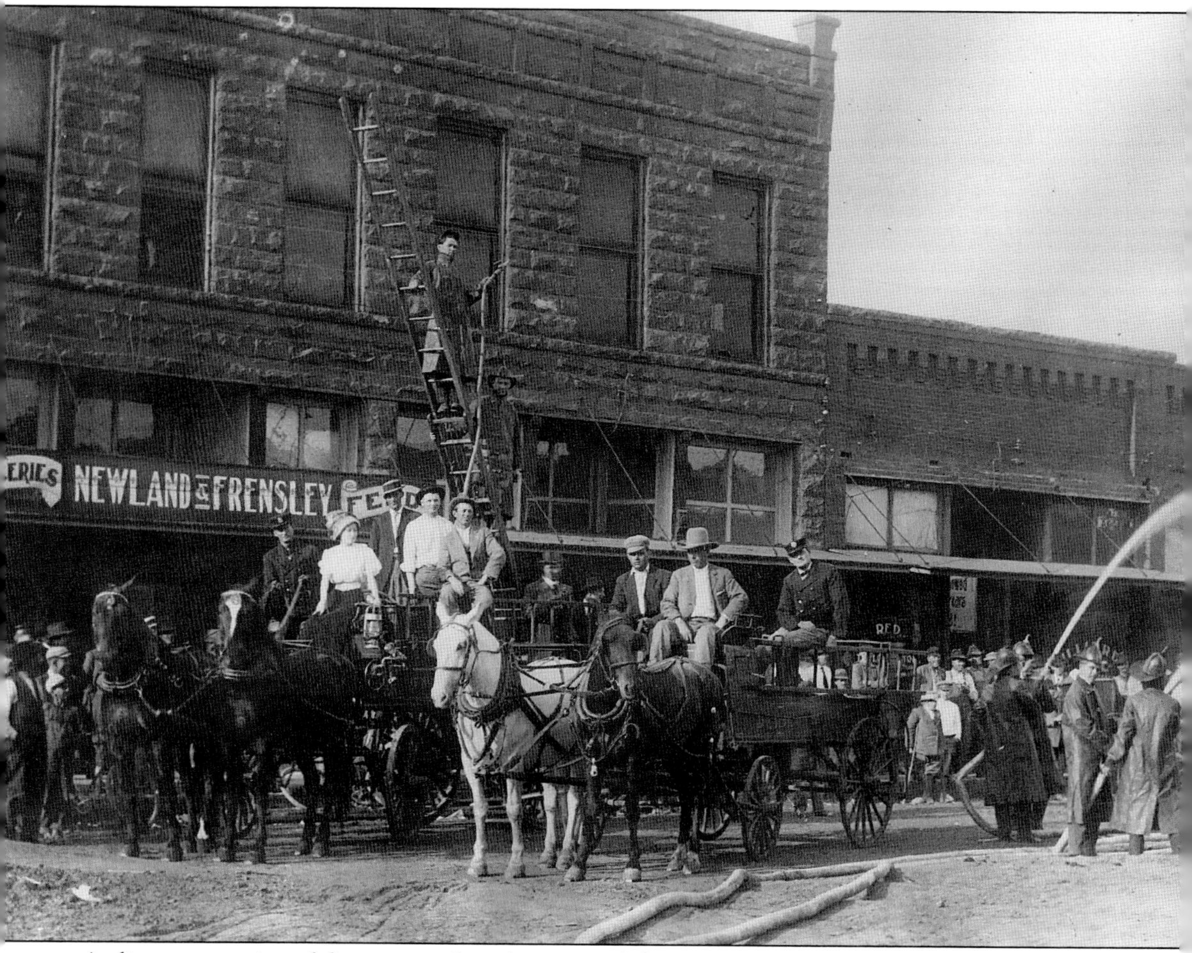

A disastrous series of fires soon after the turn of the century spurred two trends. First, new buildings began increasingly to be constructed of brick or stone, and second, the city developed an effective fire department. Pictured here in 1906, the department had two units, each drawn by two horses. As the city had fire hydrants, the department did not have a pumper. There were two full-time employees: a chief and a driver. The rest of the department members were volunteers. The two horses on the left, John and Joe, were so well trained that when the alarm sounded, they would step up on their own to where the harness hung from the ceiling, waiting to be harnessed.

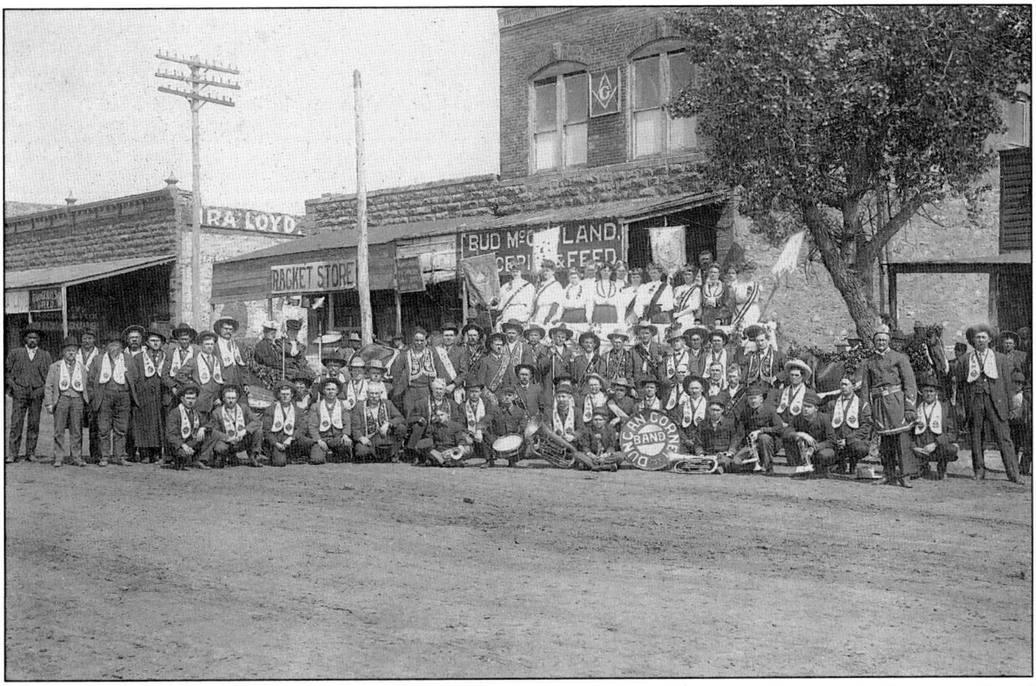

Bands continued in popularity into the twentieth century. Above is Duncan's Coronet Band photographed in front of Bud McCasland's new store at about 1905 or 1906. The band's vestments suggest a Masonic connection, made more likely as the local Masonic Lodge occupied the building's second floor. One of Comanche's most popular bands, the "Border Queen Band," is pictured below at about the same time.

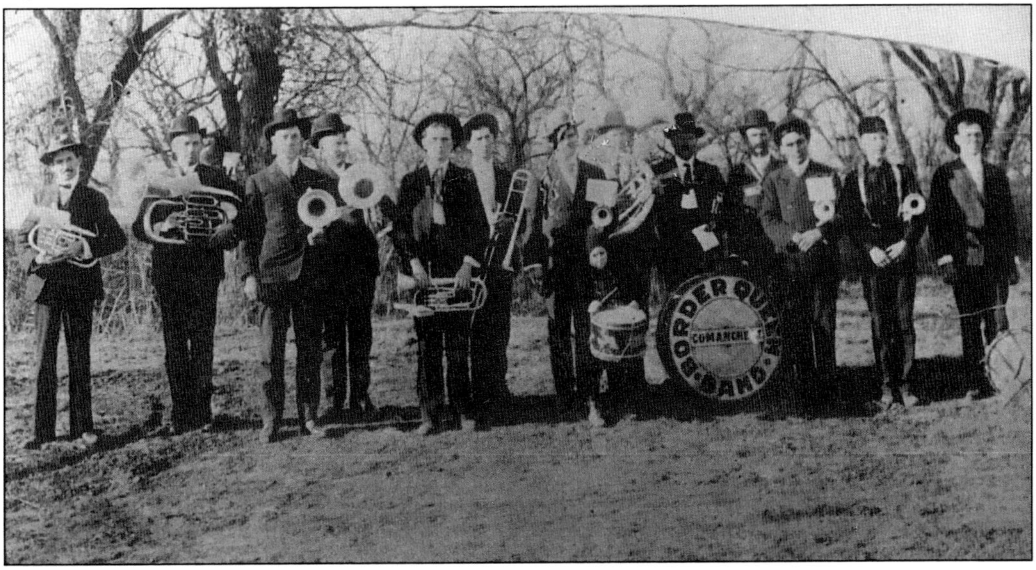

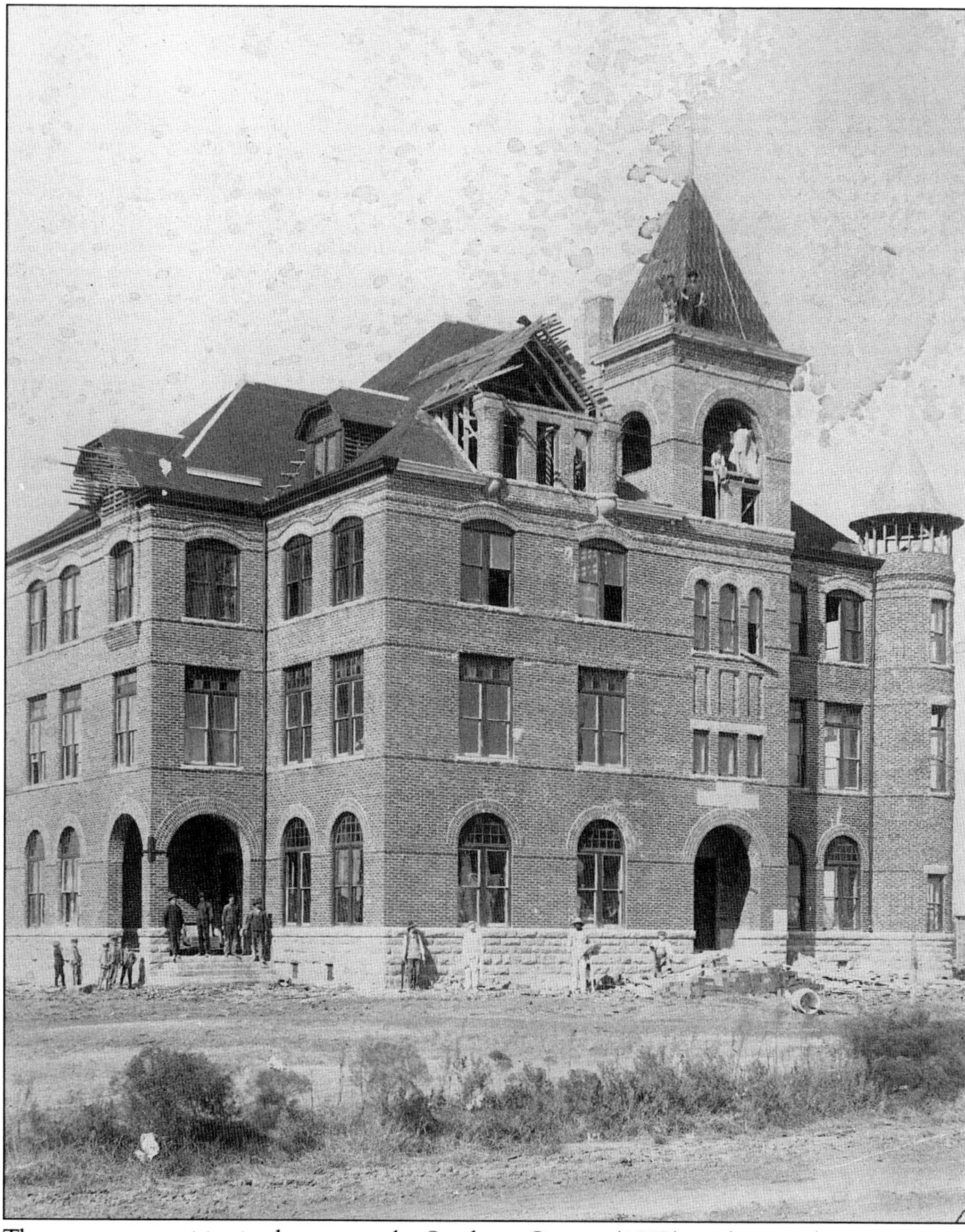

The new communities in the soon-to-be Stephens County (1907) paid particular attention to the education of their children. The size of Duncan's school suggests that the community was beginning to outstrip Marlow and Comanche in growth. Duncan's almost-completed high school is pictured in 1906. It was located on Eighth Street where the current middle school stands.

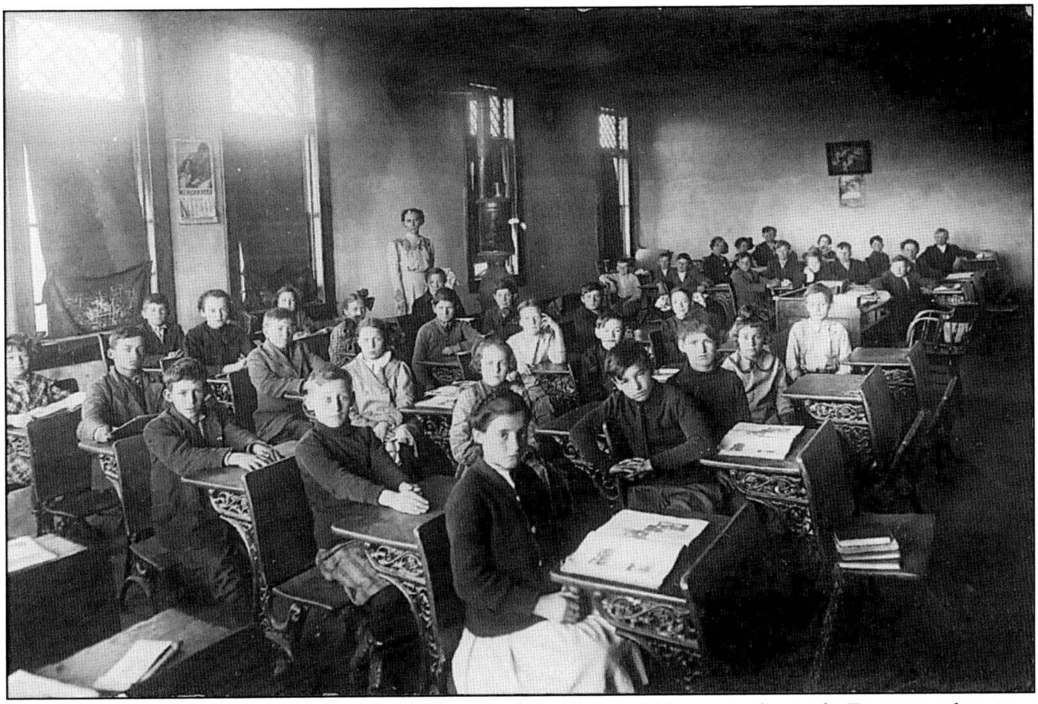

Mary Stitch, standing at the rear, was the teacher of this fifth or sixth grade Duncan class just after the turn of the century.

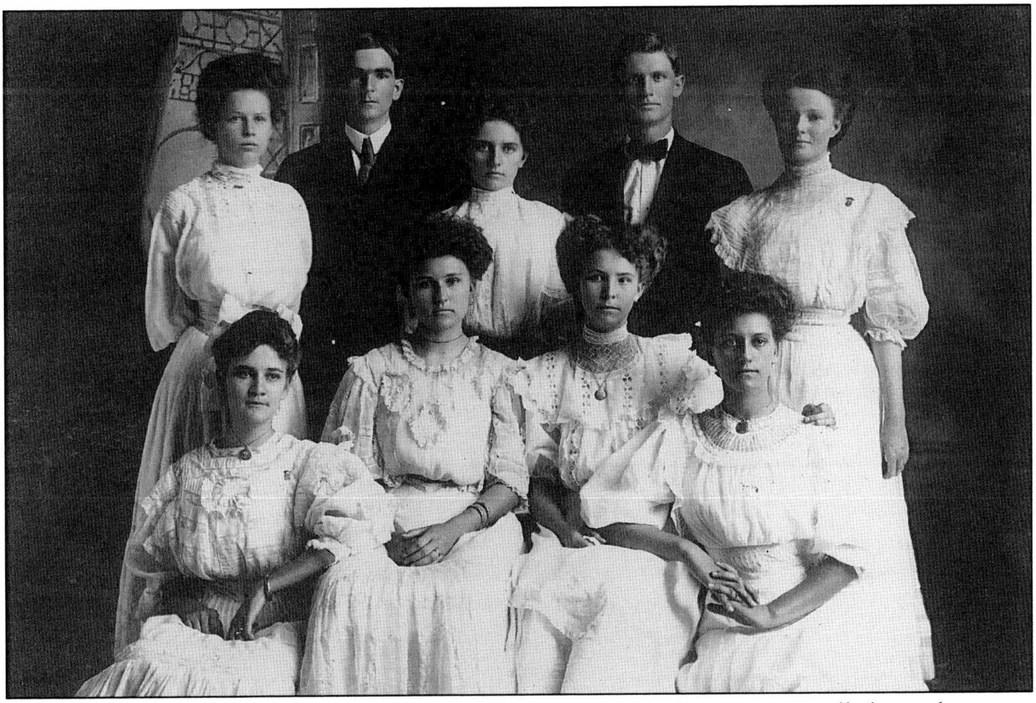

Duncan's Class of 1908, posing here for their graduation photo, was small, but subsequent classes steadily increased in size.

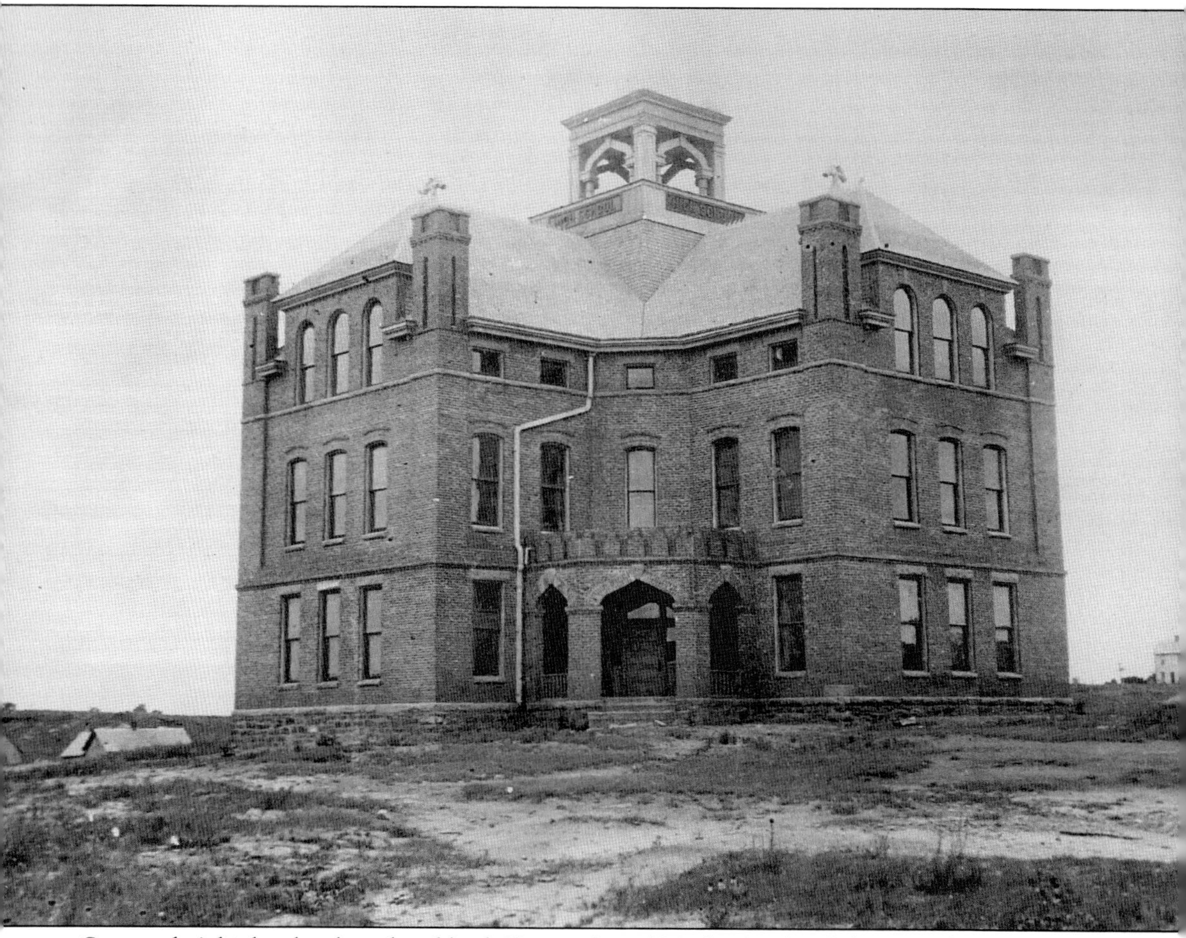

Comanche's high school predated both Duncan's and Marlow's schools by several years. Here it is shown, newly completed, in 1904.

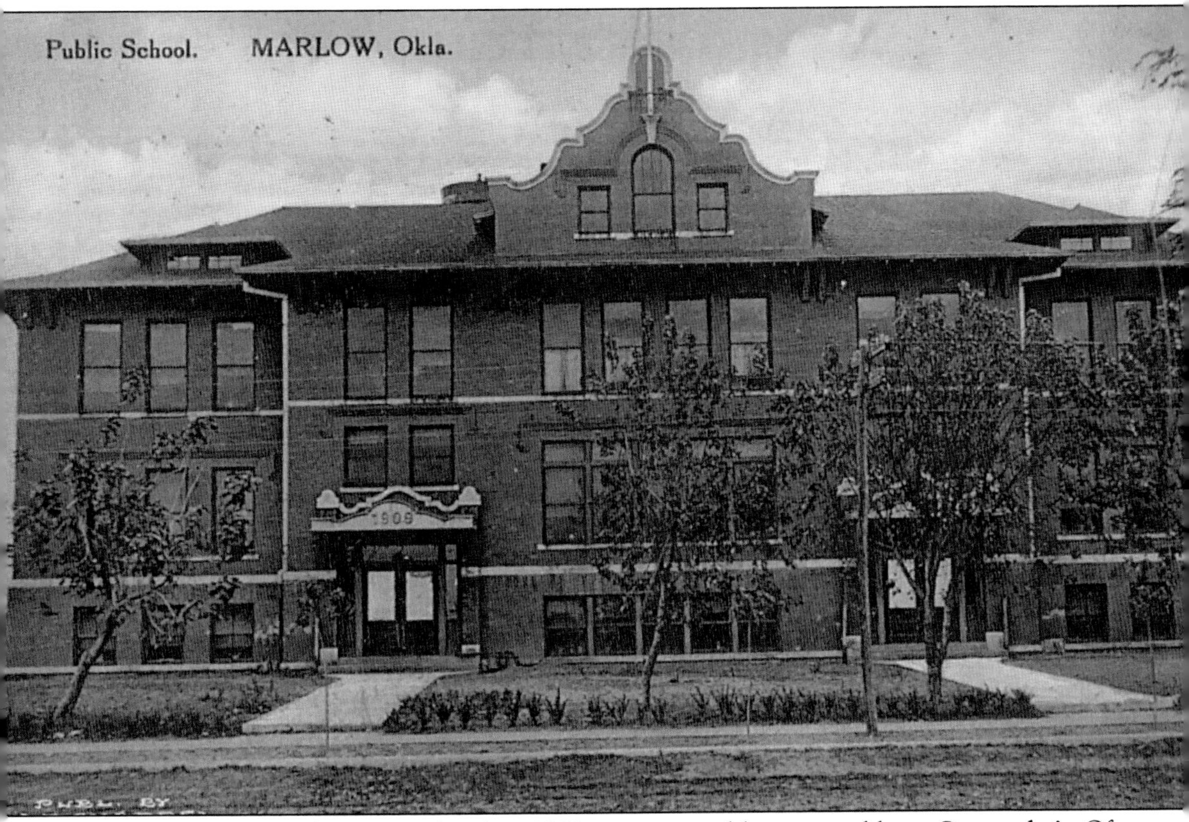

Marlow's high school was completed in 1909, in size roughly comparable to Comanche's. Of later construction, it reflects the "prairie-style" architecture that gained popularity by the end of the century's first decade.

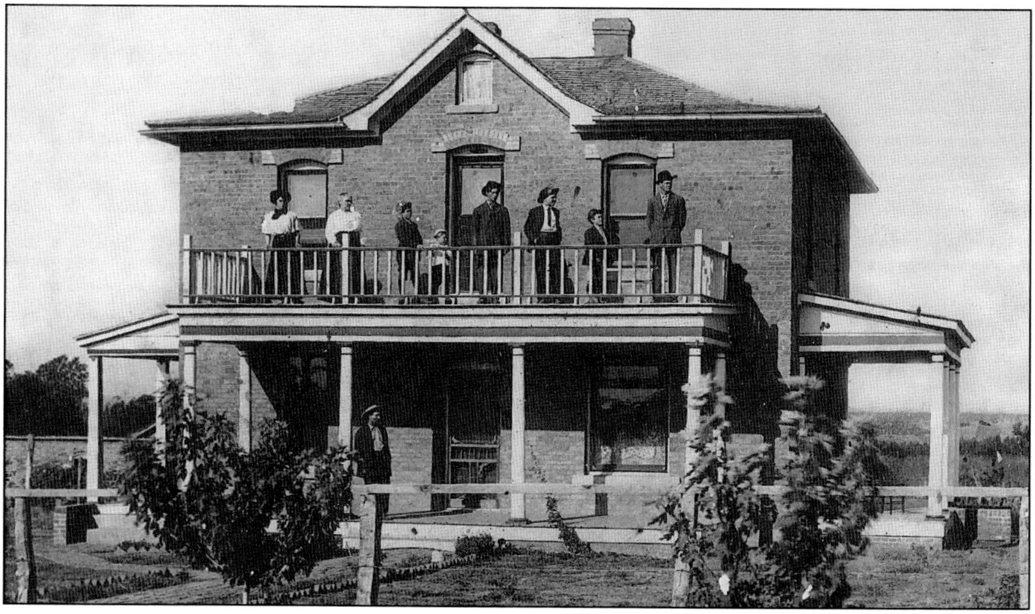

Community prosperity was reflected in the area's homes. Duncan's first brick home, constructed just after the turn of the century, was built for the Malone family by Mr. Malone, who owned Duncan's first brickyard, and Henry Jobert, an accomplished brick mason. Later, it became Duncan's first hospital when, in 1917, Dr. James Bartley purchased and remodeled it for that purpose. In 1925, with construction of a larger, more modern hospital, Bartley's hospital closed and the building was converted back to a residence.

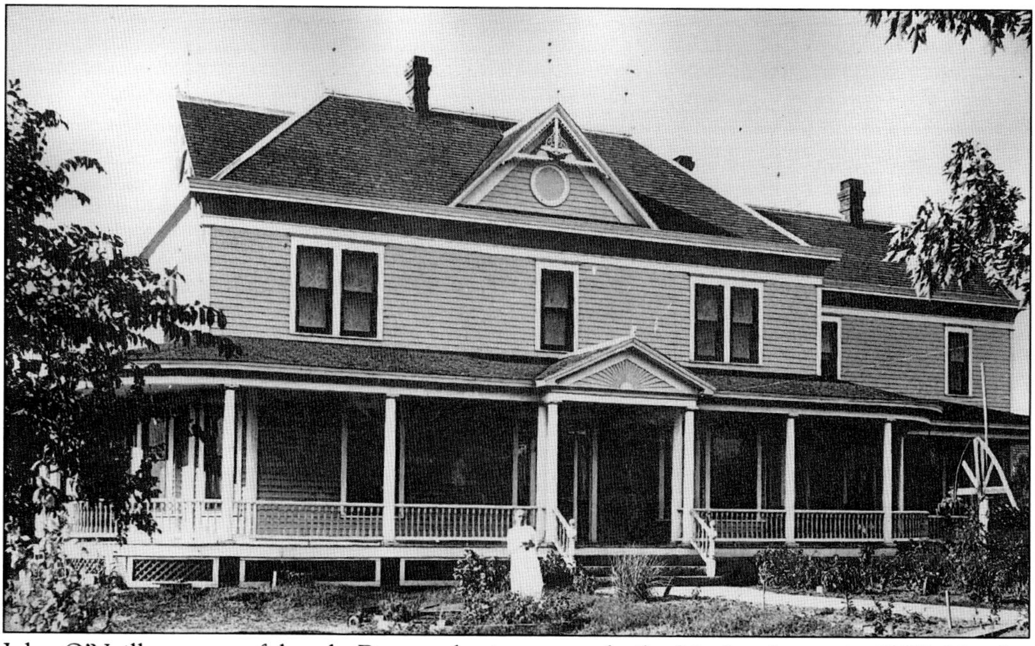

John O'Neill, a successful early Duncan businessman, built this fine home in 1907. He also opened it to the community when it became the first location for Catholic church gatherings.

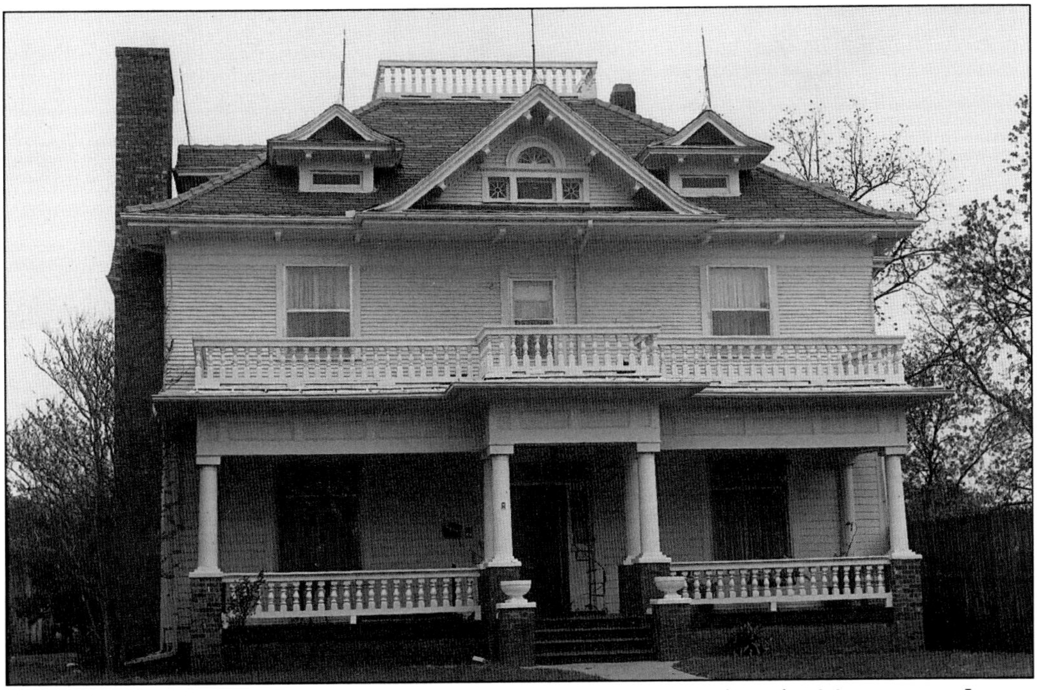

Marlow's prosperity in the first decade of the century is reflected in the Montgomery-Liman house, built in 1909.

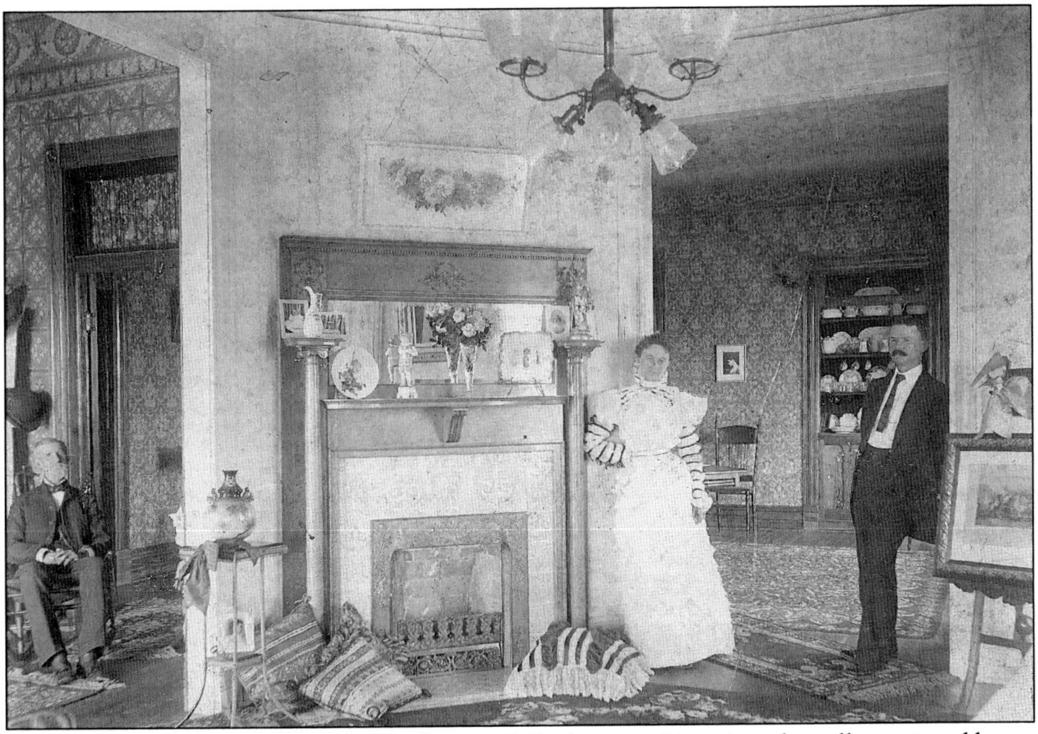

This unidentified photograph reveals the tastefully decorated interior of a well-appointed home located somewhere in Stephens County.

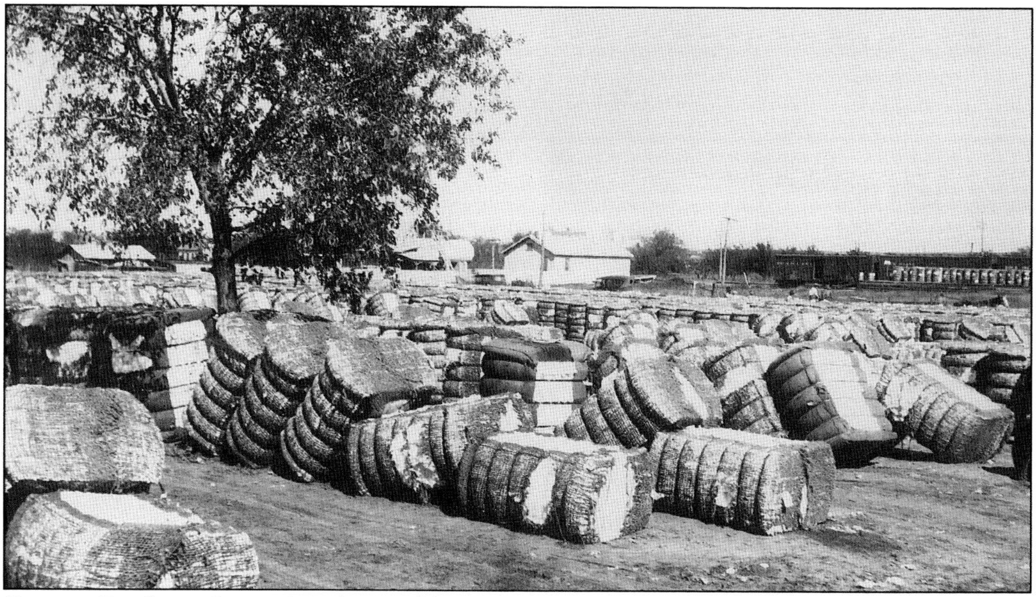

Cotton, Stephens County's "white gold," was reaching its peak as a cash crop by the end of the first decade. Evidence of its importance to the county is seen in the field of cotton bales awaiting loading on the Rock Island.

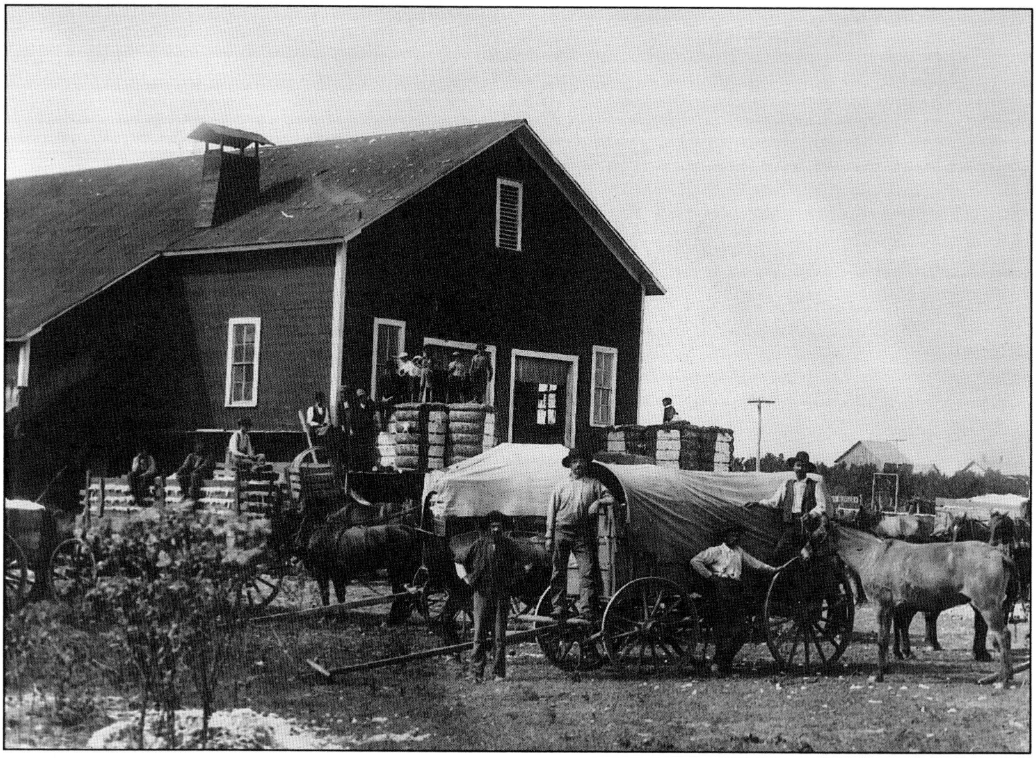

By the end of the decade, Duncan listed five cotton gins among its businesses. Comanche, likewise, had five, and Marlow, a similar number. By the early 1920s, Marlow had 13 gins in operation. Frank Fuqua's gin in Duncan, above, is shown about 1906.

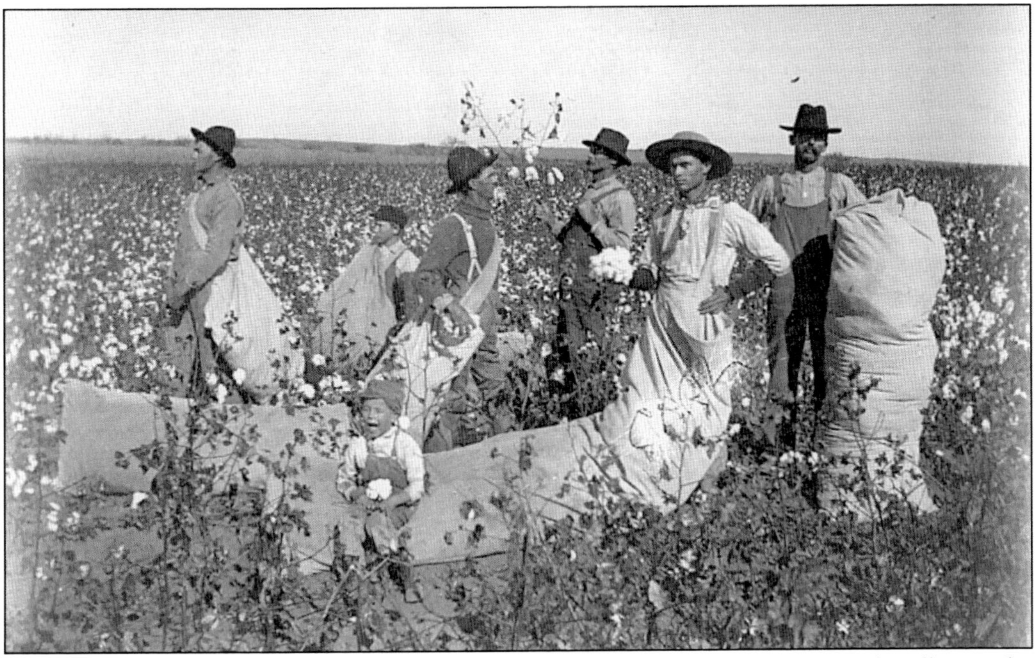

Picking cotton by hand, as illustrated by the Albright family above, continued well into the middle of the twentieth century. Nevertheless, agricultural mechanization appeared early in Stephens County, probably just after the century's turn. It was evident for certain by 1908, the date of the threshing machine pictured below working on the Albright farm. It was located 5 miles southwest of Marlow. The steam-powered thresher was owned and operated by Ben Hlavaty.

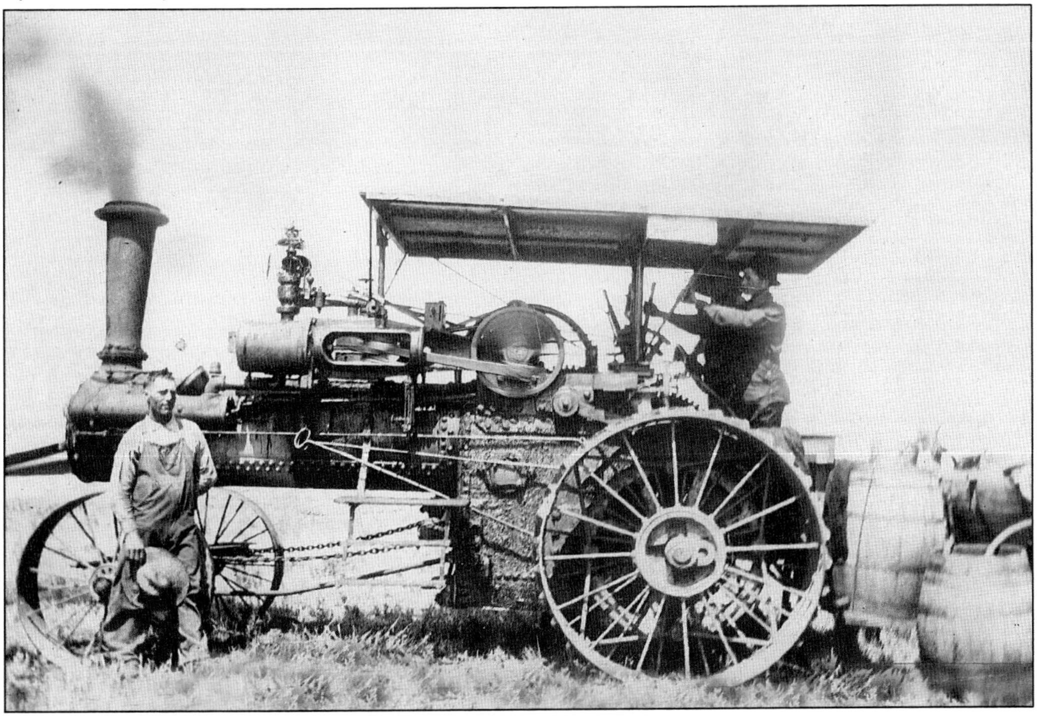

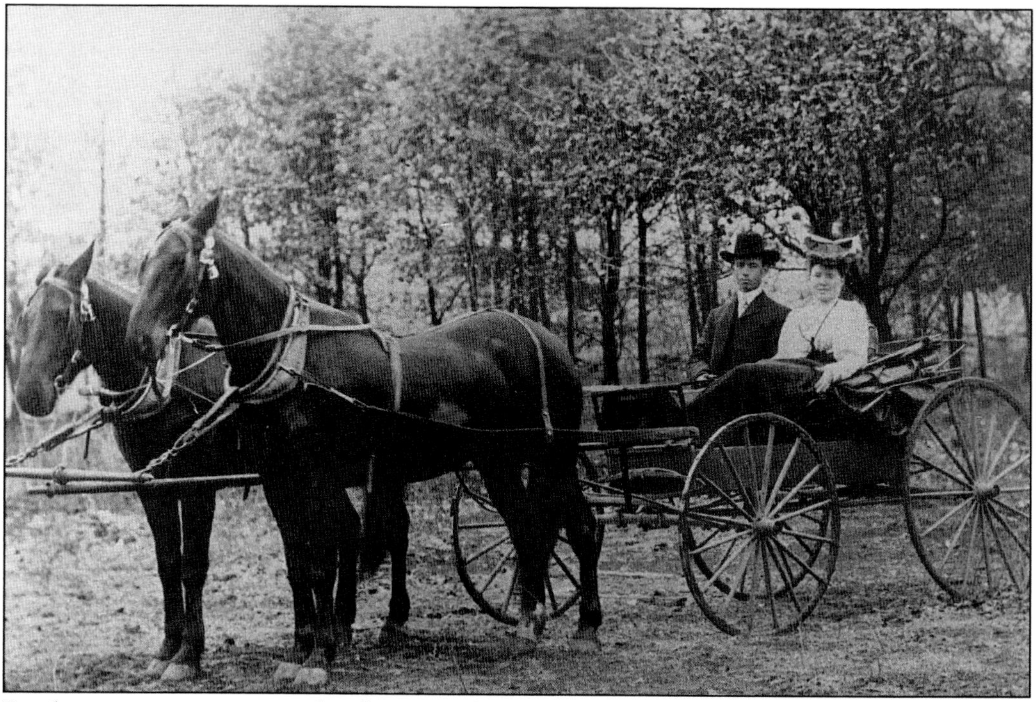

Sunday outings were a popular diversion during this period. Mr. and Mrs. Harold Moore of Alma, above, and Leonard and Lenora Bumpas, below, show off their Sunday finery.

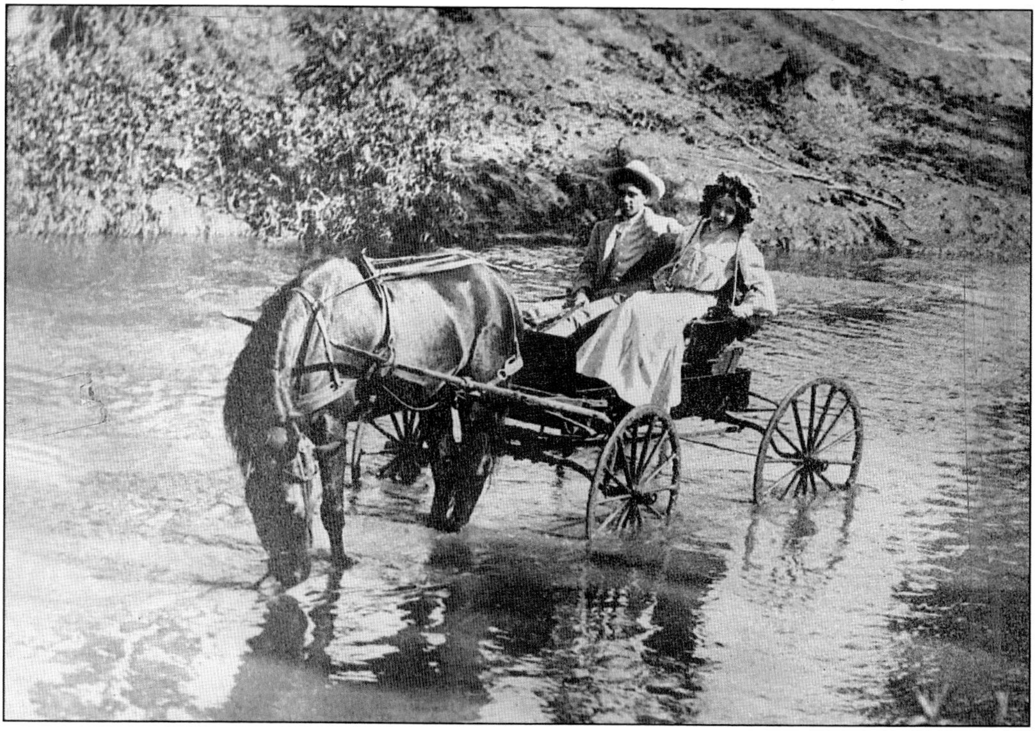

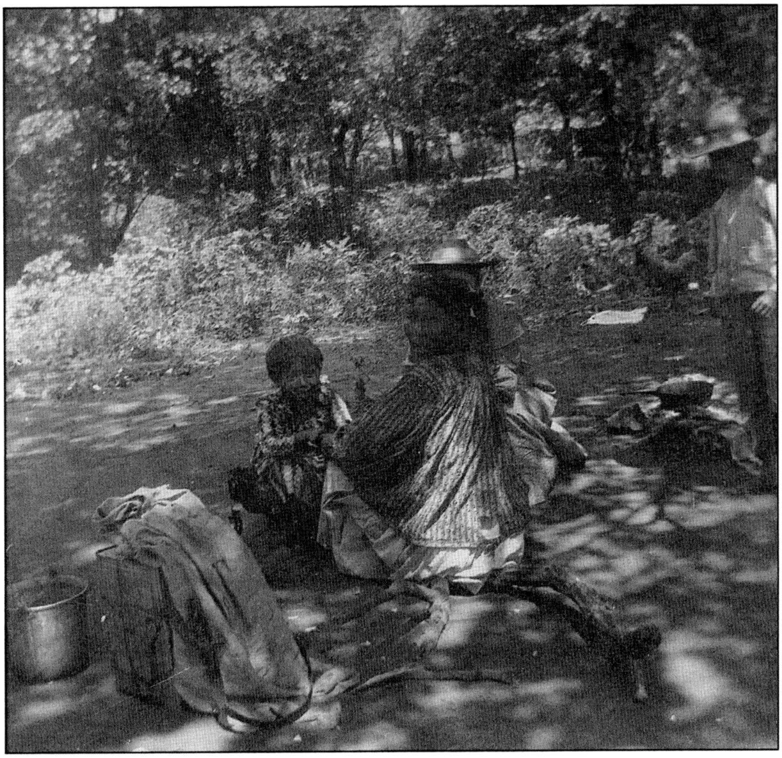

Though not often referred to in day-to-day histories of the county, Native Americans were nonetheless a familiar sight. Many were landowners and ranchers, having taken a land allotment before the territory was open to general settlement, and they became prominent citizens. The photos on this page show two Native American families from the area in the early 1900s.

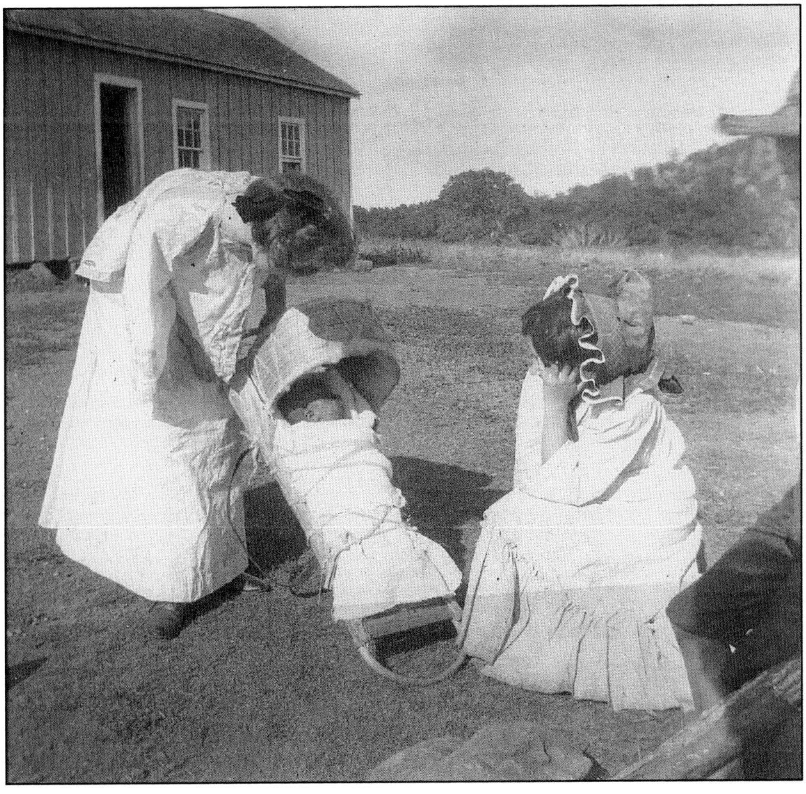

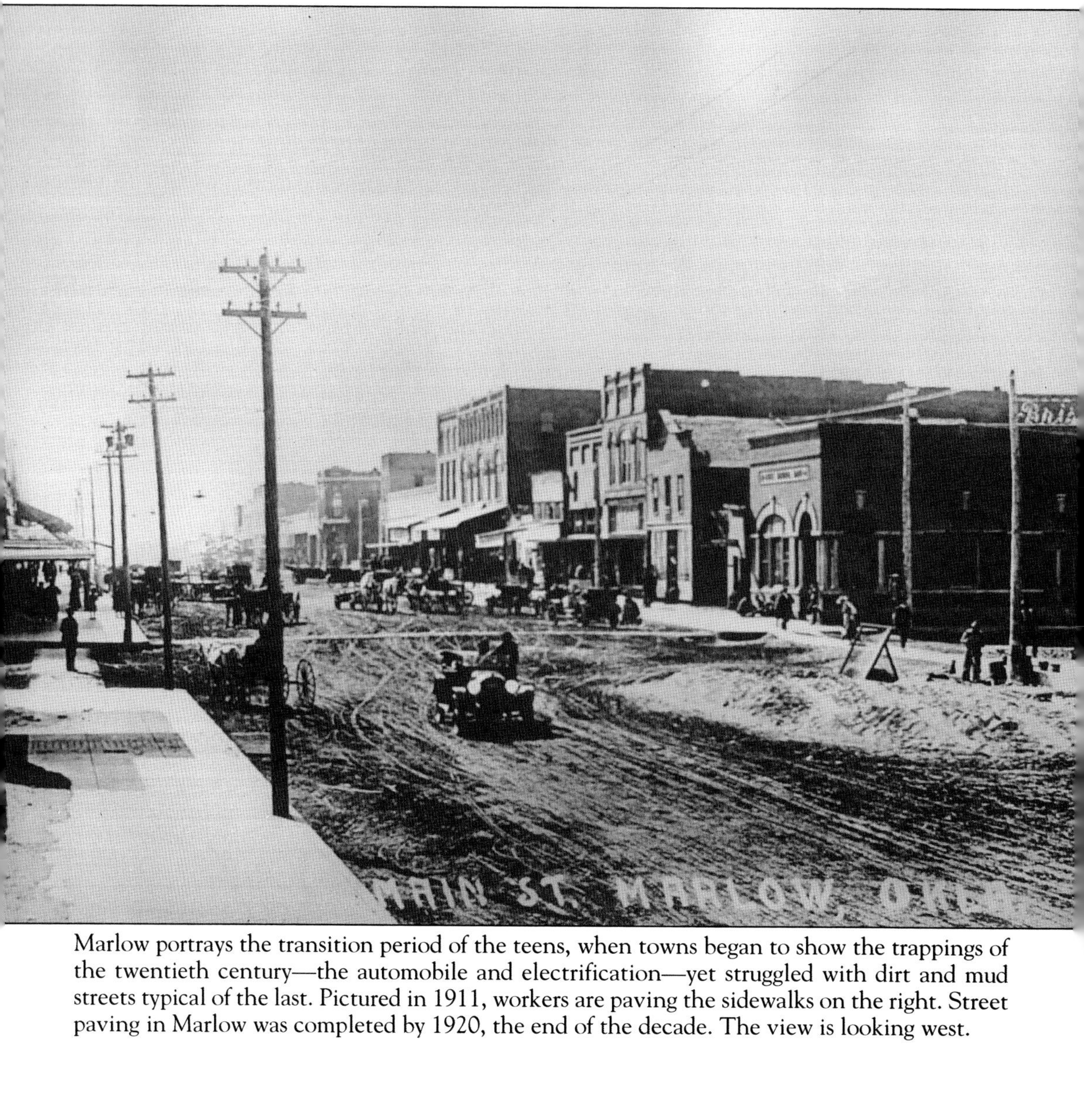

Marlow portrays the transition period of the teens, when towns began to show the trappings of the twentieth century—the automobile and electrification—yet struggled with dirt and mud streets typical of the last. Pictured in 1911, workers are paving the sidewalks on the right. Street paving in Marlow was completed by 1920, the end of the decade. The view is looking west.

Three

CONSOLIDATION AND GROWTH

THE TEEN YEARS

The teen years were in many respects a transition period for the county and its communities as mechanization entered into farming, the automobile shortened distance times, communications became quicker, oil was discovered, and world events had a greater impact; yet most of the county remained pretty much a reflection of the past century.

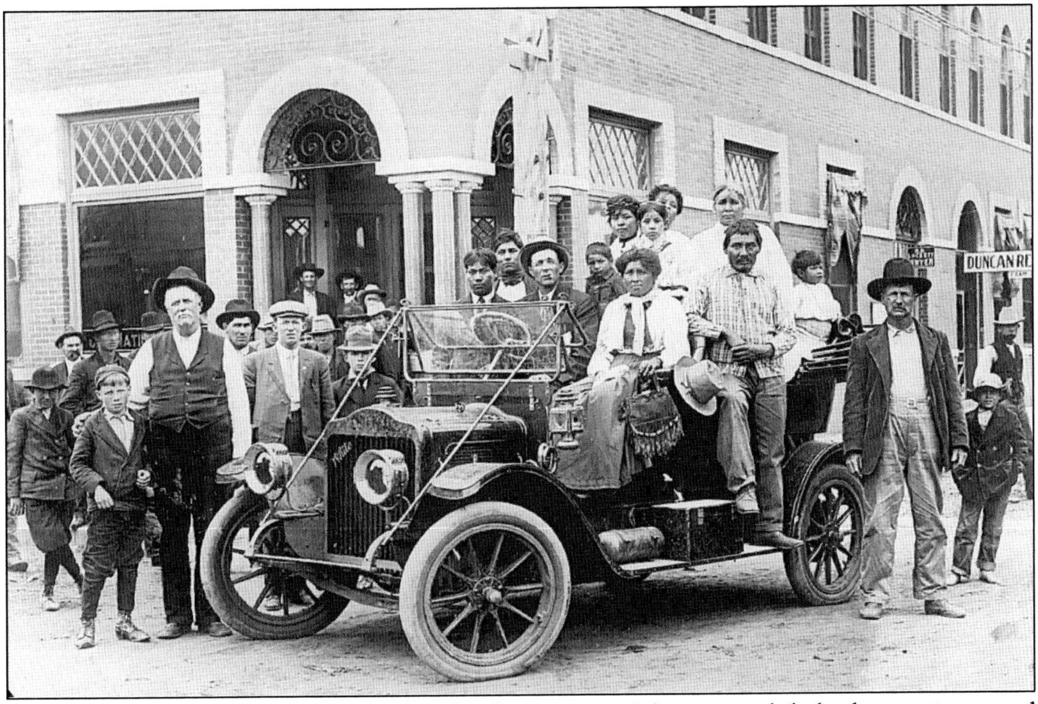

Captured here is the essence of the decade: the coming of the automobile both as an improved means of transportation and as a symbol of prosperity. The photo appears to have been taken in about 1916 in front of Duncan's City National Bank at the corner of Main and Eighth Streets.

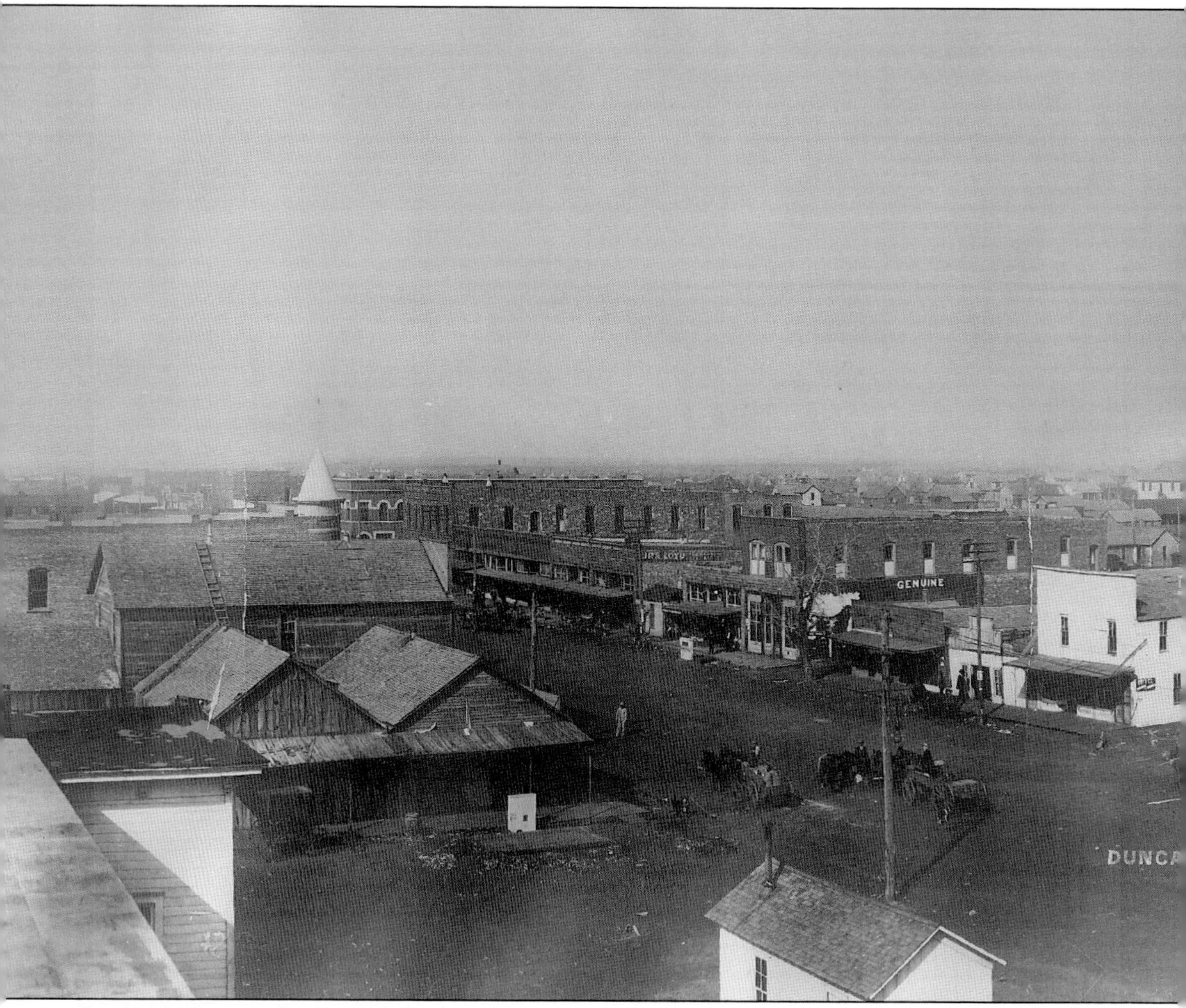

By 1910, Duncan had established itself in the configuration that would last for almost a half-century. Note the turret of the city hall left of center. It remained in use until a new building was constructed in 1951, and was torn down in 1962. The view looks northwest from Seventh and Main Streets.

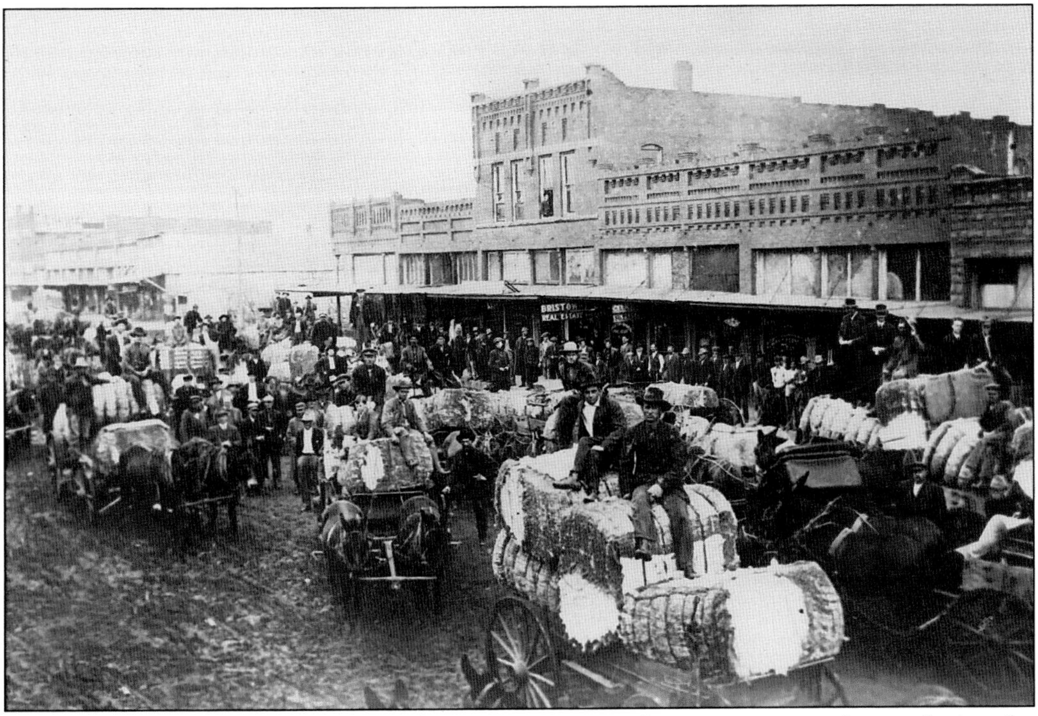

Main Street of Comanche in 1914 shows a prosperous, busy community. It was during the decade of the teens that the cotton industry reached its peak in Stephens County.

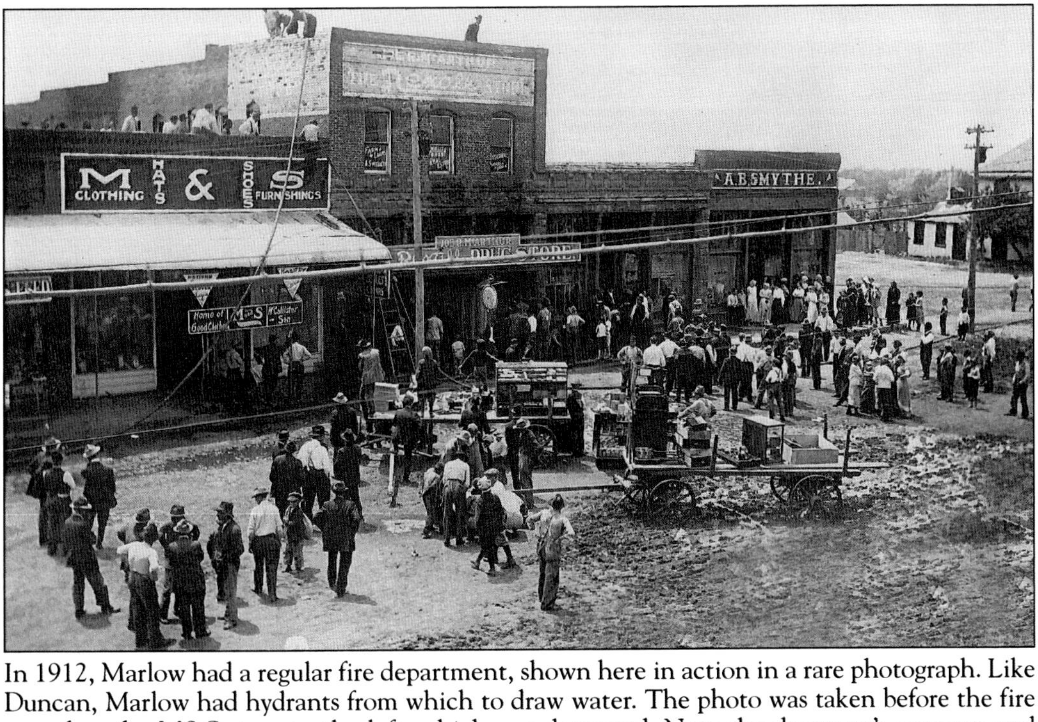

In 1912, Marlow had a regular fire department, shown here in action in a rare photograph. Like Duncan, Marlow had hydrants from which to draw water. The photo was taken before the fire spread to the M&S store to the left, which was destroyed. Note the drugstore's counters and merchandise on the wagons and in the street.

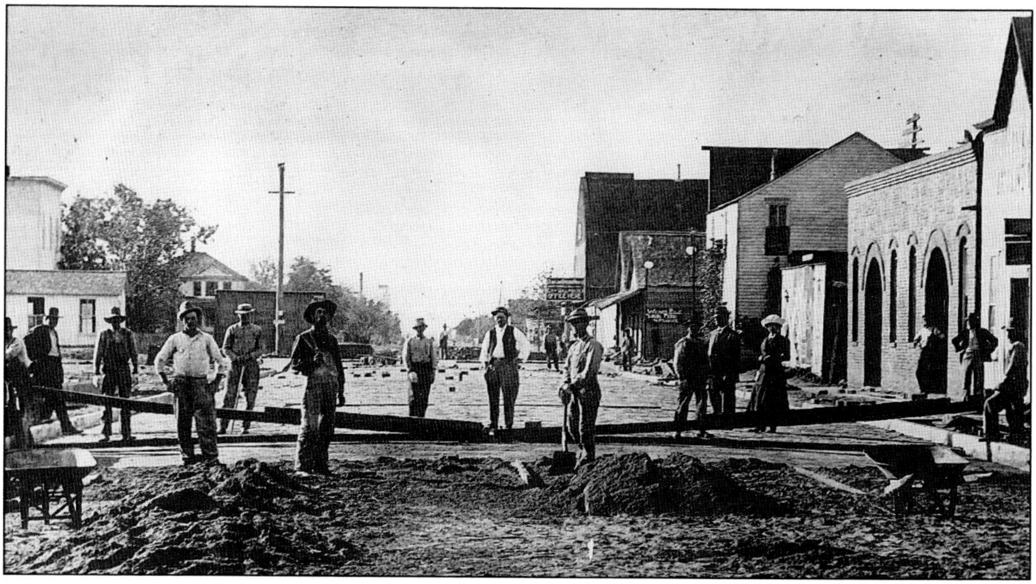

Public works continued during the decade in all three towns. Above, Duncan is laying brick on Seventh Street in about 1911, while below, Comanche is preparing a stretch of future Highway U.S. 81 for paving in about 1919.

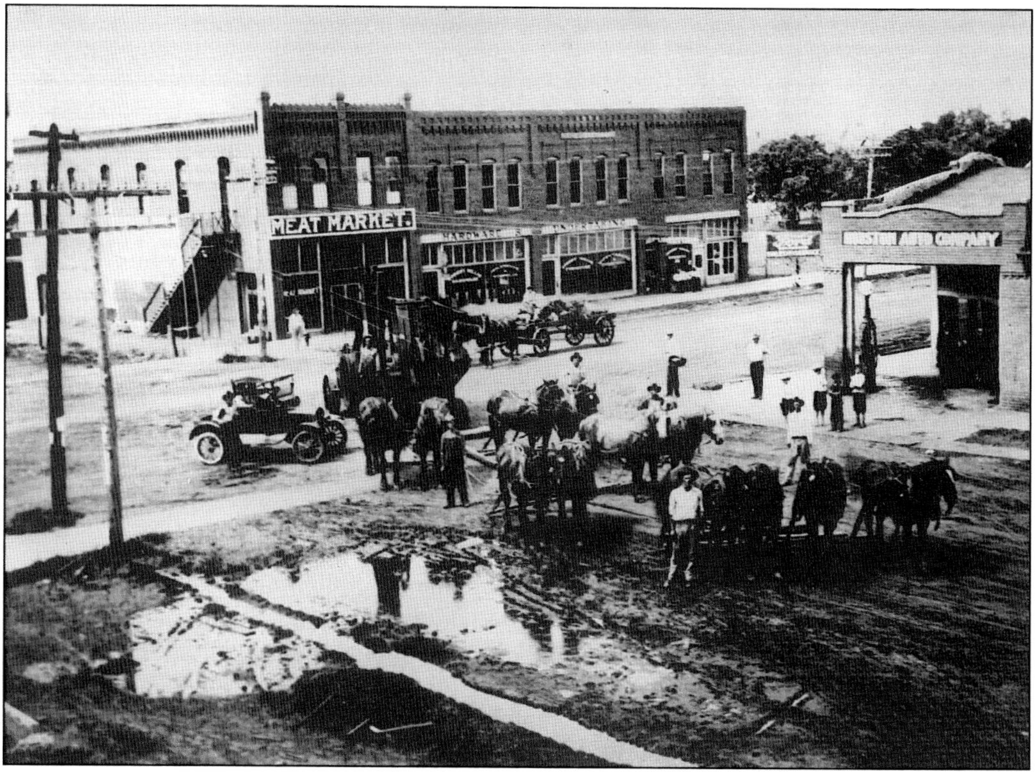

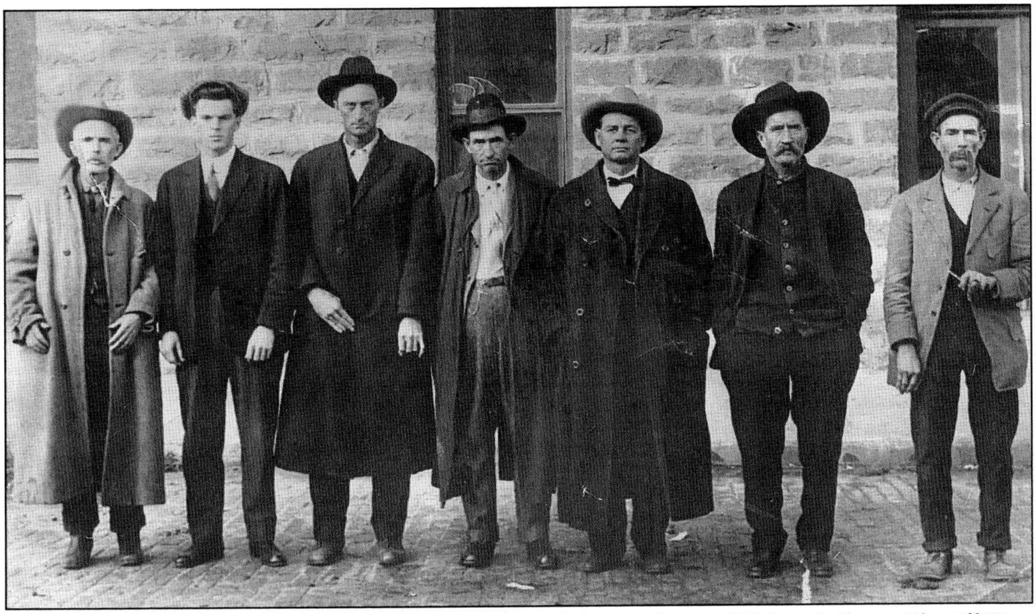

Stephens County peace officers are pictured, from left to right, in 1913 as follows: Sheriff Tom Bray, Deputy Lynn Boykin, unidentified, Deputy Bob Pearson, Deputy A.V. Moore, jailer Press Latham, and custodian Jack Latham.

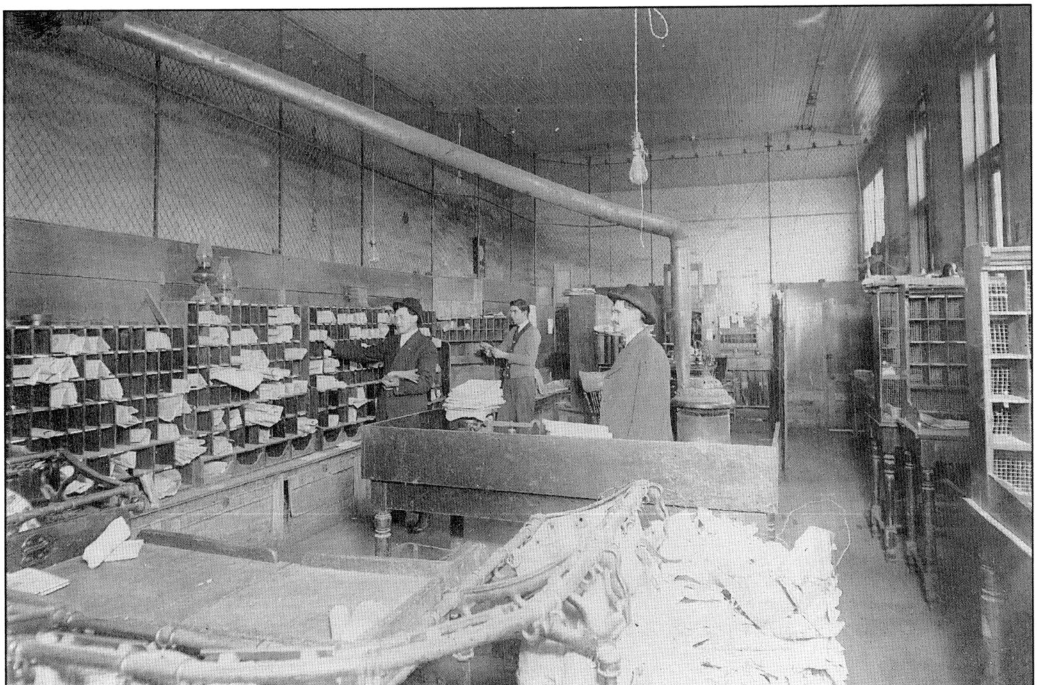

An interior view of Duncan's post office from about 1912 shows, from left to right, postal clerks Charles Broadbent and Alonzo Wharton. The third man is unidentified.

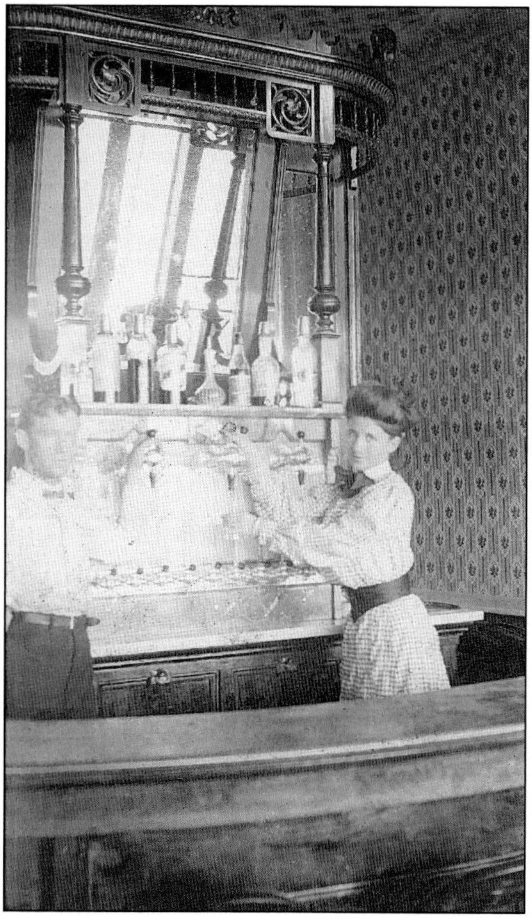

Ice cream parlors and restaurants came into great popularity during this period. Pictured to the left around 1912 is a soda fountain in Marlow, and below is Wallace Williams' Bakery and Ice Cream Store on Duncan's Main Street in 1910 or 1911.

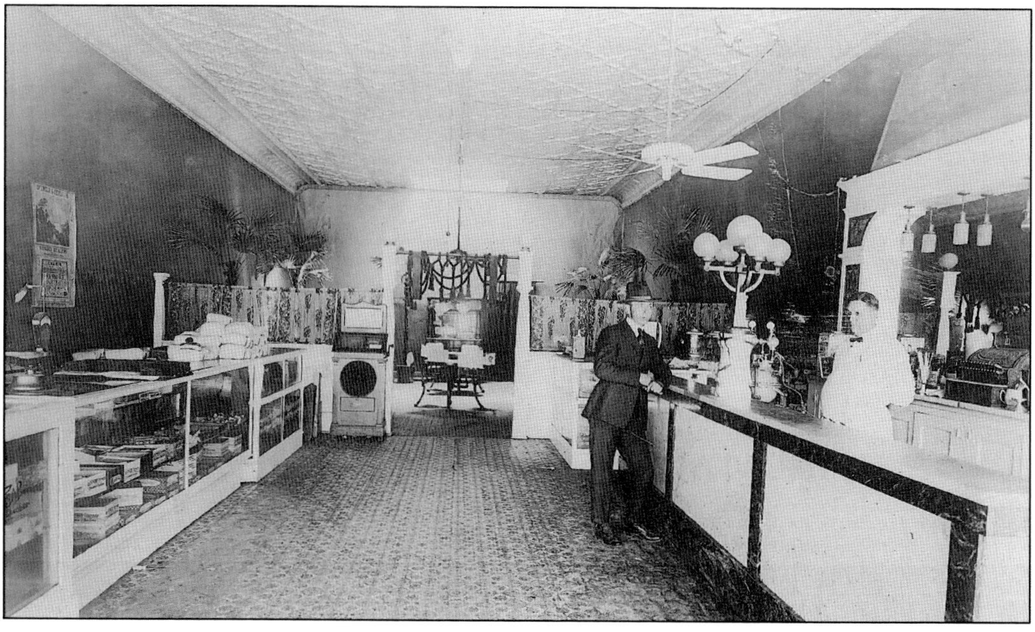

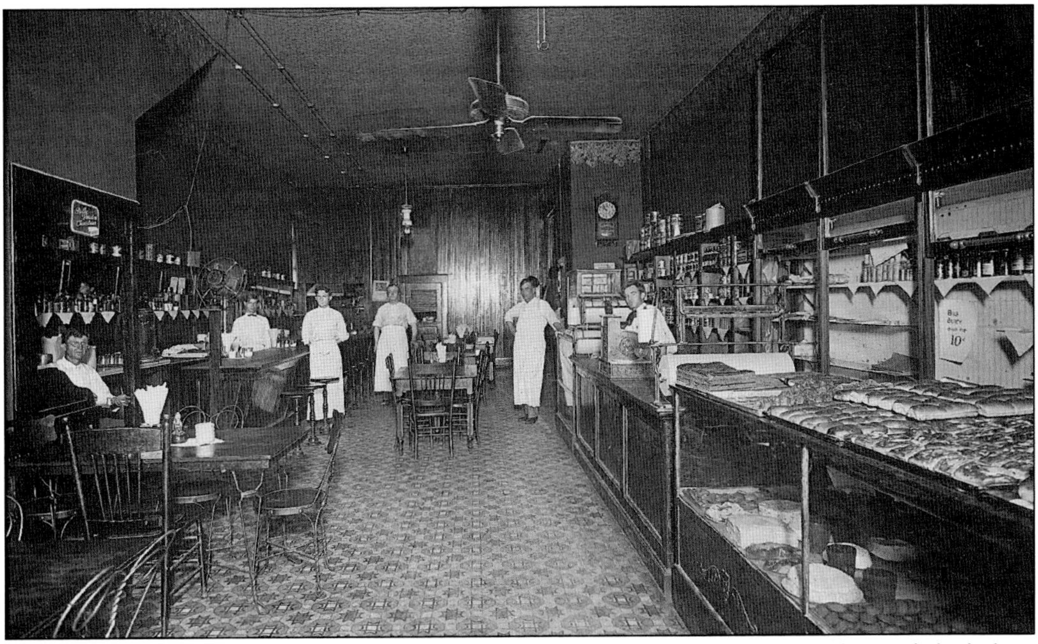

Above is an unidentified bakery and restaurant, perhaps located in Marlow, while below, Duncan's Midway Hotel's café is pictured in 1915.

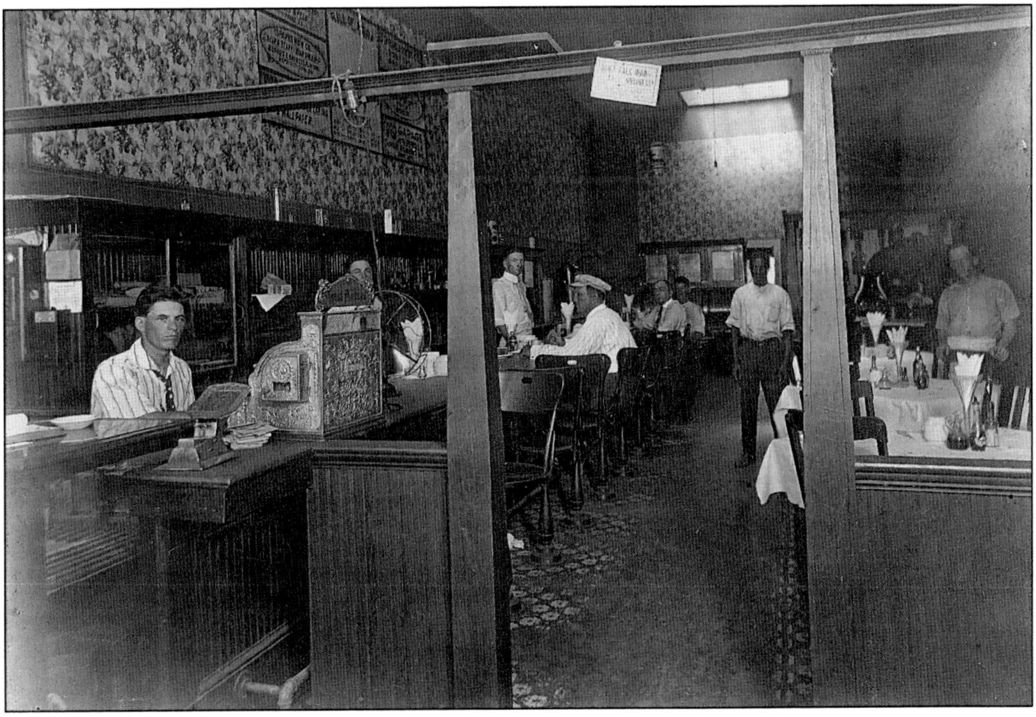

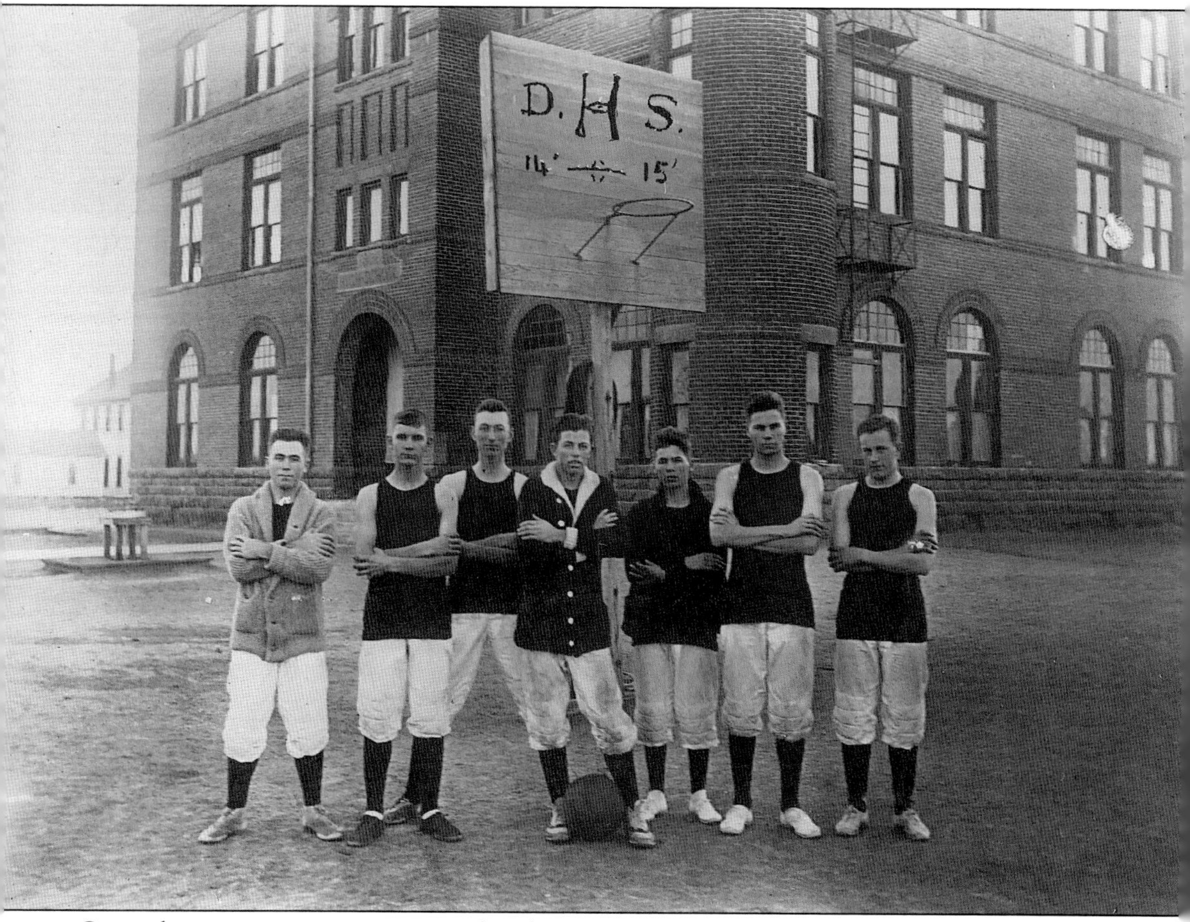

Sports became an important part of each community's school programs during this decade. Duncan High School's basketball team is pictured in 1915.

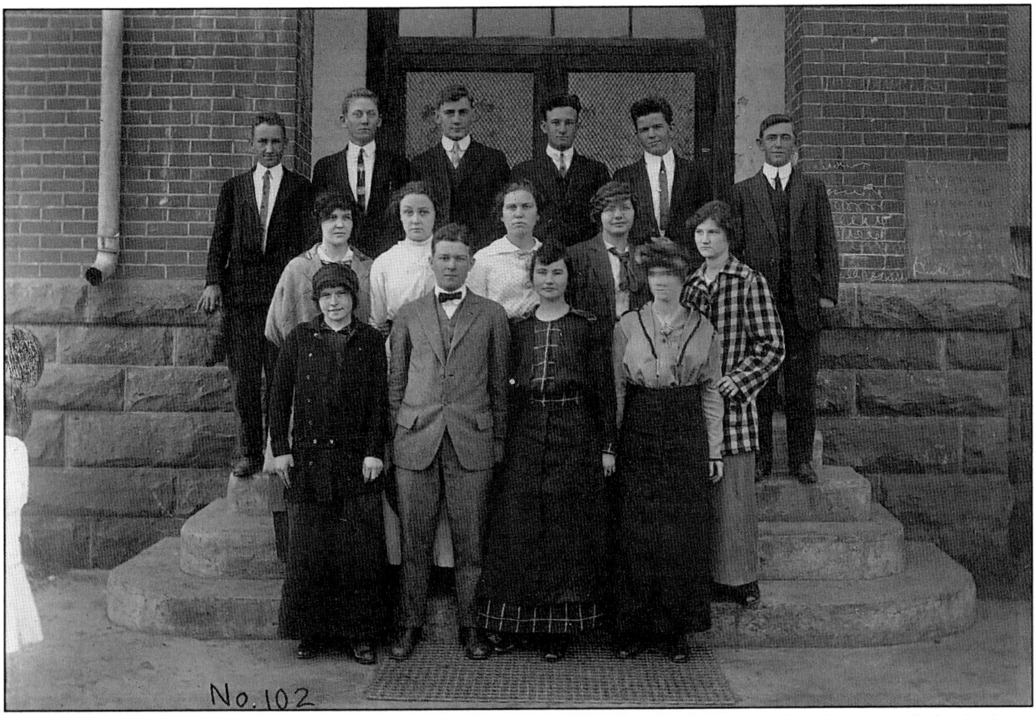

Duncan High School's junior class of 1915 pose for their photograph above, while below, Duncan High School's student body gather for an assembly in 1913.

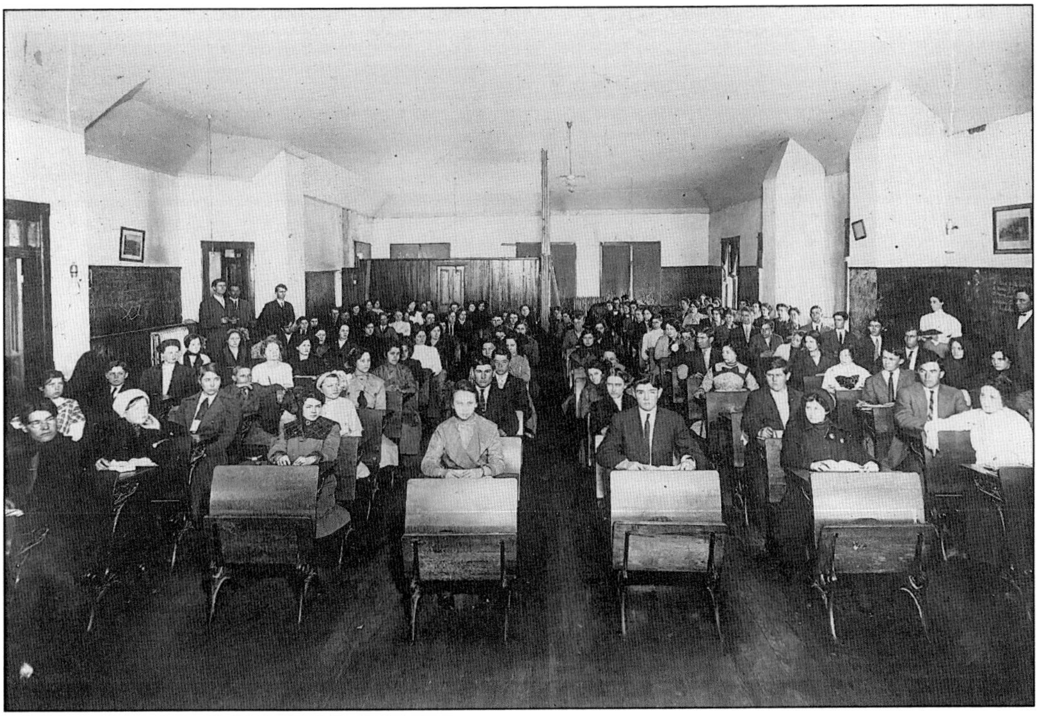

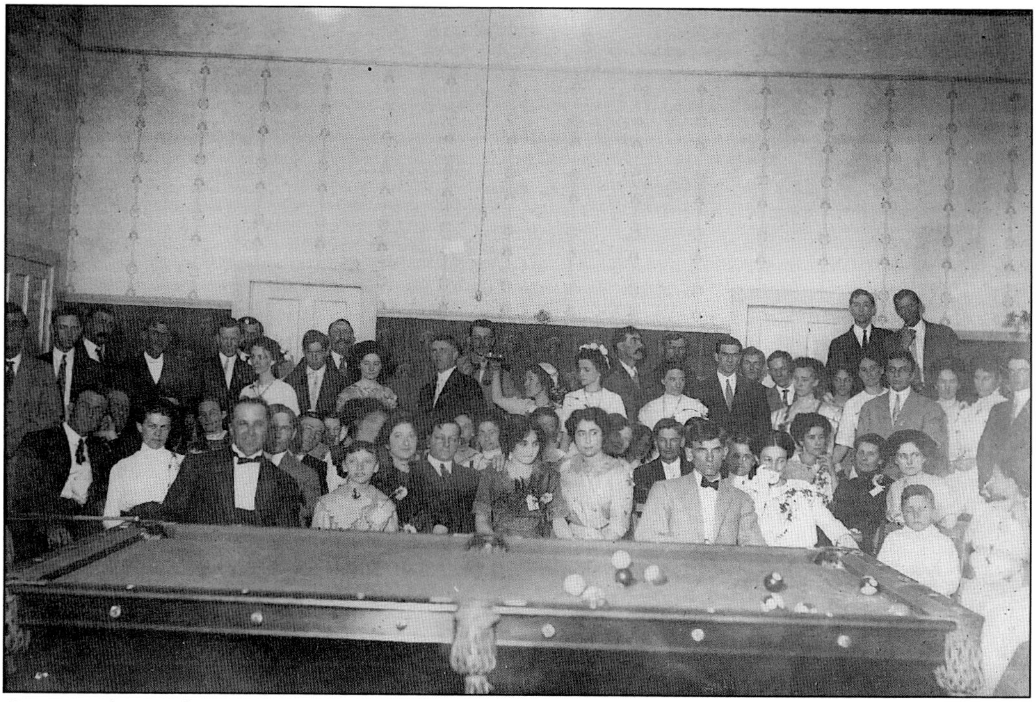

Civic and social organizations developed in each of Stephens County's communities, as illustrated by the opening of Duncan's Moose Lodge in 1911. The occasion was a family affair.

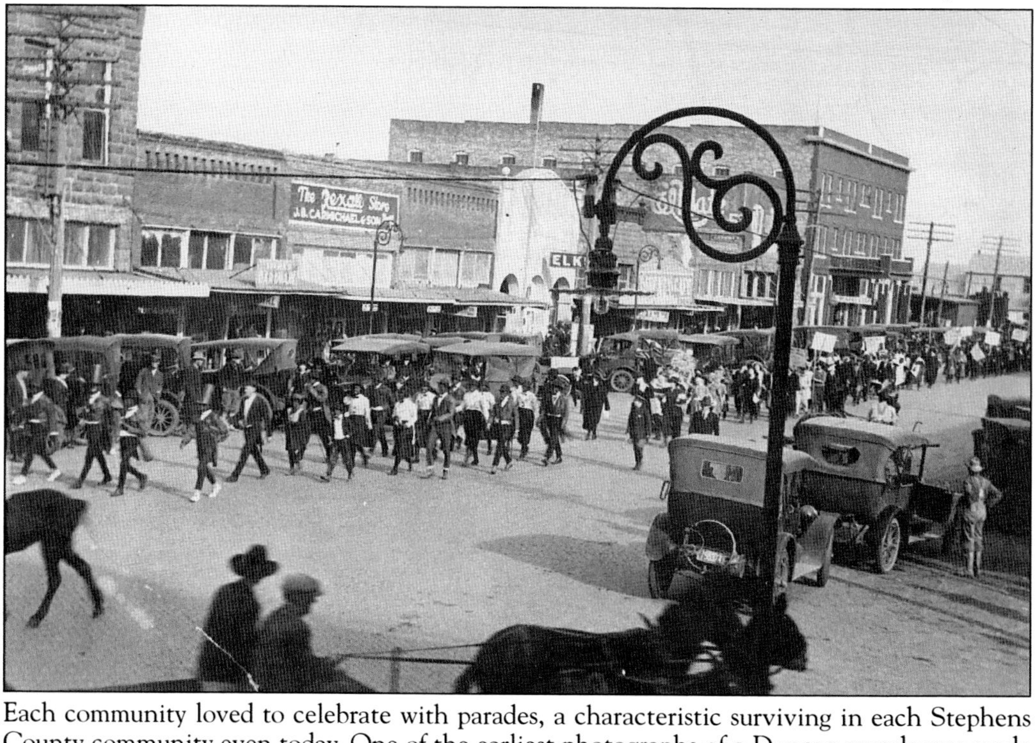

Each community loved to celebrate with parades, a characteristic surviving in each Stephens County community even today. One of the earliest photographs of a Duncan parade was made in 1919. This view is to the northeast from Eighth and Main Streets.

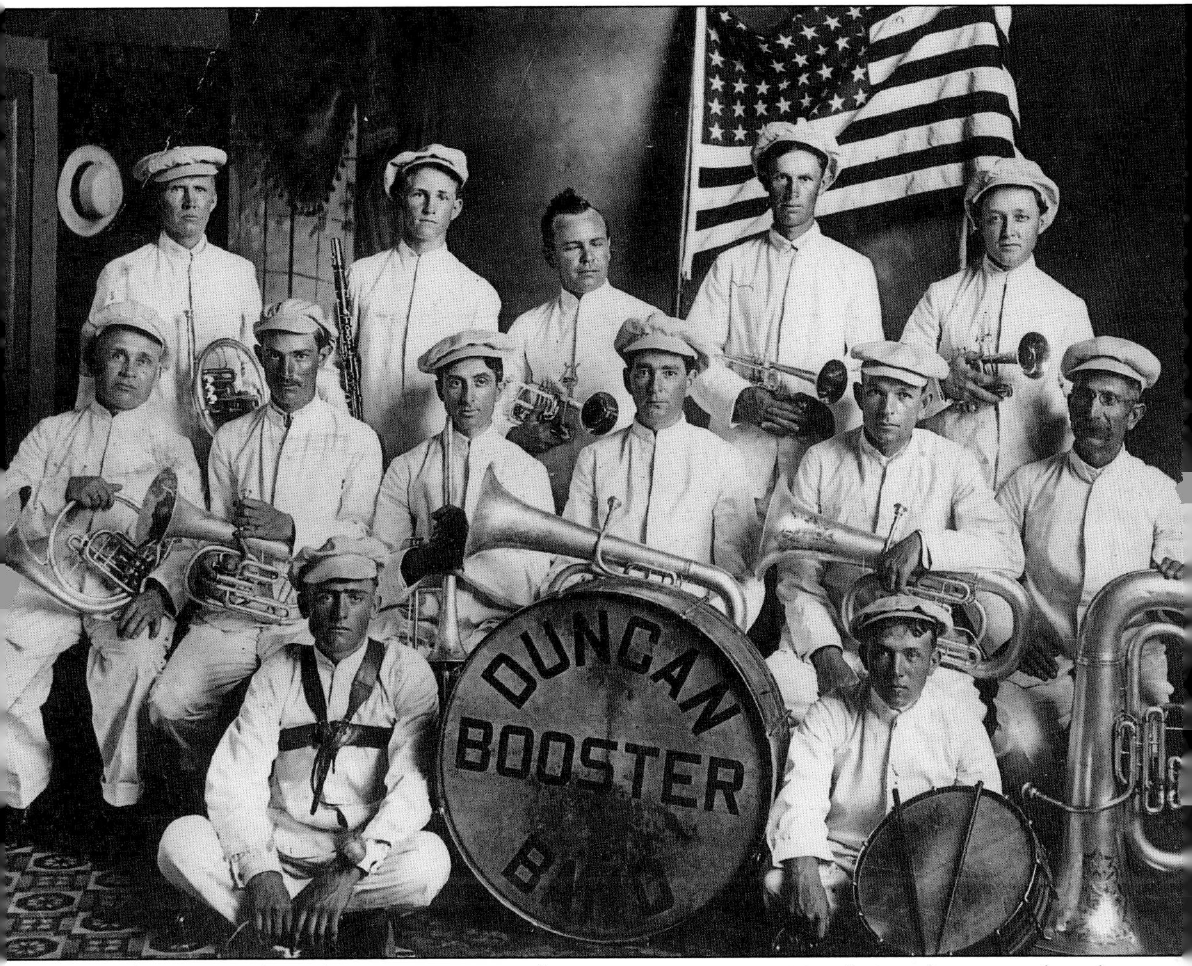

Bands continued to play an important role in community activities during the teens, though their role began to decline soon after the end of the decade. Duncan's last band, the Duncan Booster Band, is pictured in 1917. They disbanded in the 1920s, but not before traveling to Kansas City in a special rail car to perform. Pictured from left to right are the following: (front row) Clyde Davenport and Leo Howe; (middle row) G.A. Howe, Fred Johnson, Leonard Bumpas, H.L. Wharton, Ernest Markham, and Allen Butterbaugh; (back row) Mr. Hupp, Ed Langham, Ross Sampson, Buddy Johnson, and Charley Broadbent.

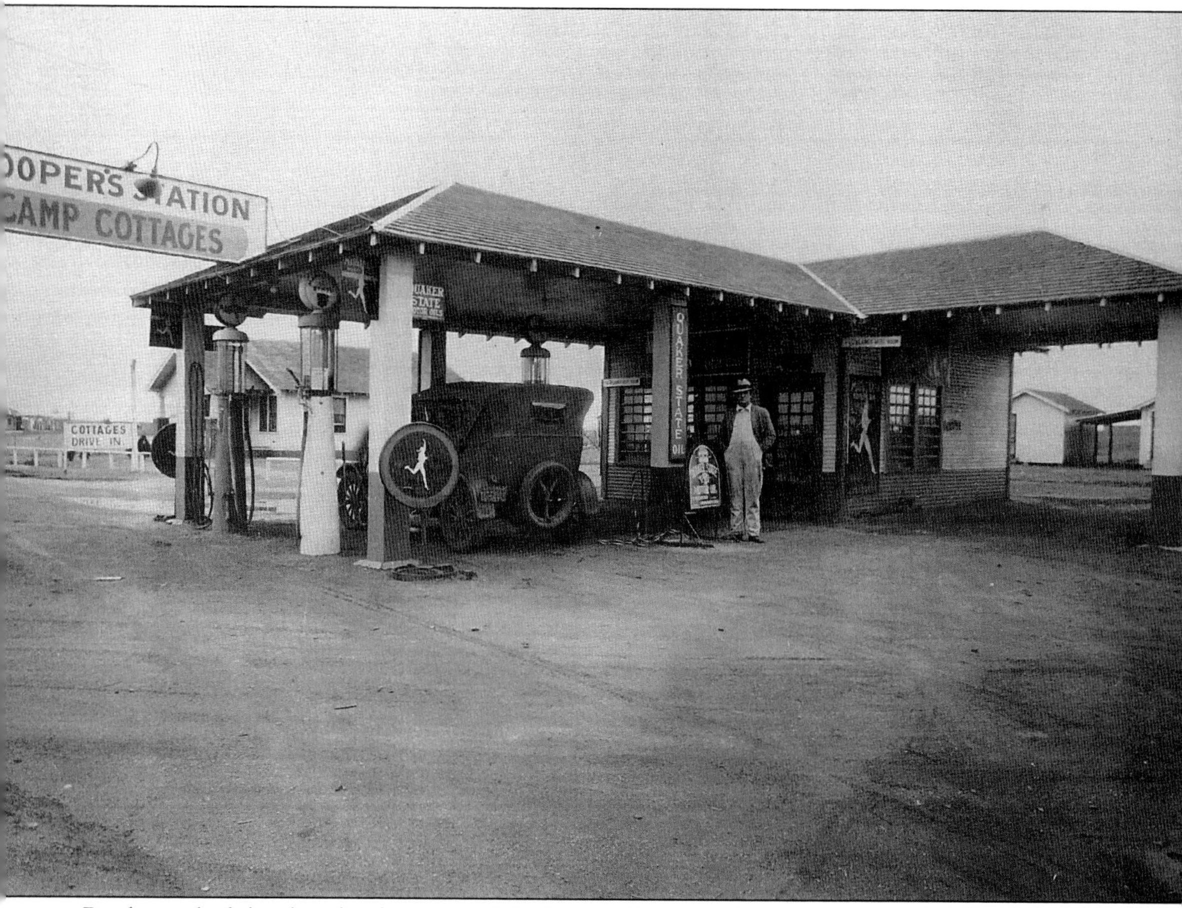

By the end of the decade, the automobile had made a significant impact in Stephens County, and enterprises to service the vehicles and passengers sprang up across the county. The filling station and overnight cottages, the forerunner of today's motel industry, became the essence of this new age. Cooper's Station and Camp Cottages, located on the highway south of Marlow, serves as a classic example. Mr. Cooper is pictured with his touring car.

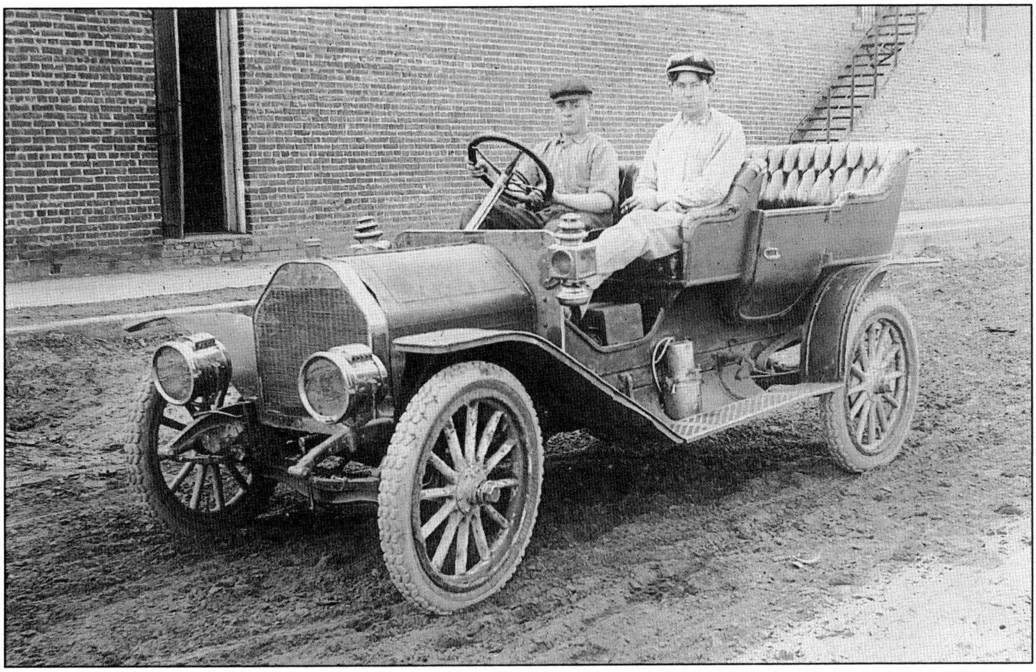

B.O. Johns and E.E. Bearce pose in a new 1913 Buick from one of Duncan's several auto dealers, while below, Duncan's new fire engines are pictured ready in the firehouse.

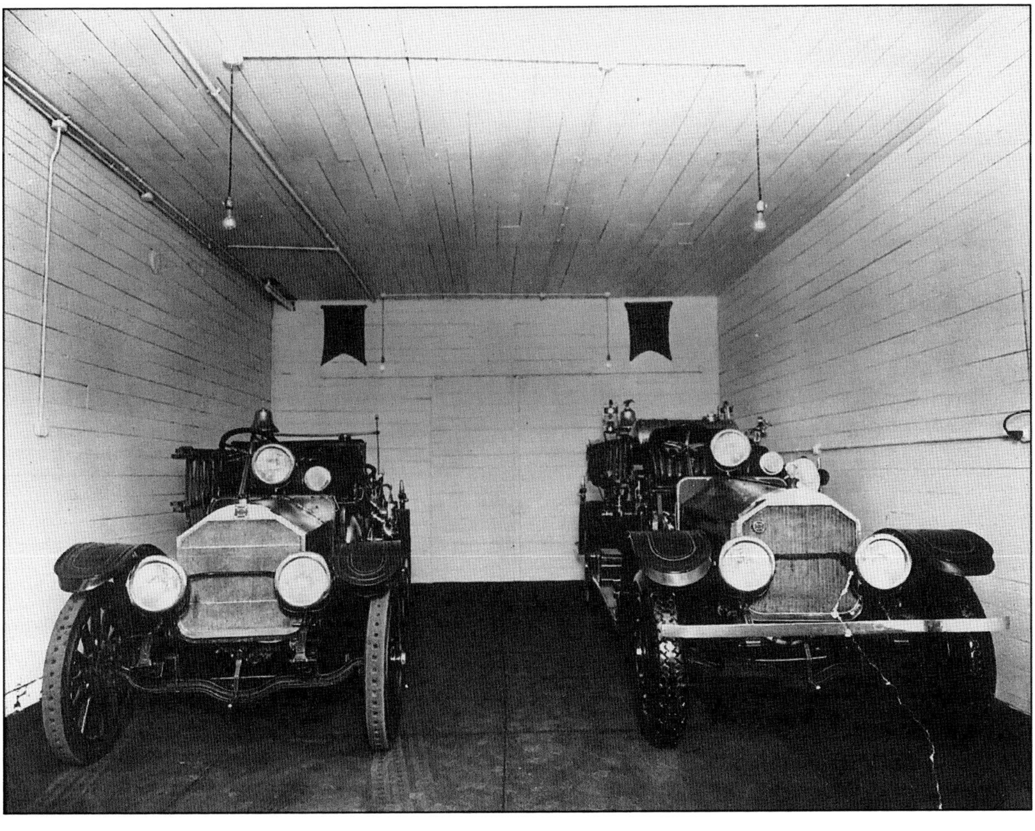

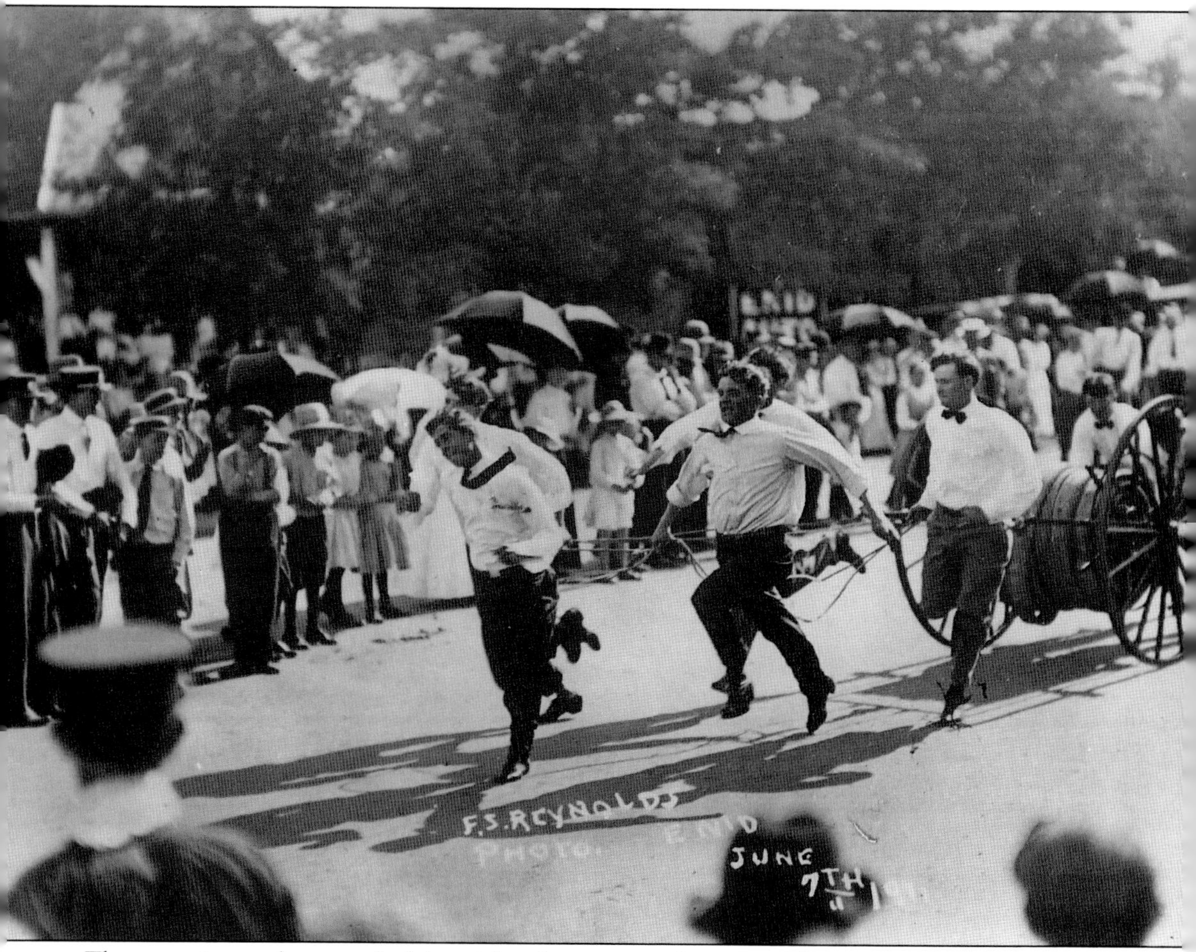

The crowning and most colorful social and recreational event of the year in Stephens County, from the early 1900s until the mid-1920s, was without a doubt the Comanche Carnival held each summer. In its heyday, as many as 25,000 people passed through the gates of the three-day carnival. The Rock Island ran excursion trains from Enid, Oklahoma, in the north, and Ft. Worth, Texas, to the south, to fill the demand for transportation. Sporting events; horse, sulky, and wagon racing events; rodeo stunts; Indian War Dances; side-shows; amusement rides; foods of all kinds; and, by 1913, "airship" rides were anticipated and enjoyed by the attendees. The famous Quanah Parker, the last of the Comanche War Chiefs, and the equally famous Geronimo, the last of the Apache War Chiefs, were frequent early-day participants, along with famous cowboy stars like Tom Mix. The photograph above captures the spirit of the carnival. Volunteer firemen races pitted community against community, and added to the excitement. Duncan's crew race to the finish line in 1911.

Bart King, Charlie King, and Fred King, from left to right, stand next to their race horse, Old Apron Face, ridden by Skinner Walker.

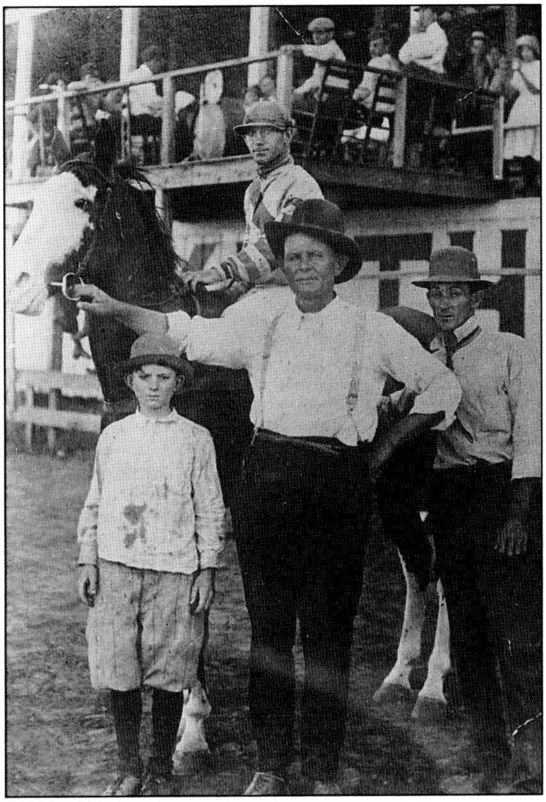

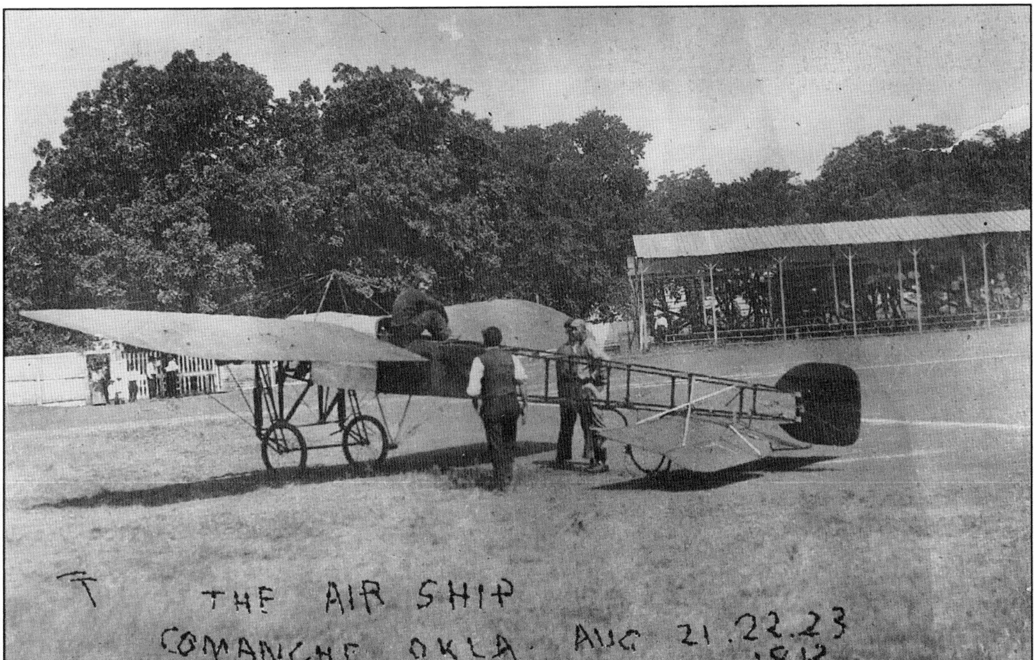

The first aeroplane to be featured at the carnival is shown on August 21, 1913. Aeroplanes were largely still a novelty in these early years of aviation development.

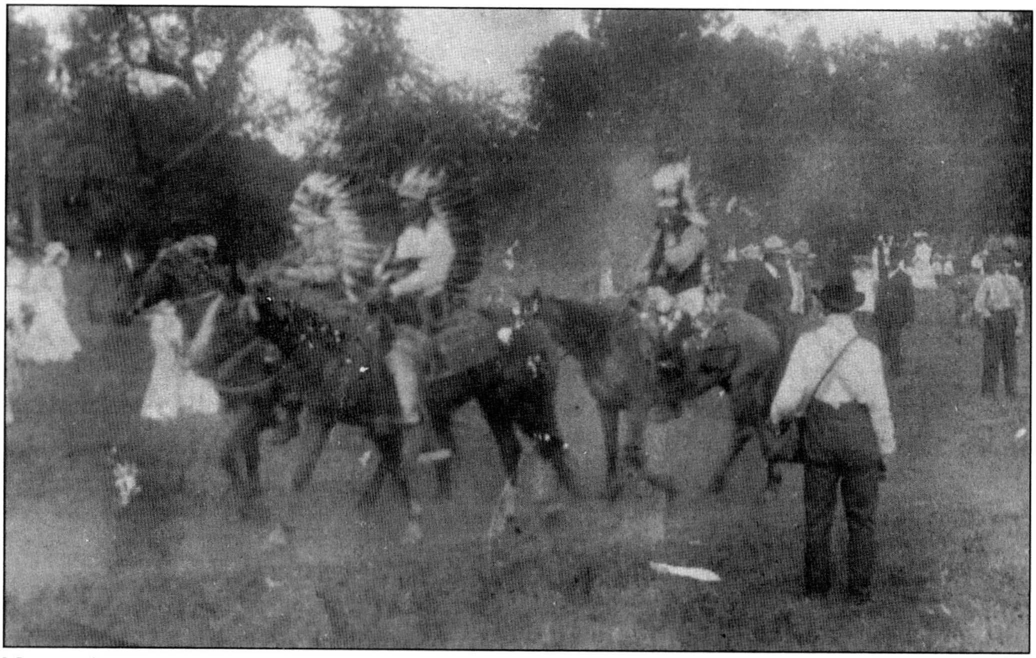

Native Americans were an important part of the Comanche Carnival from its 1901 onset. They were avid participants in the festivities, as shown above, and performed in races and colorful dances. They arrived a week before the carnival to assist in erecting facilities, and were given several beeves, which they butchered, dressed, and hung to dry on the hills to the east where many camped (below).

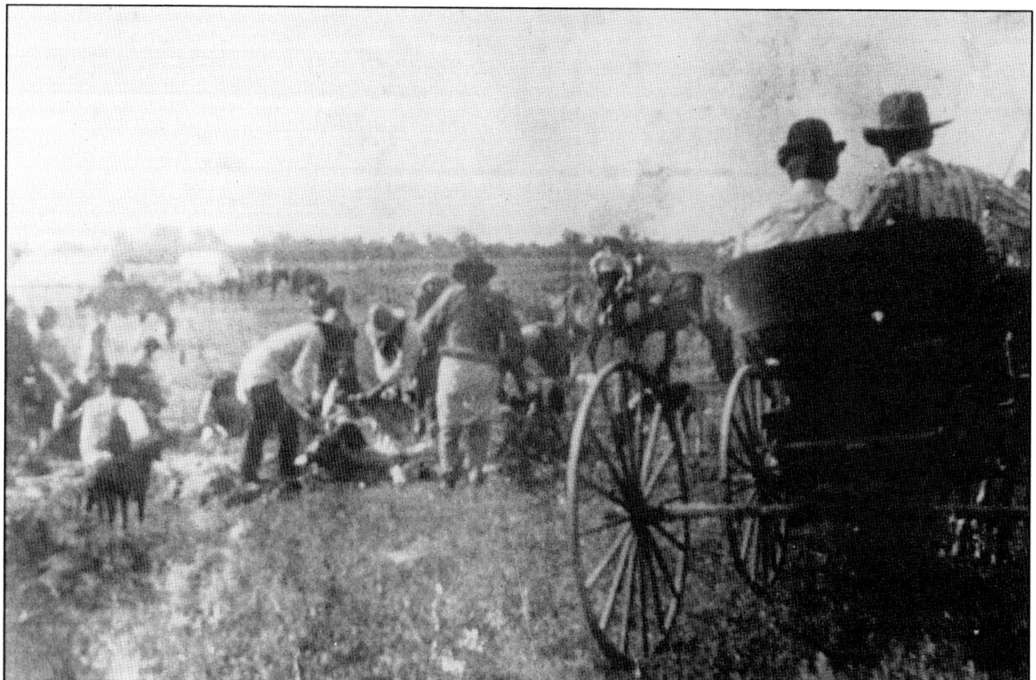

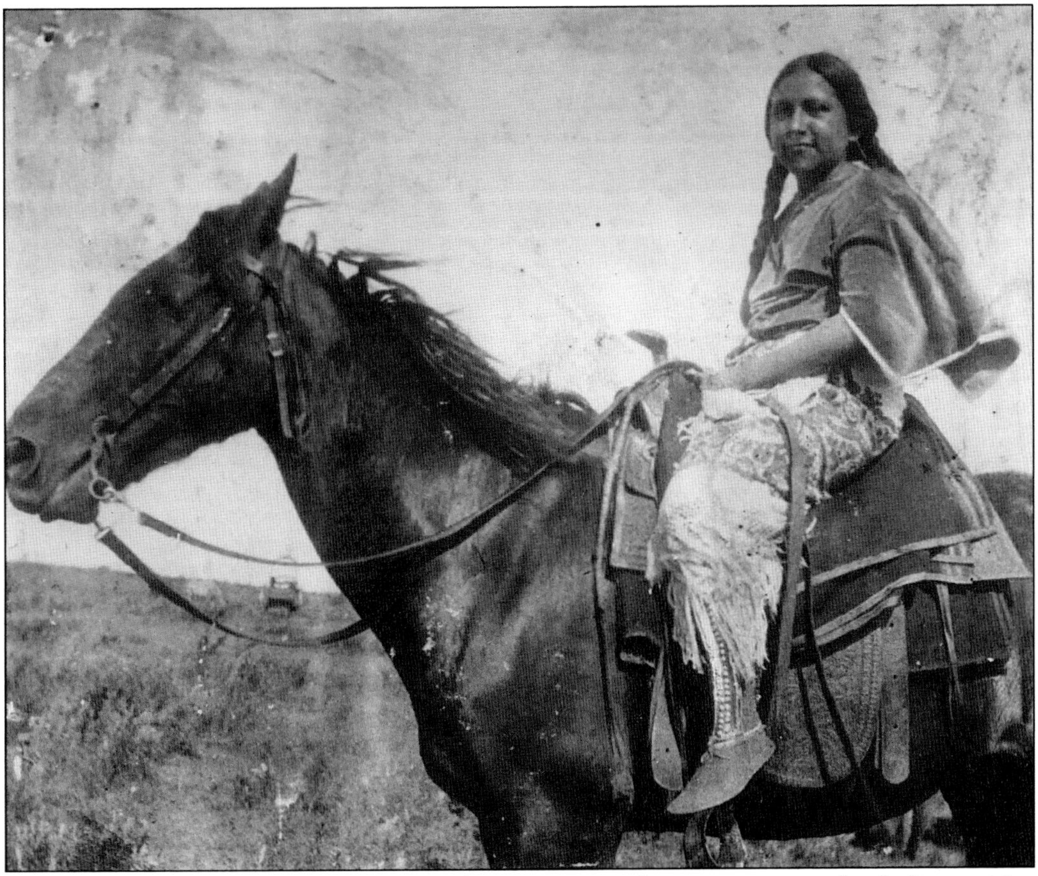

There is no doubt that the carnival's attendees were as much an attraction to this Indian maiden as were the Indians to visitors.

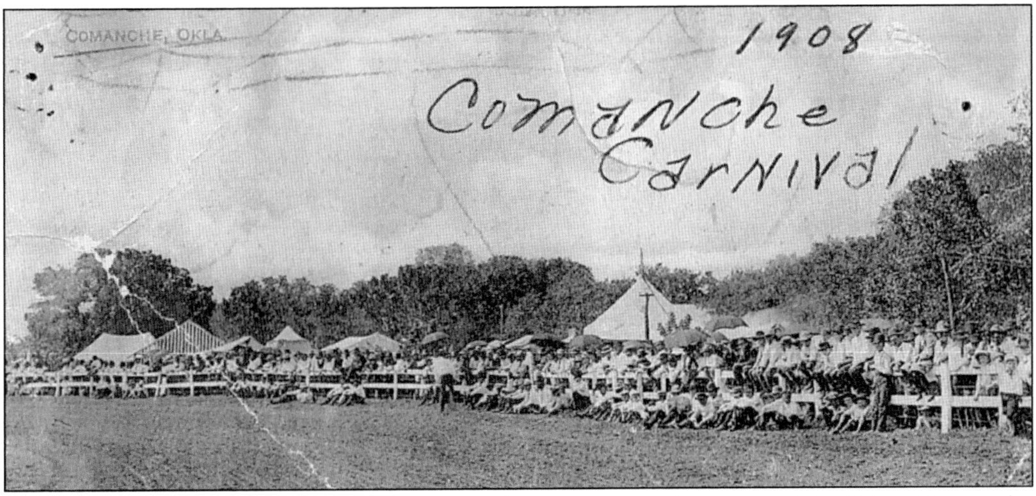

In the message on this postcard's reverse side, portraying the carnival in 1911, Comanche druggist D. Warren invites visitors "to make our Store your principal stopping place. We have the coolest and most comfortable place in town and have Ice Cream and Cold Drinks that will satisfy your thirst and relieve your fatigue."

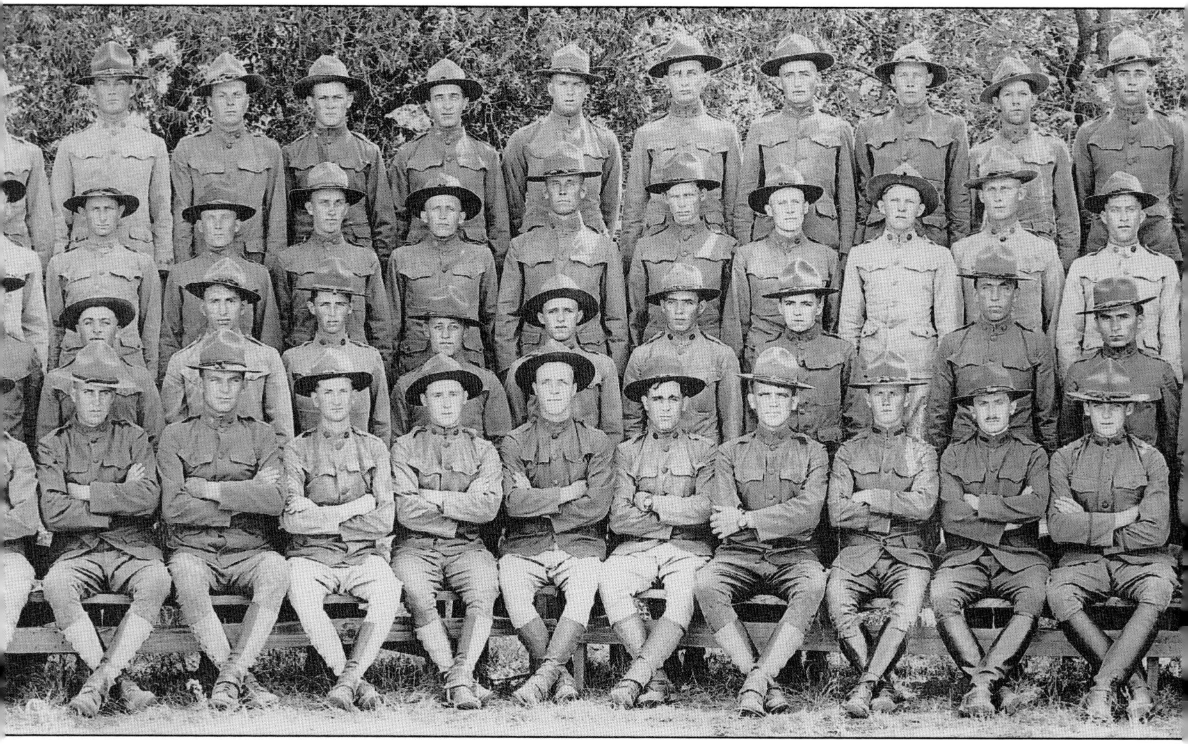

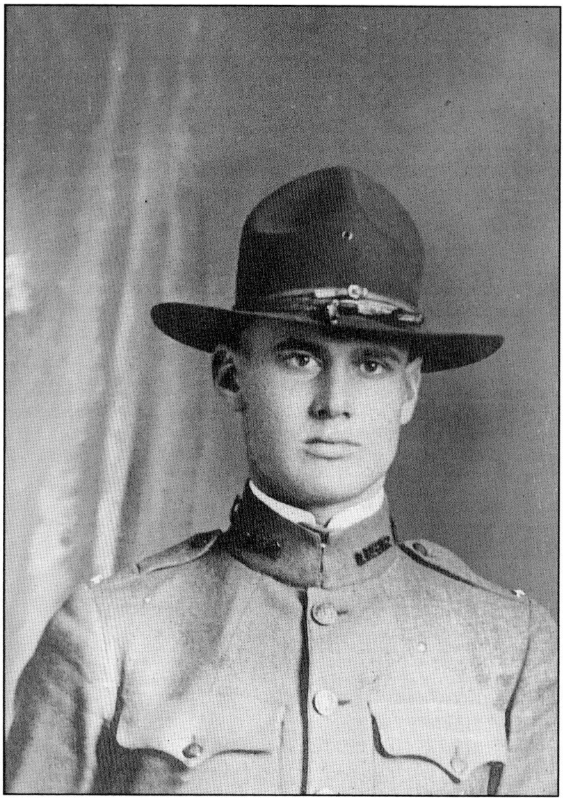

A world-defining event, World War I likewise had an impact in Stephens County. Duncan High School's yearbook for 1919 lists 94 students, graduates, and faculty who served, including 2 killed and

First Lieutenant Thomas H. McCasland, a local resident, volunteered for service. A member of the 90th Artillery Division, 2nd Corps, he saw action in the Argonne. (Photo courtesy of the McCasland family.)

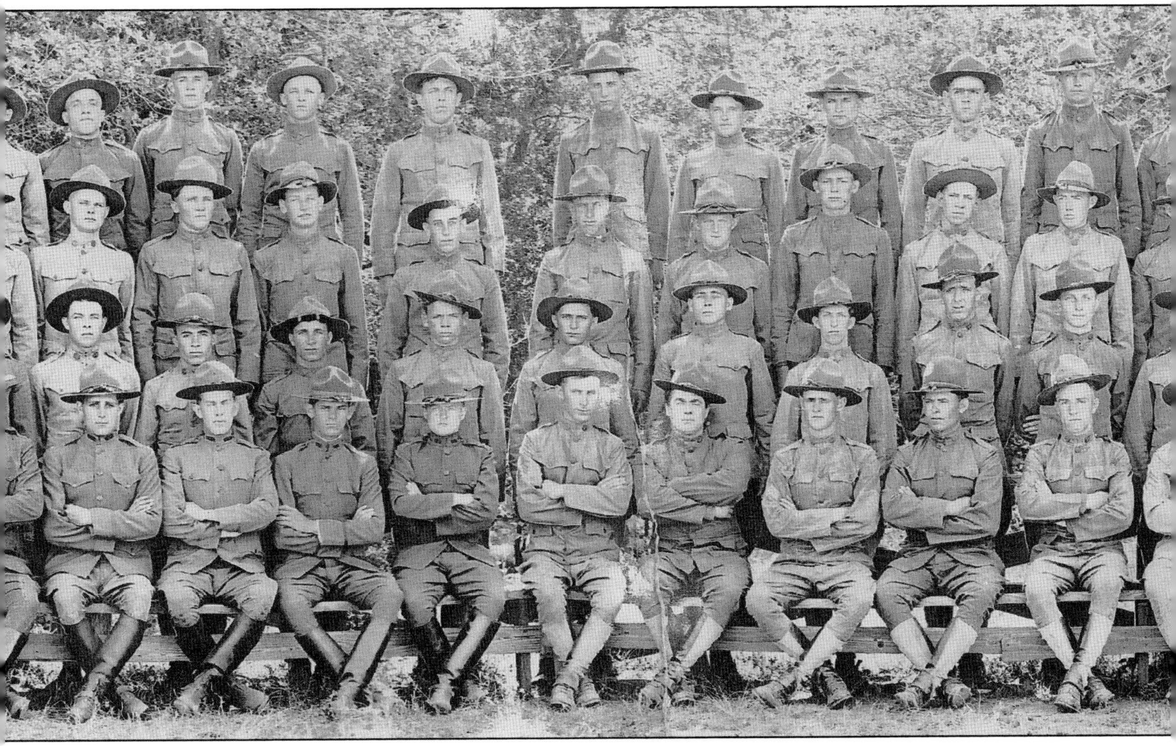

3 wounded. Marlow and Comanche counted a proportionate number of men in their communities who served in the Great War. Pictured above in 1918 is a unit in which many Stephens County soldiers served.

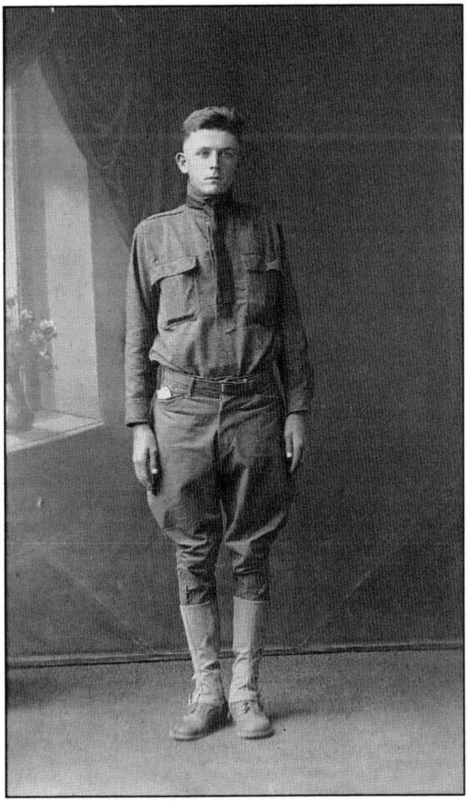

Henry C. Dixon represents the many citizens of Stephens County who served in the enlisted ranks during the Great War.

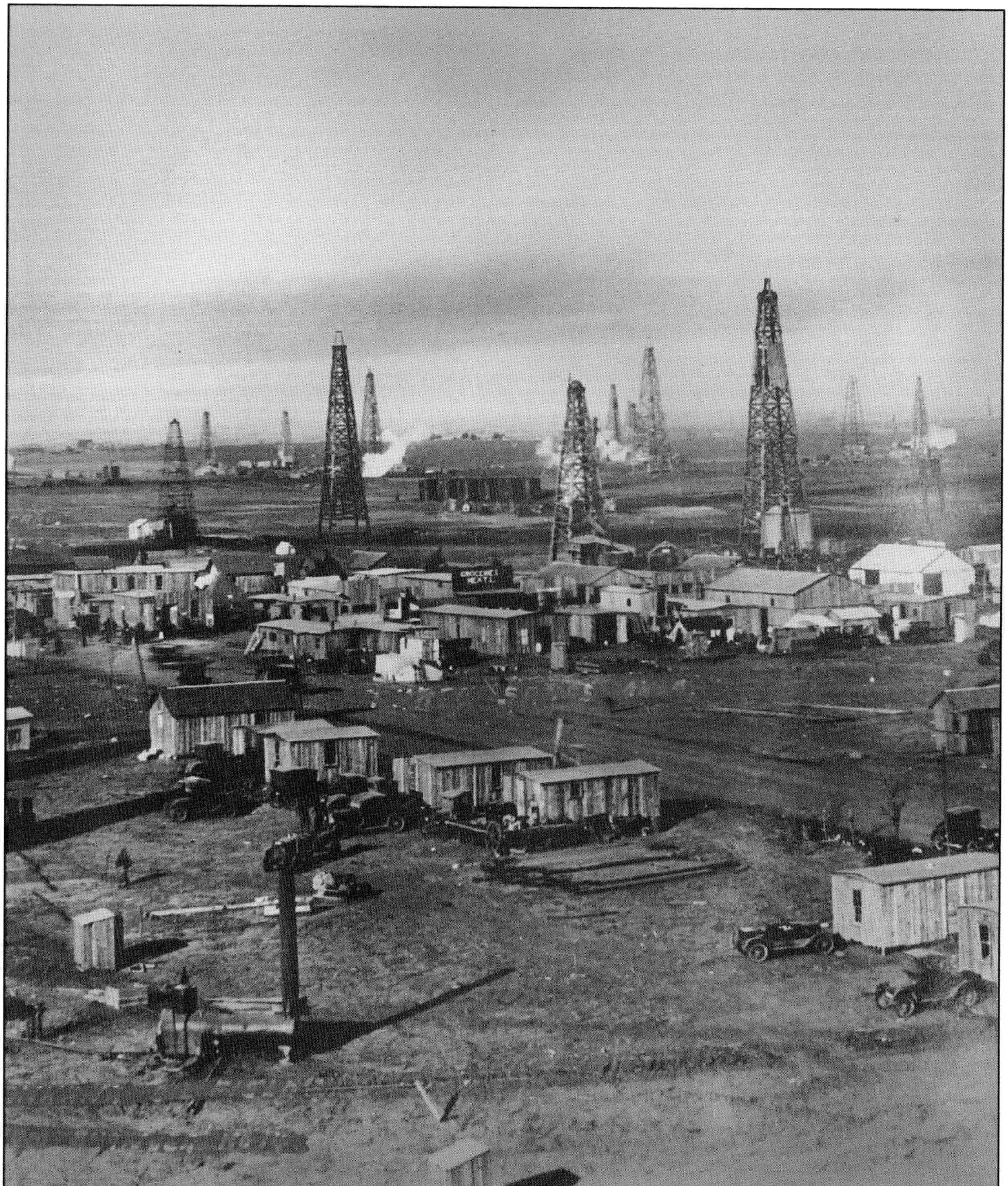

This oil field and shanty town were part of the Empire oil field, one of many that sprang up in the county overnight with the discovery and development of the oil industry.

Four

THE OIL BOOM AND PROSPERITY

THE 1920S

The "Roaring Twenties" were every bit that in Stephens County with the coming of the oil industry. Oil brought prosperity, reflected in Main Streets, fine homes, well-stocked merchandise stores, and bustling enterprises. The county's oil fields became and remained Oklahoma's highest producing areas well until the 1980s.

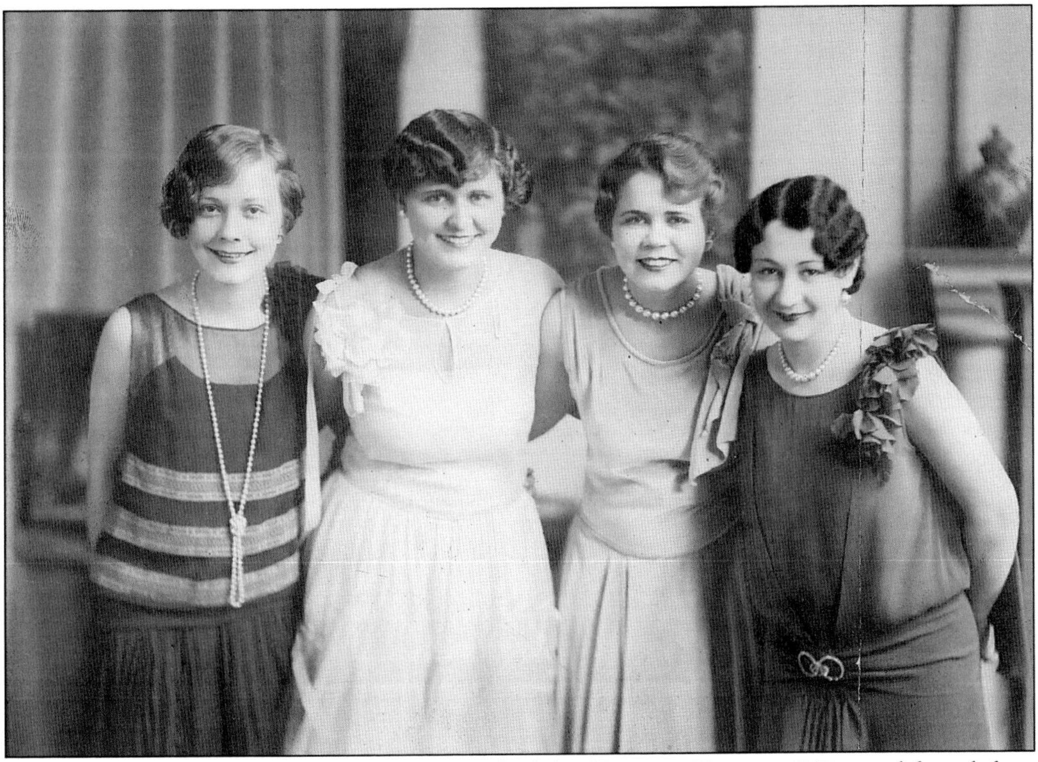

Four happy coeds reflect the optimistic mood of the "Roaring Twenties." Pictured from left to right are the following: Isabel Clark, Eva Doty, Leota Tomer, and Nell Gilbert.

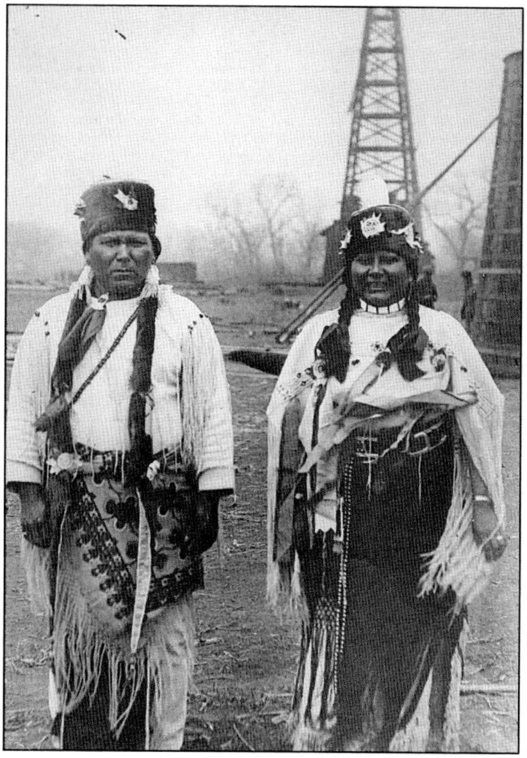

O Nah Dy and his wife stand before the well that bears his name. Located in the southwest part of the county, this well, discovered in 1918, became the first to produce oil of a commercial volume and led to additional explorations that opened several large pools.

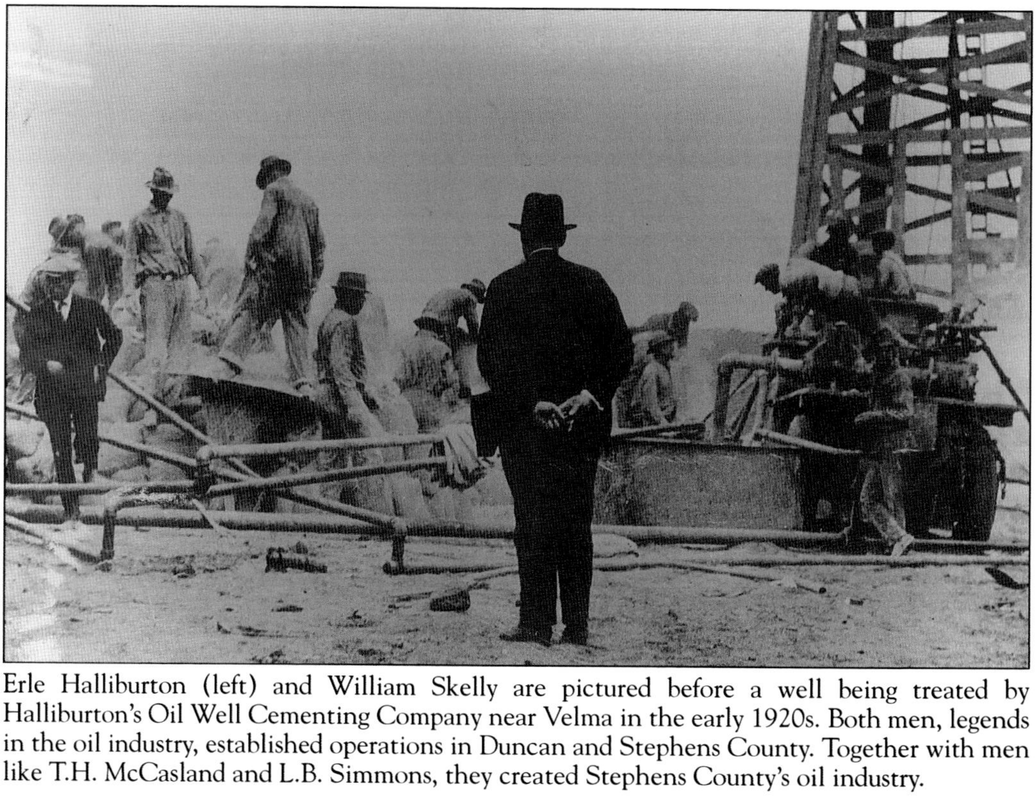

Erle Halliburton (left) and William Skelly are pictured before a well being treated by Halliburton's Oil Well Cementing Company near Velma in the early 1920s. Both men, legends in the oil industry, established operations in Duncan and Stephens County. Together with men like T.H. McCasland and L.B. Simmons, they created Stephens County's oil industry.

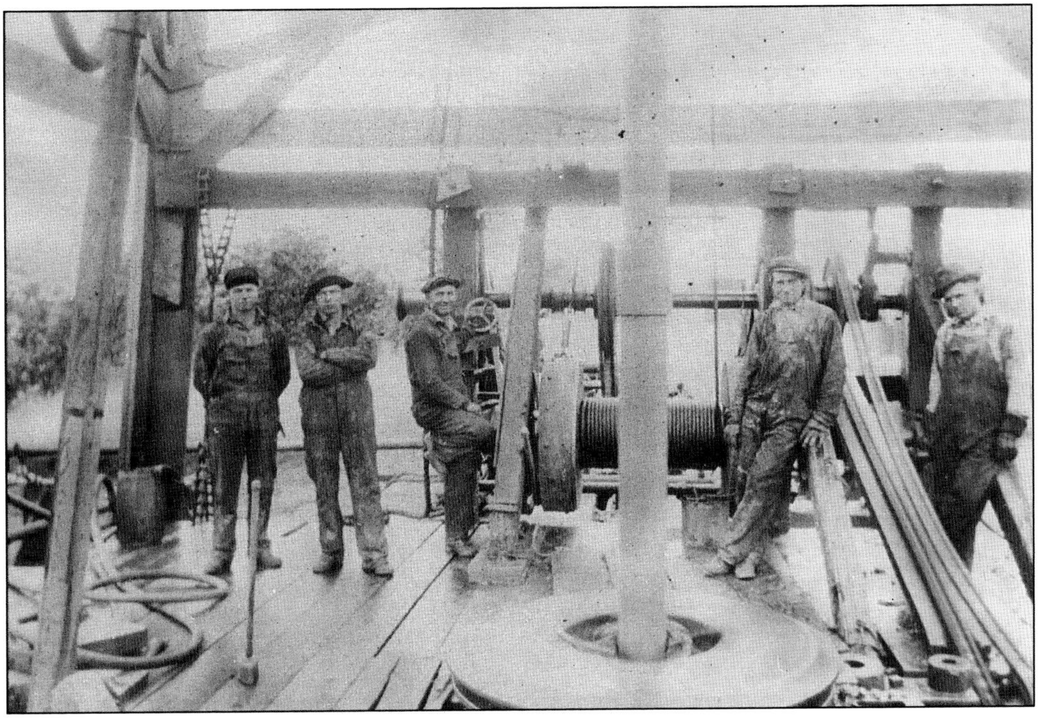

These oil workers pose at their drilling platform near Duncan.

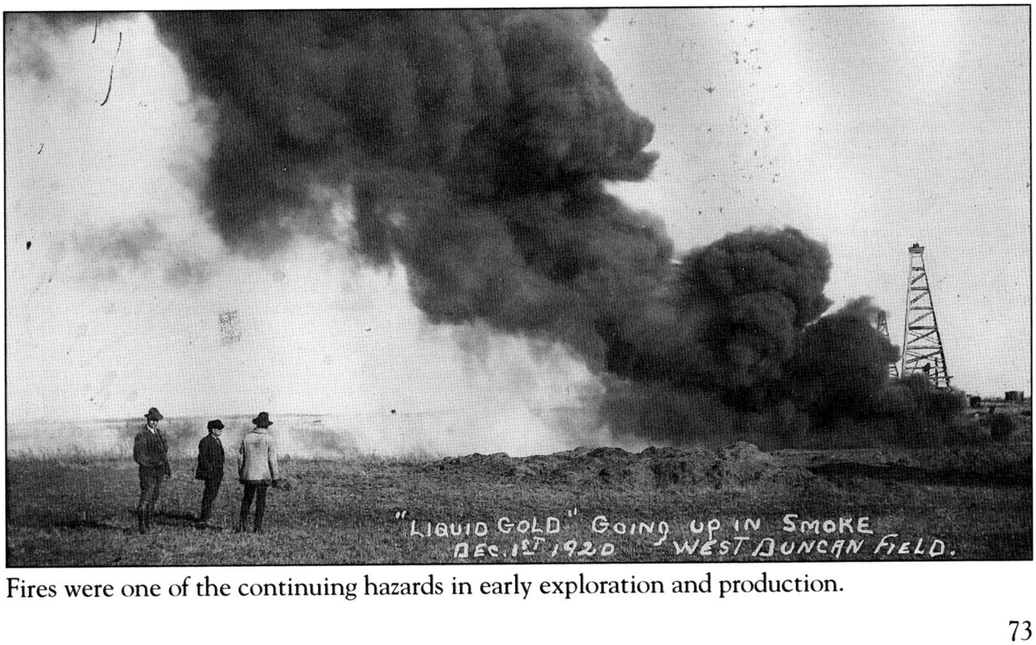

Fires were one of the continuing hazards in early exploration and production.

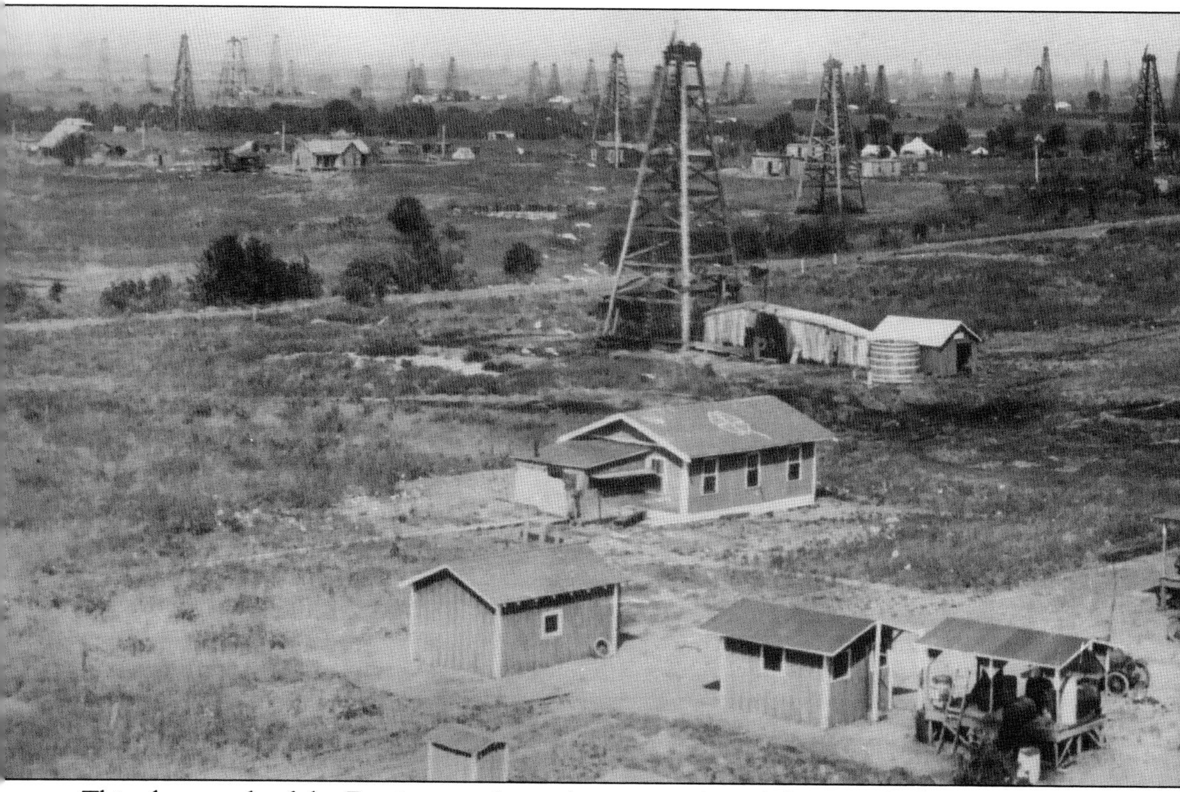

This photograph of the Empire area shows the magnitude and density of oil exploration and

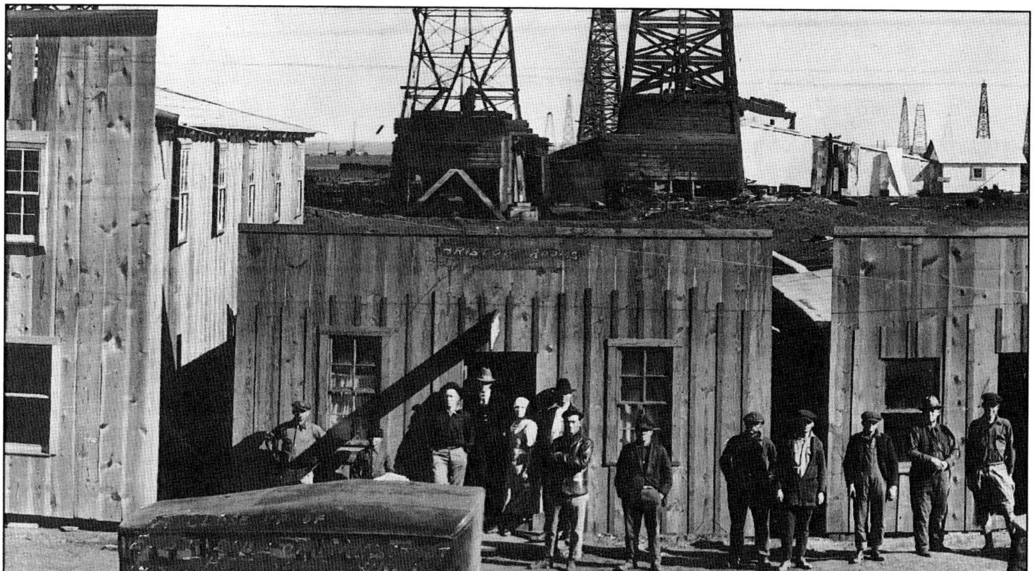

At first, the oil boom towns offered little of comfort to the oil workers as illustrated by this early photograph.

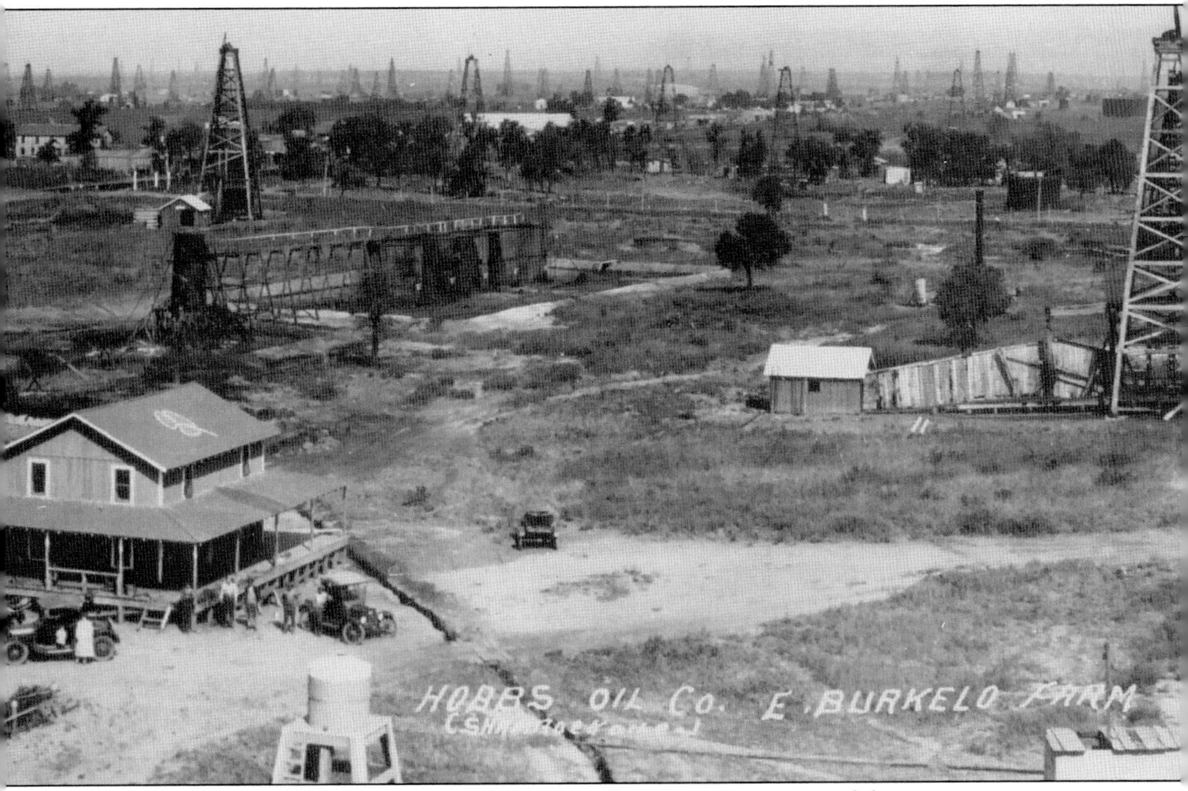

production across the county. It was also repeated in the eastern part of the county.

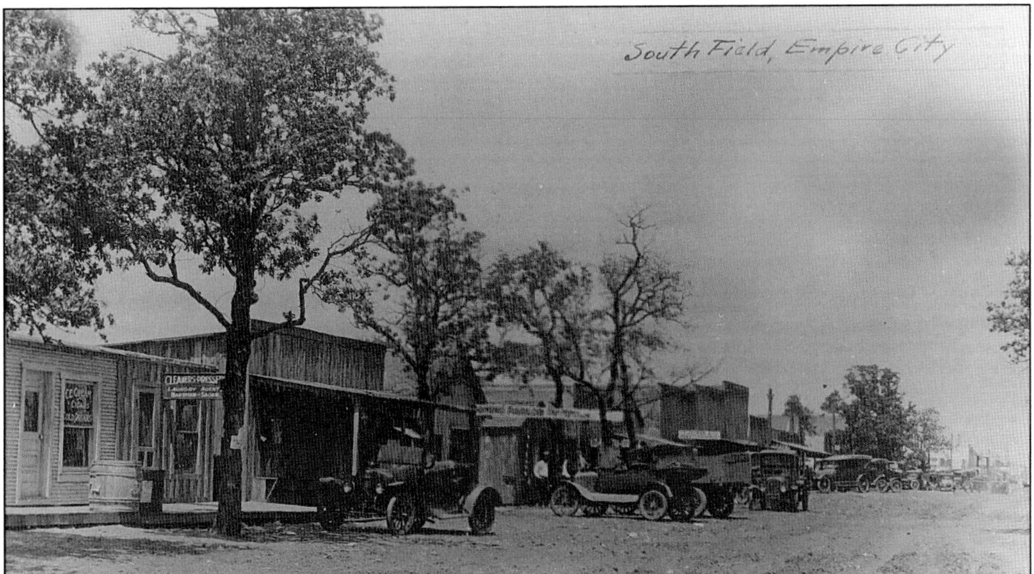

Later, the boom towns grew and took on a somewhat more permanent appearance as Empire City illustrates in the mid-1920s. Note the long main street and many vehicles. At the end of the boom, however, little remained of these towns but a few foundations. They died as quickly as they sprang up.

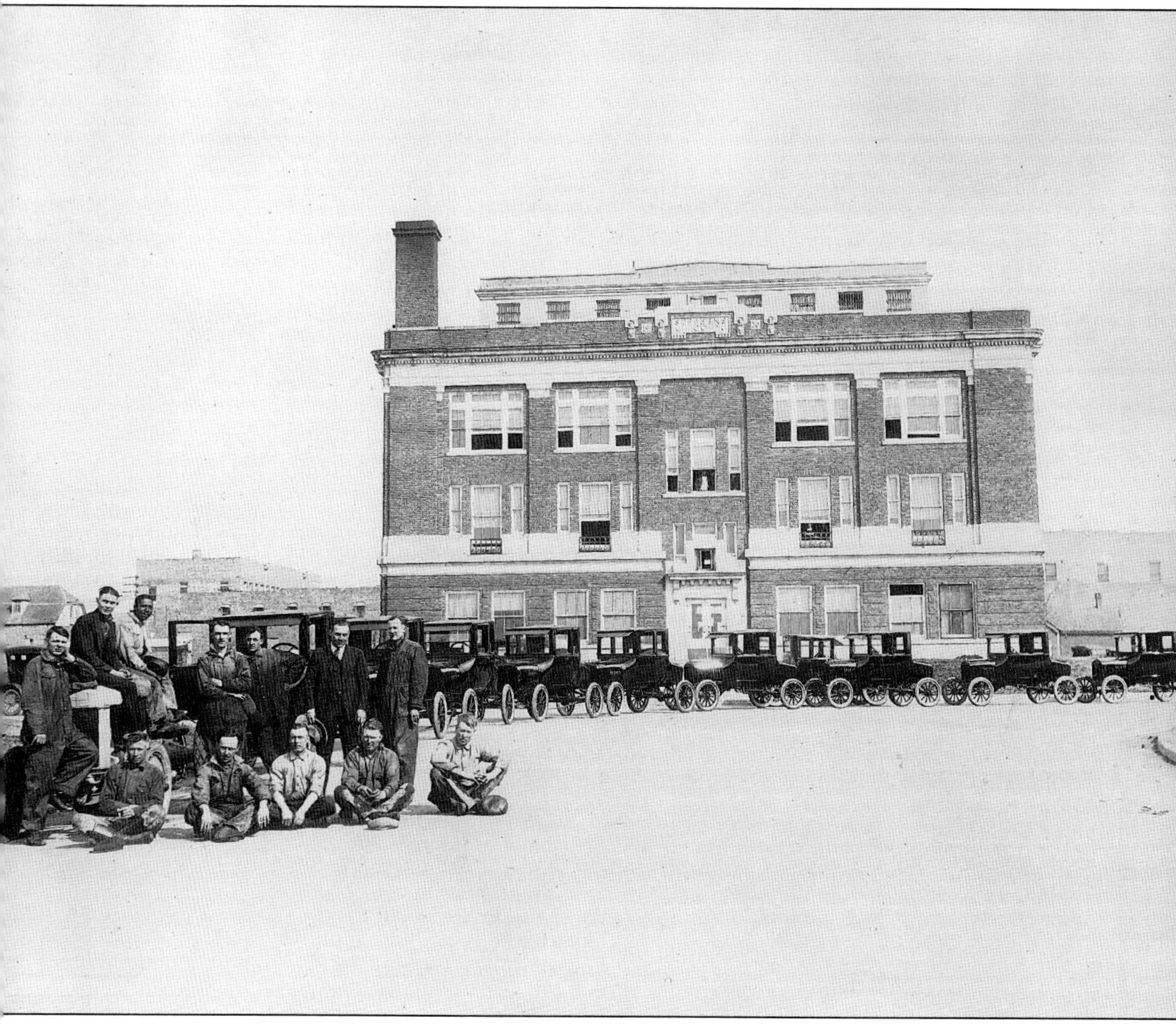

The oil boom years brought prosperity to the county and its communities. Nowhere is this better illustrated than in this early-1920s view of the new county courthouse and a load of new Model-T Fords just delivered to the Duncan Auto Company.

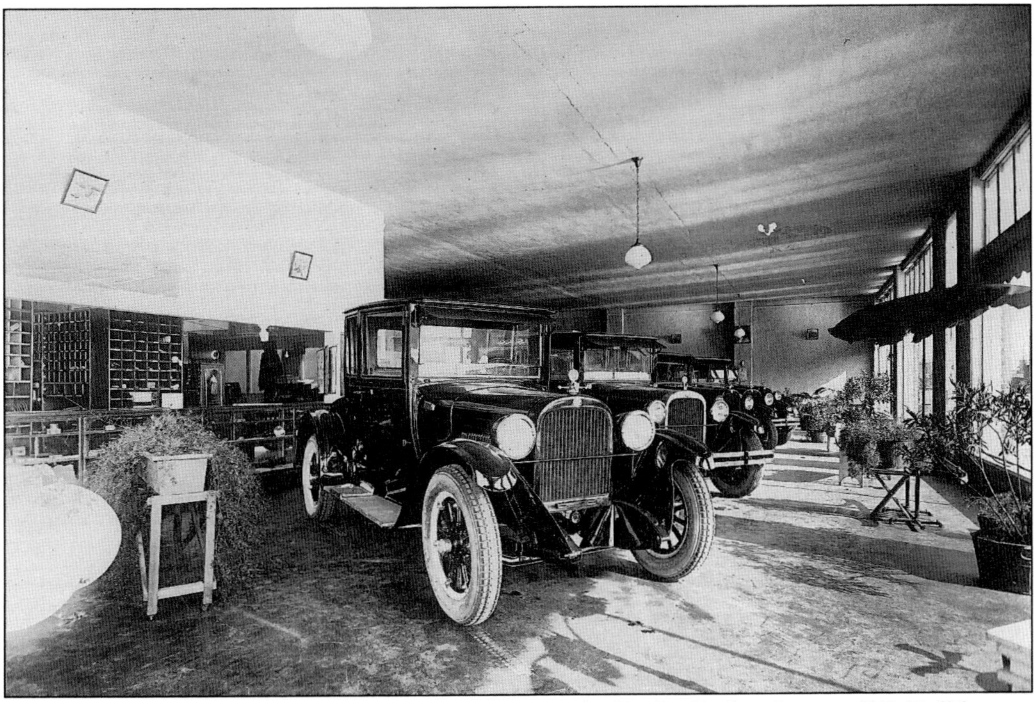

Among other prospering auto dealers in Duncan was the Beeler Dodge Agency. E.P. Halliburton is said to have come in and ordered 20 of these new Dodges for his employees. Below, a busy, crowded Main Street in Duncan suggests good times for merchants.

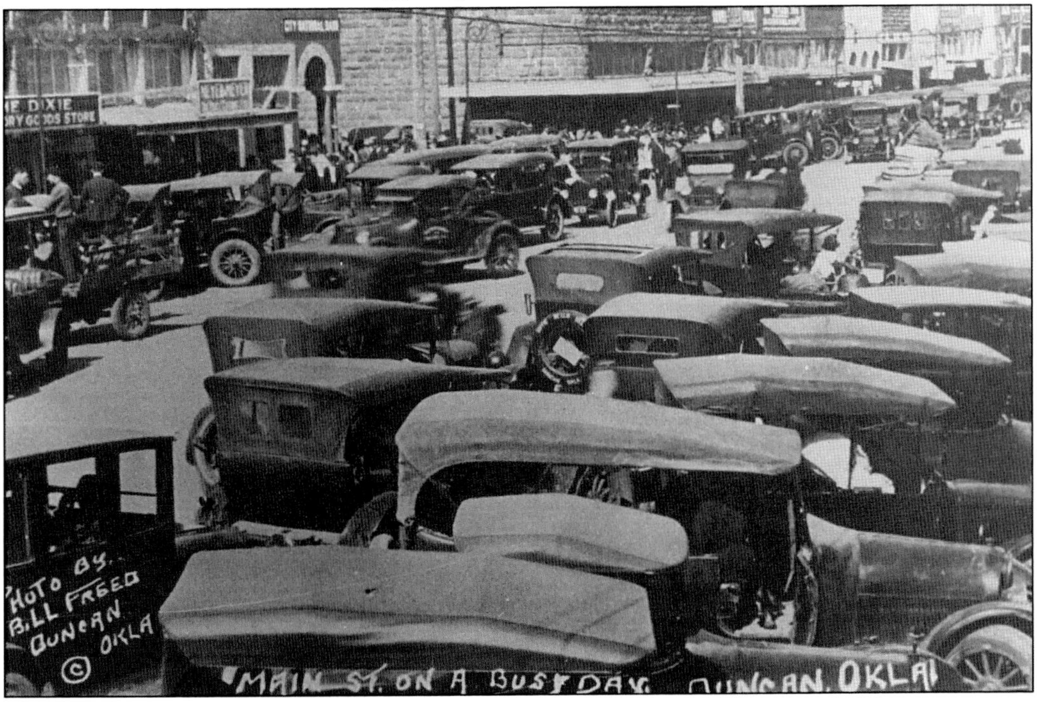

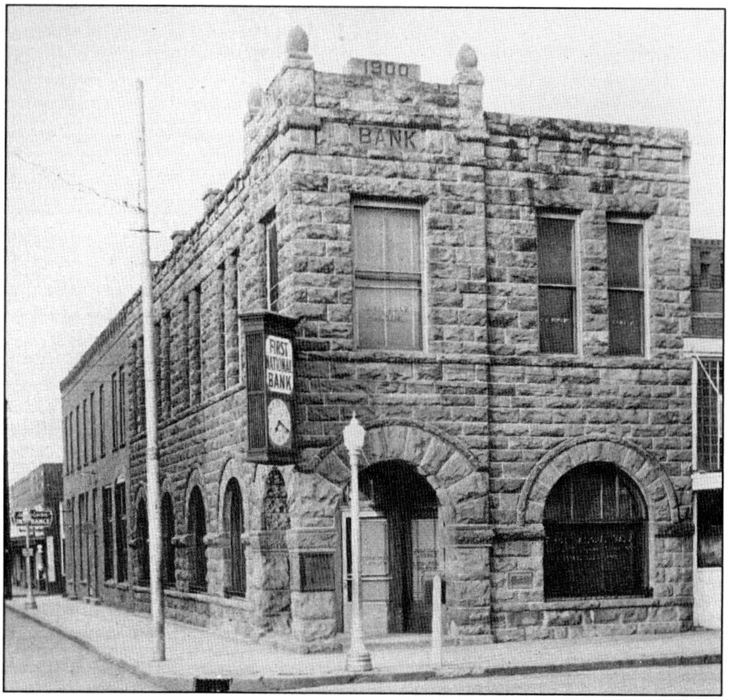

Two of the county's mainstay financial institutions were the First National Bank, shown left and below in its period splendor, and the City National Bank, on the facing page. Interior photographs were made of both in the mid-1920s.

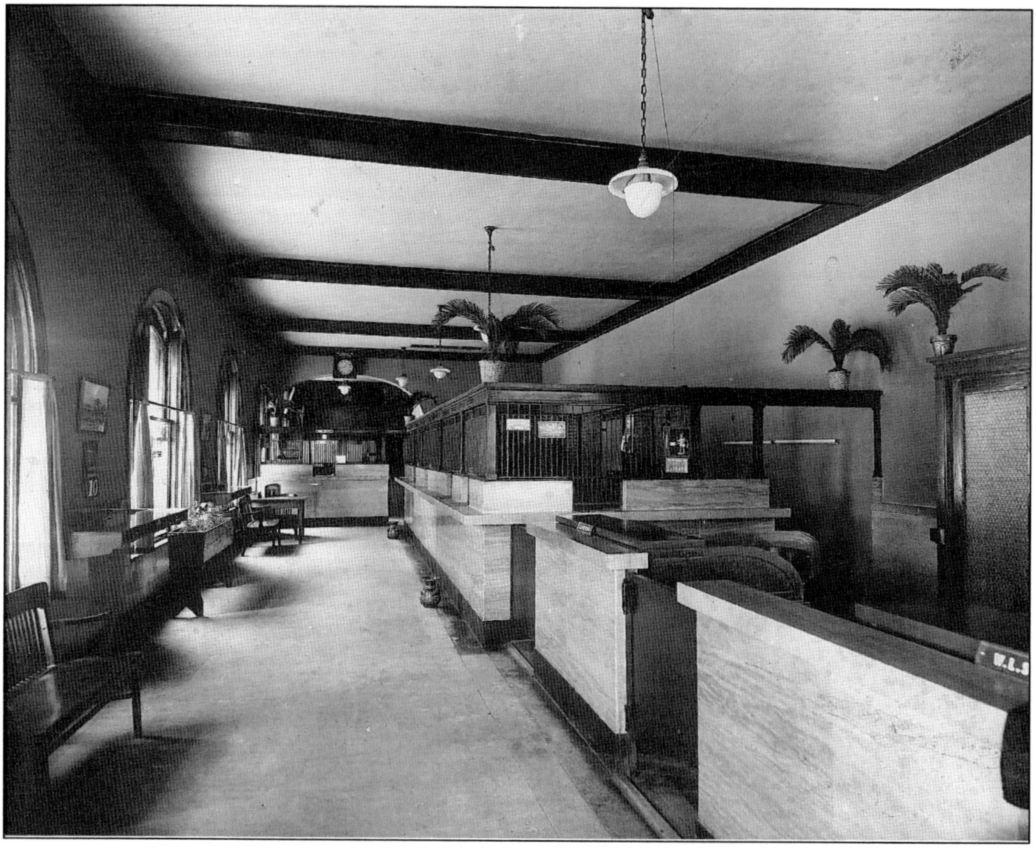

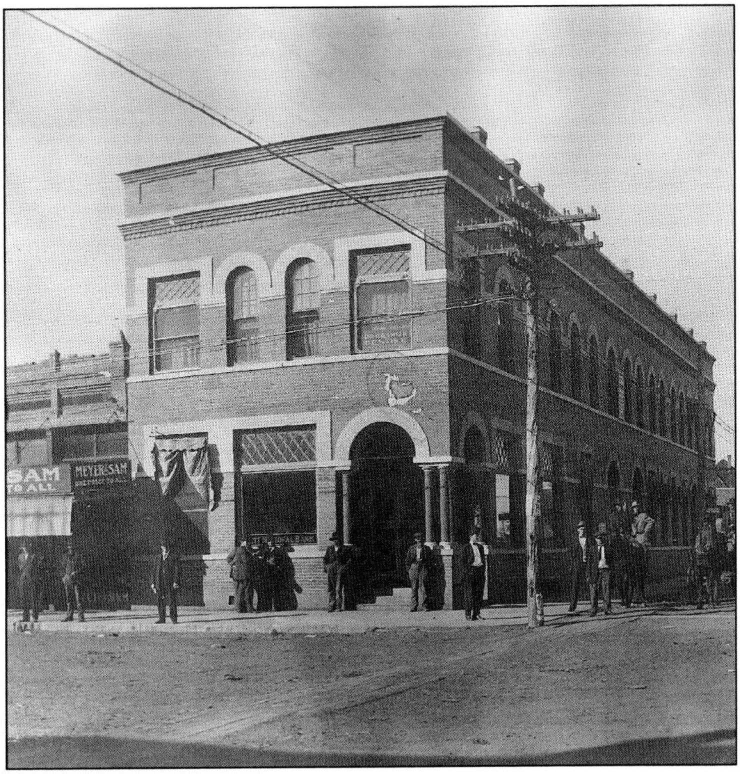

The City National Bank building, at right, survives today. Below is a view of the bank's interior in the 1920s.

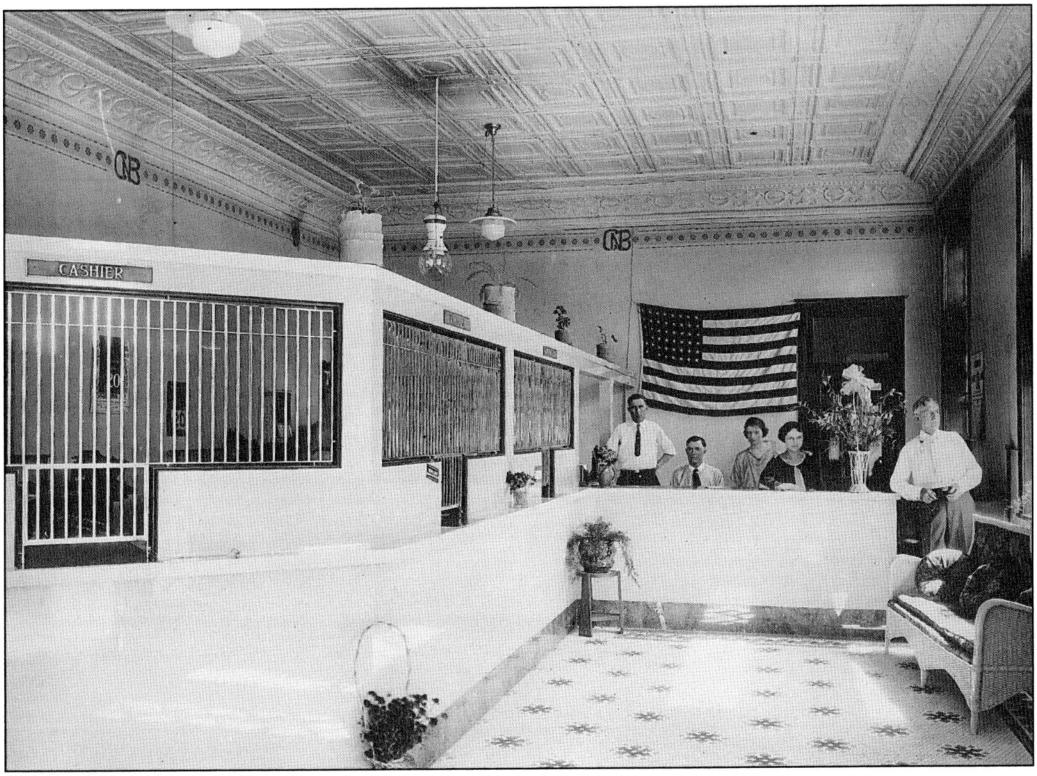

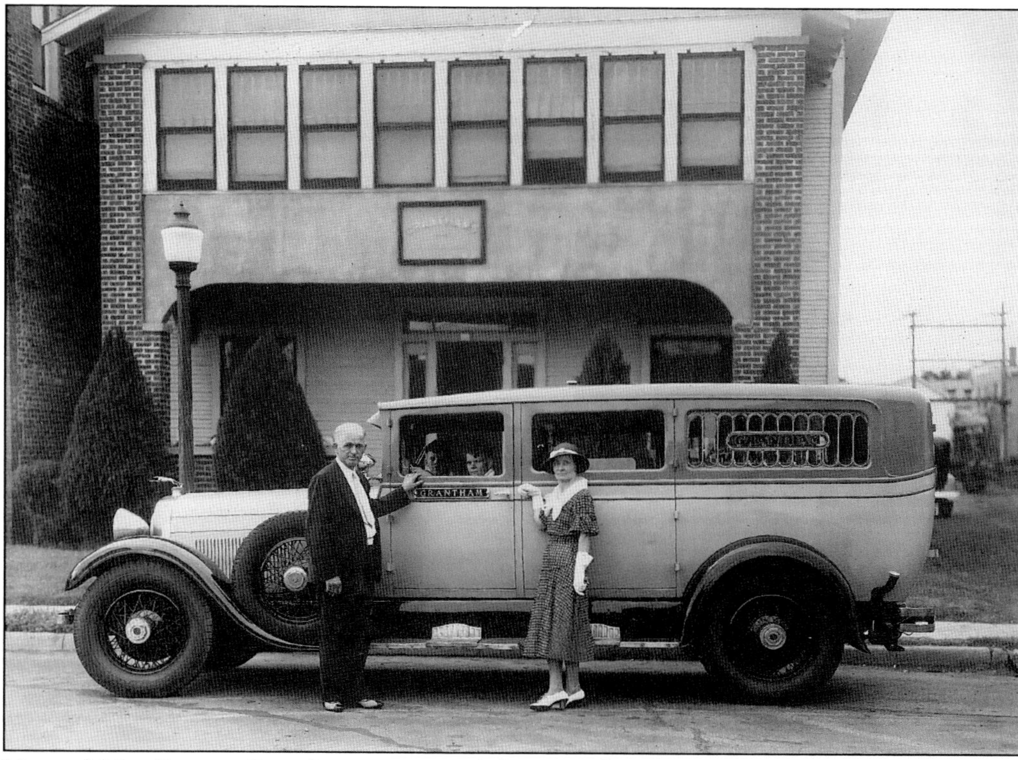

Mr. and Mrs. Beeson Grantham, owners of the Grantham Funeral Home, display their new hearse in the late 1920s. Below, Mr. Reynolds, at right, poses in his music store with his mother; John Eddleman, an employee; and Ella Mae Cates, who is sitting at the piano. These are among Duncan's business enterprises that flourished during the decade.

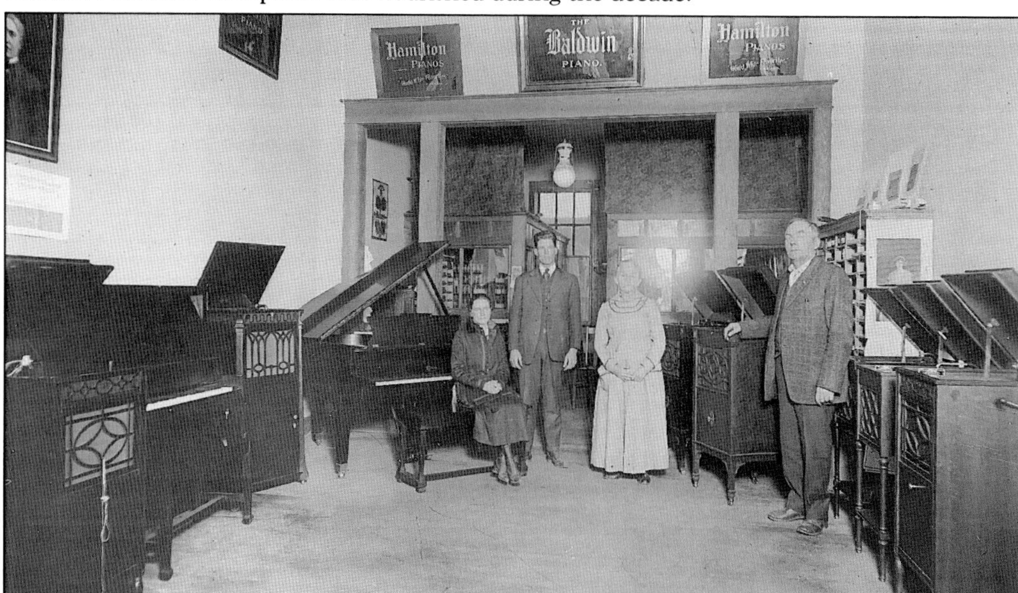

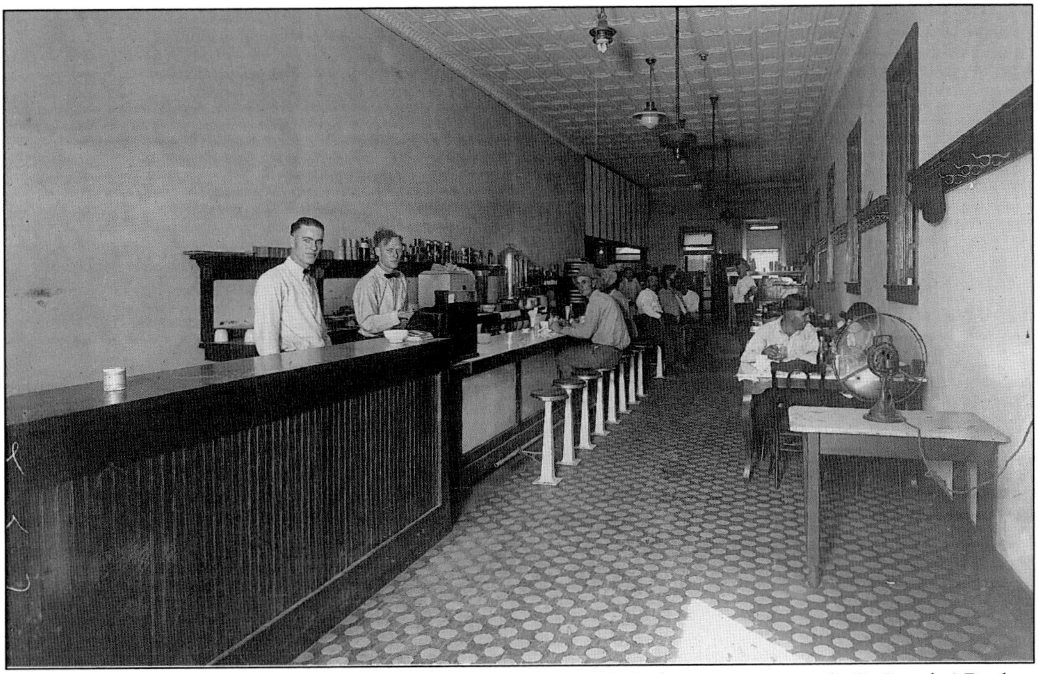

The Met Café in Duncan serves customers in 1921, while below, visitors to O.C. Sparks' Barber Shop in Marlow enjoy his services.

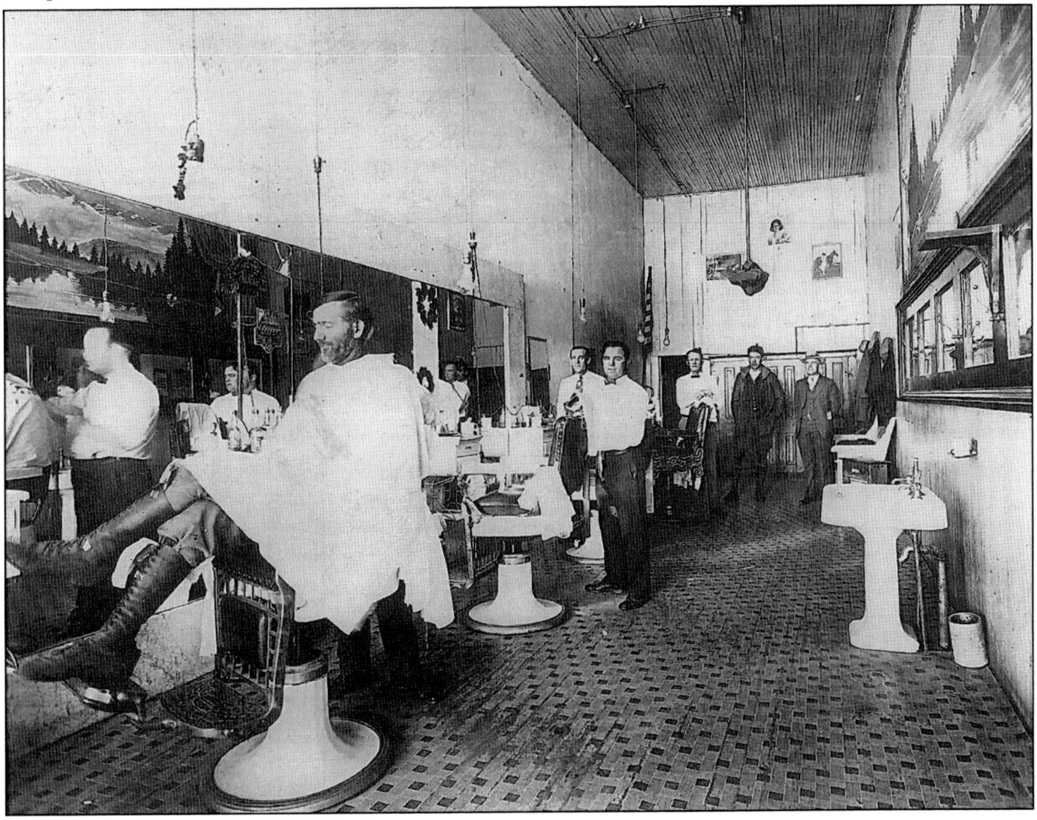

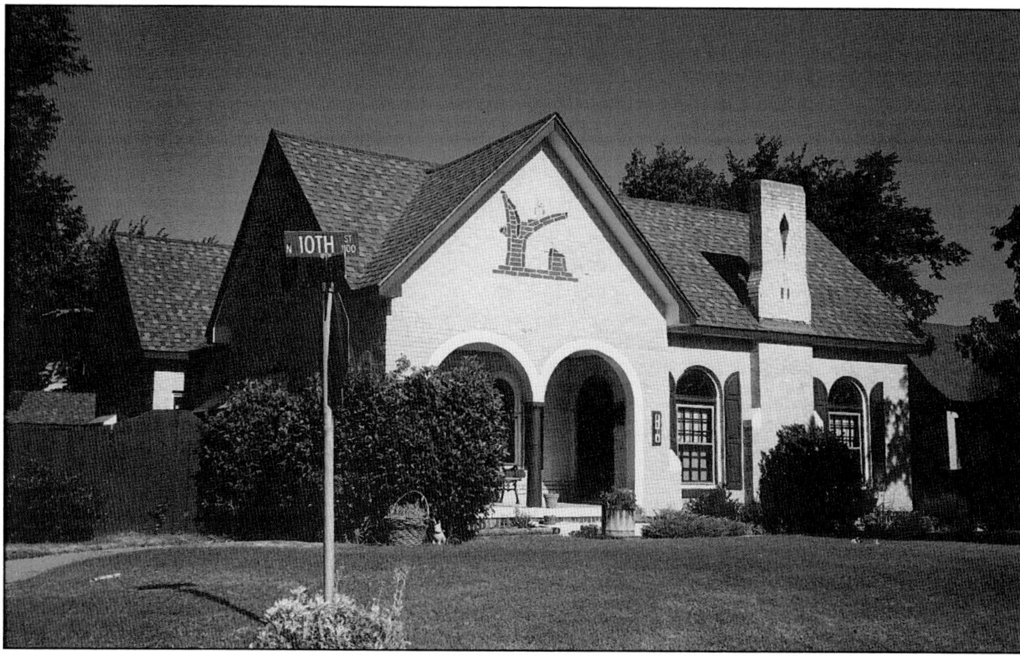

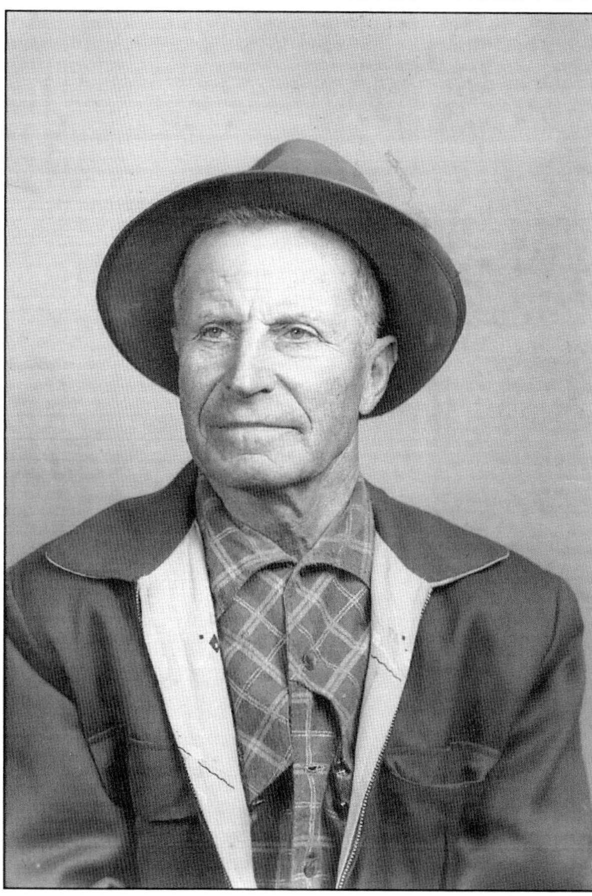

A true mark of a community's prosperity is the high quality of its homes, even middle-income homes. Duncan residents built many fine homes in the prosperous 1920s, many the work of skilled masons like Lucian Haas, pictured left. Haas learned his trade from Duncan's first skilled mason, Henry Jobert, and personalized each of his houses with a bit of decorative brickwork. The results of his skills are evident even today in these surviving examples. note the owl in the decorative tree above. (Mr. Haas' picture courtesy of his family.)

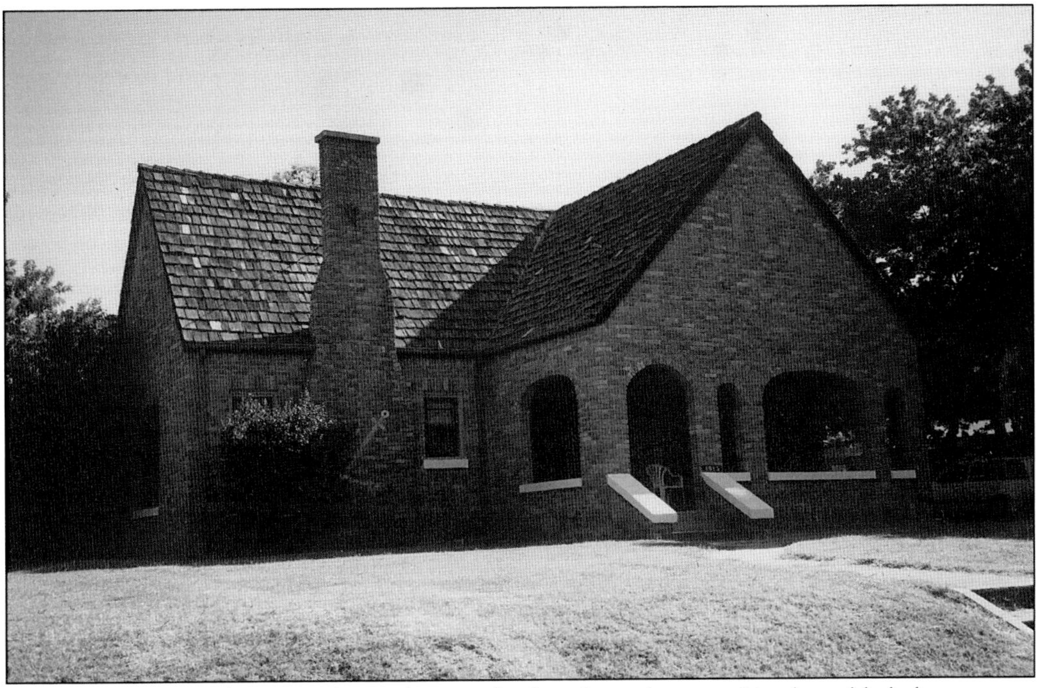

Mr. Haas' skills are shown in the anchor on the fire place above and in the gable below.

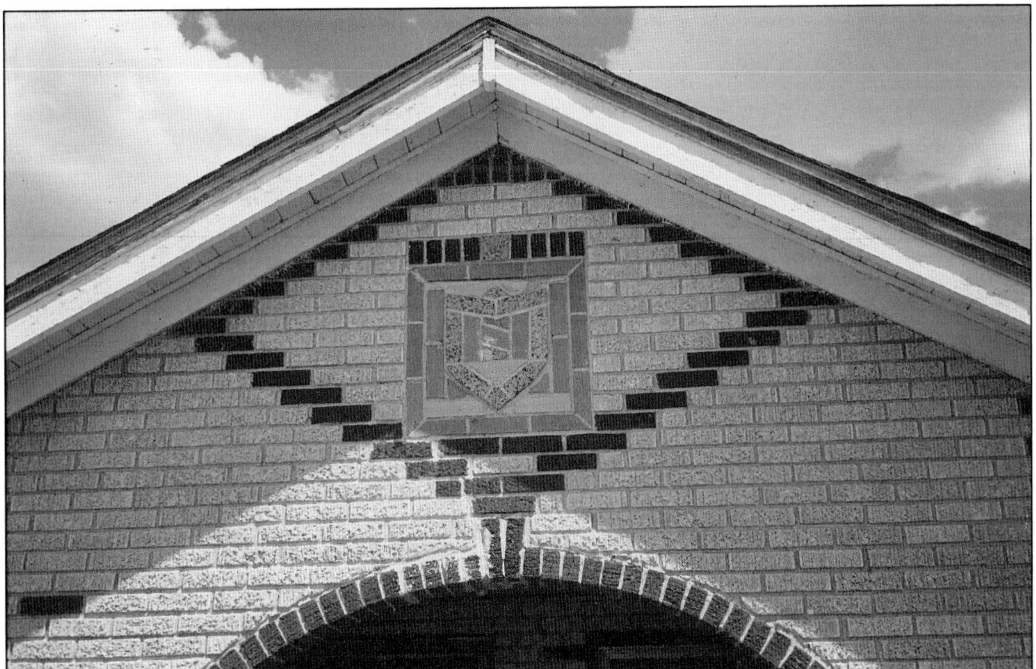

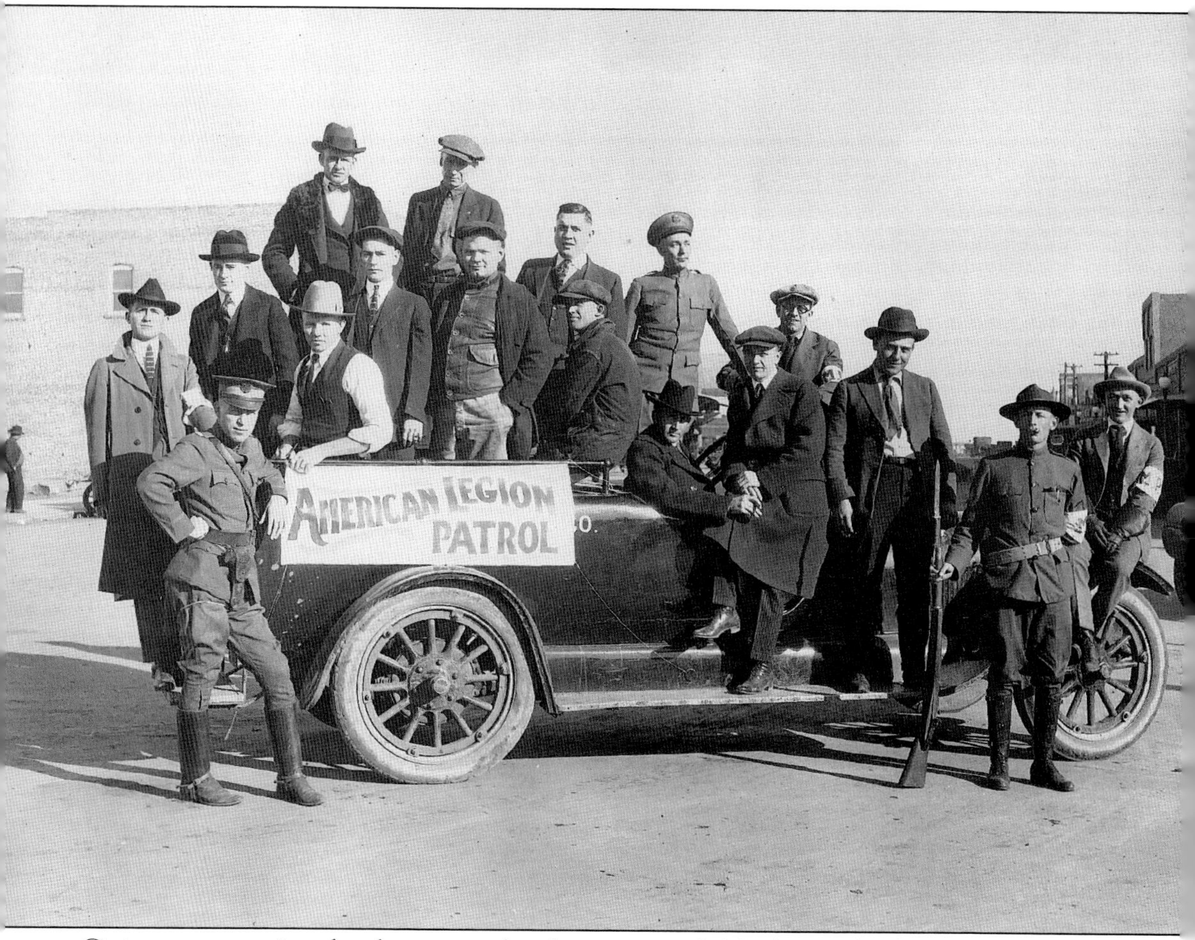

Civic groups continued to be a part of each community's life during the decade. Pictured on above is the American Legion Patrol, comprised of the county's World War I veterans.

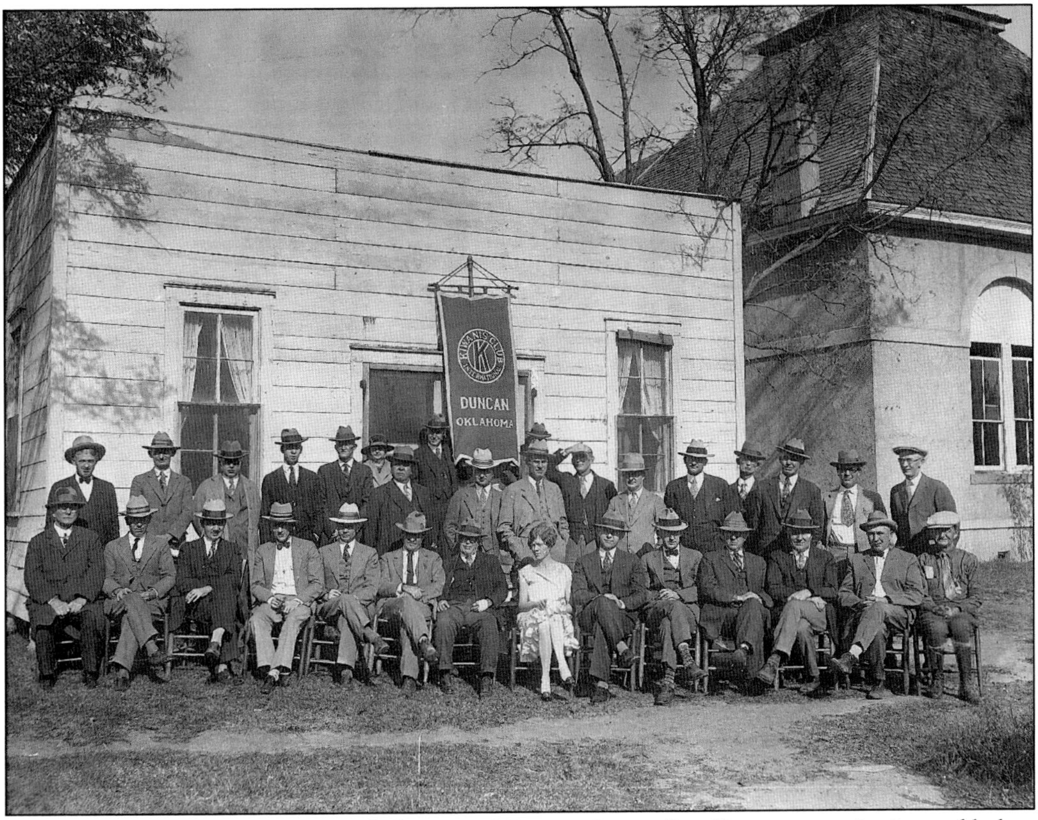

Duncan's Kiwanis Club is pictured above, and Duncan's own Boy Scouts troop is pictured below during an "Anti-Puncture" campaign to rid the roads of puncture-causing debris. Automobile tires in the 1920s were very susceptible to punctures.

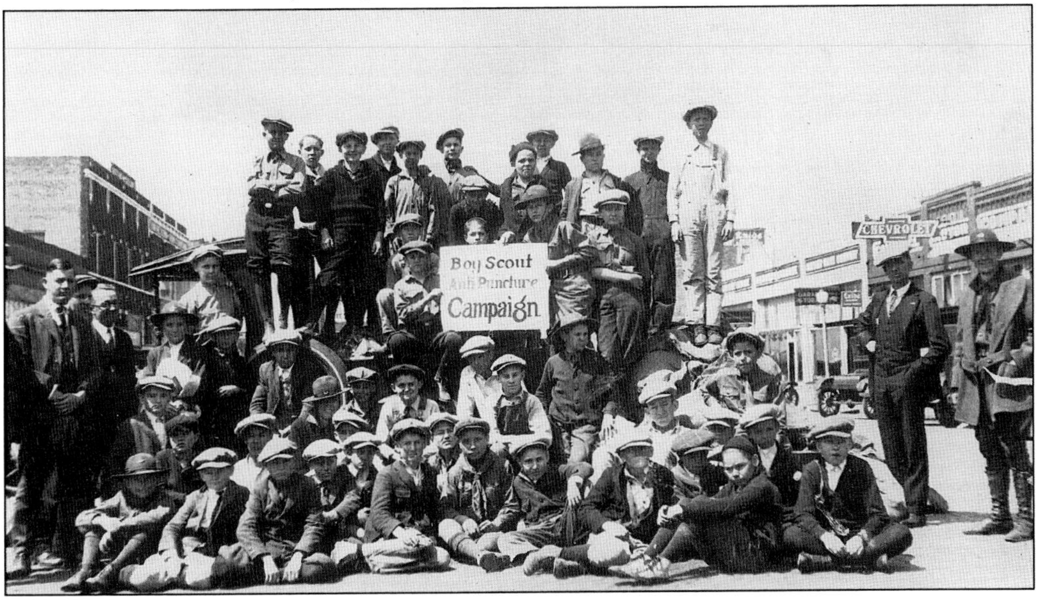

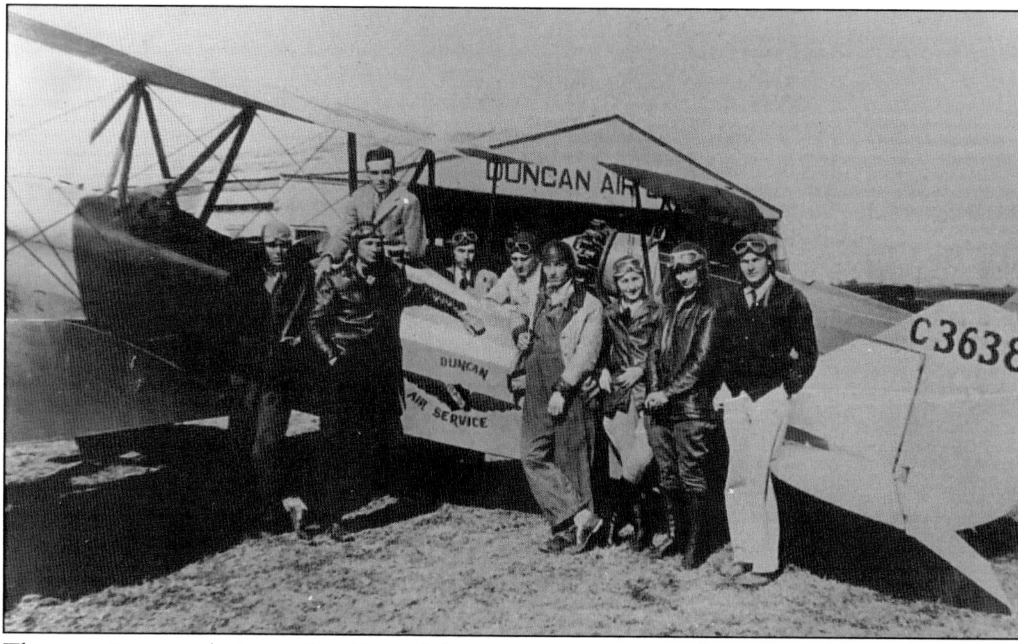

The growing popularity and utility of American aviation in the 1920s played a significant role in Duncan. The community's airfield hosted a flying school, pictured above. Owned by John Halliburton, the World War I training aircraft provided training for many of Stephens County's early aviators.

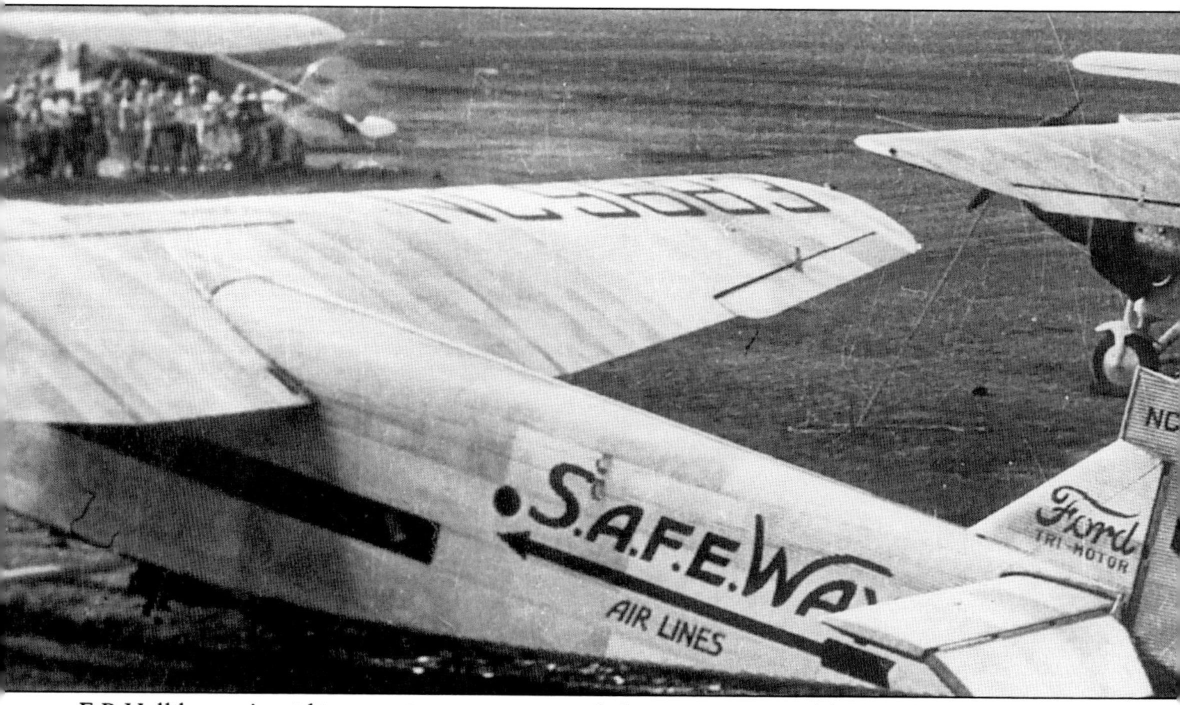

E.P. Halliburton's avid interest in aviation extended to recognition of the need for a safe, reliable air transportation system. In April 1929, he founded S.A.F.E. Airlines, or Southwest Air Fast Express, one of the first in the nation. With eight Ford Trimotors, it was a success. Over its

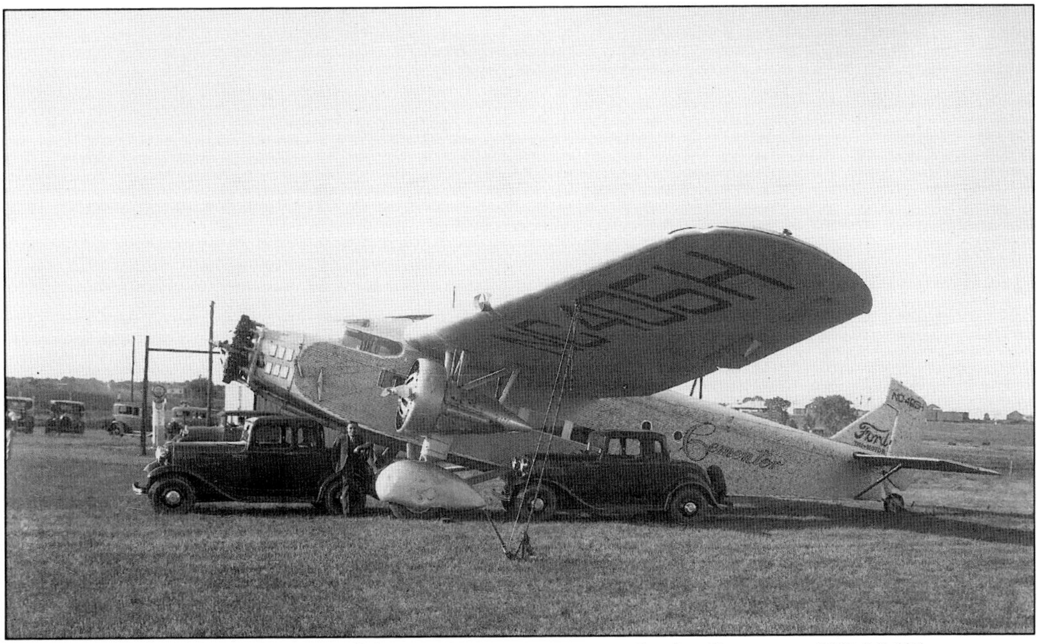

Duncan's airfield was host to Halliburton's company aircraft, the *Cementer*. E.P. Halliburton was an early advocate of aviation, and his company became one of the first in the nation to acquire a corporate aircraft. Mr. Halliburton is pictured with his aircraft in the late 1920s.

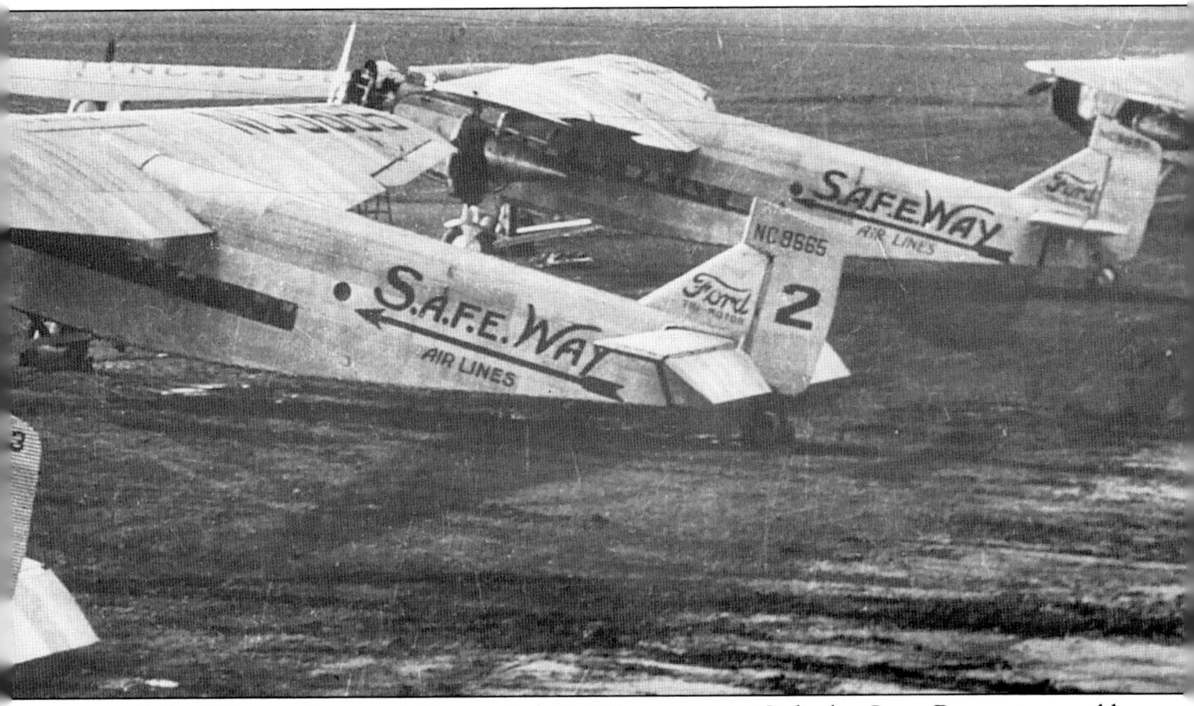

brief life of 18 months, the airline carried 48,000 passengers. Only the Great Depression could stop its operations.

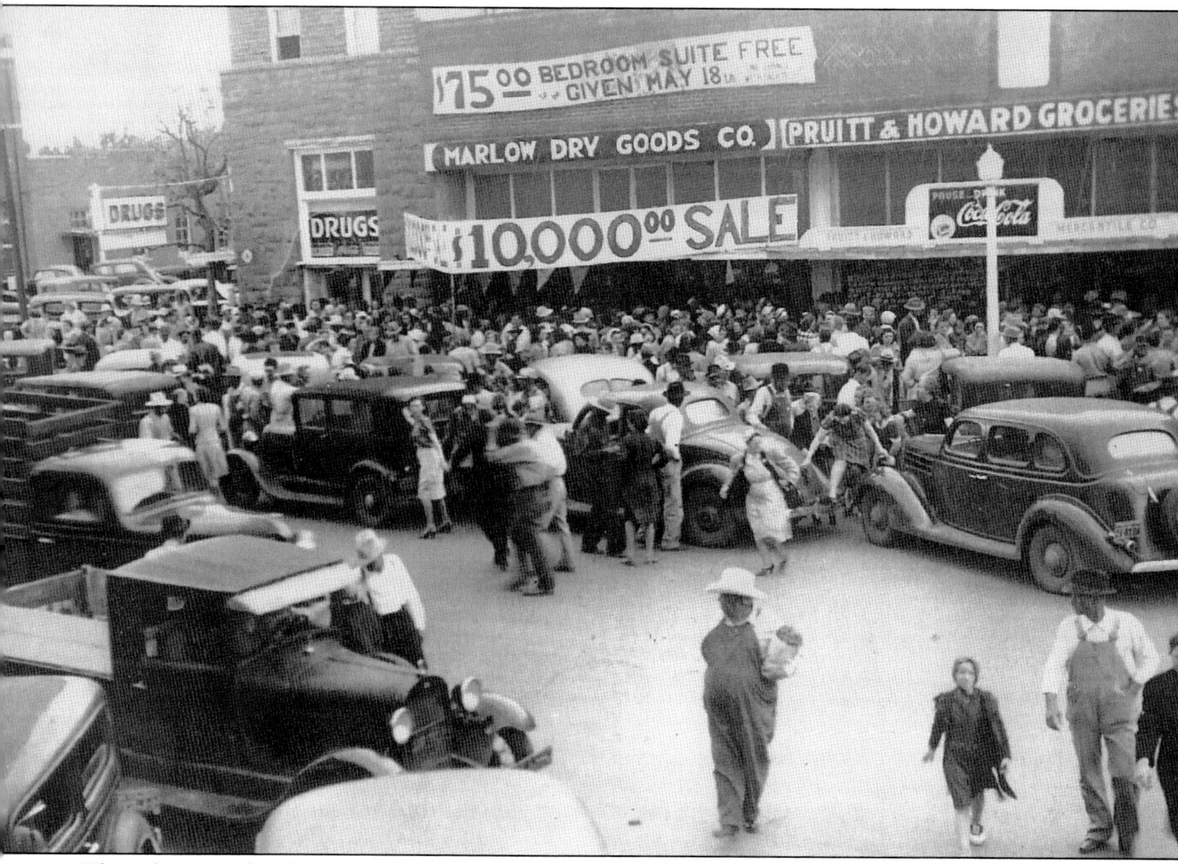

The photograph above in many ways epitomizes the Great Depression. In this image, a crowd throngs in front of the Marlow Dry Goods store in hopes of winning the $75 bedroom suite being offered.

Five

From Prosperity to Depression and Recovery

The 1930s

The Depression hit rural Oklahoma particularly hard. Though its effects were clearly felt in Stephens County, even at lower prices and lower production, the oil industry provided a base that made life less difficult for many. For those less fortunate, however, the communities responded with assistance and support.

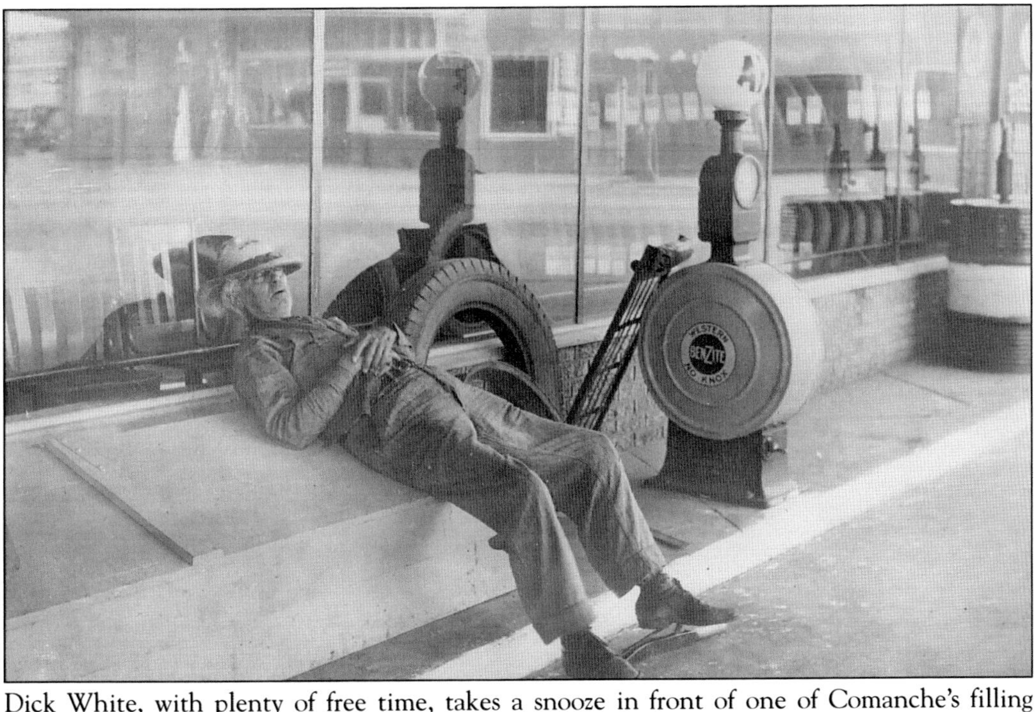

Dick White, with plenty of free time, takes a snooze in front of one of Comanche's filling stations as he waits for customers for his harness and shoe shop across the street.

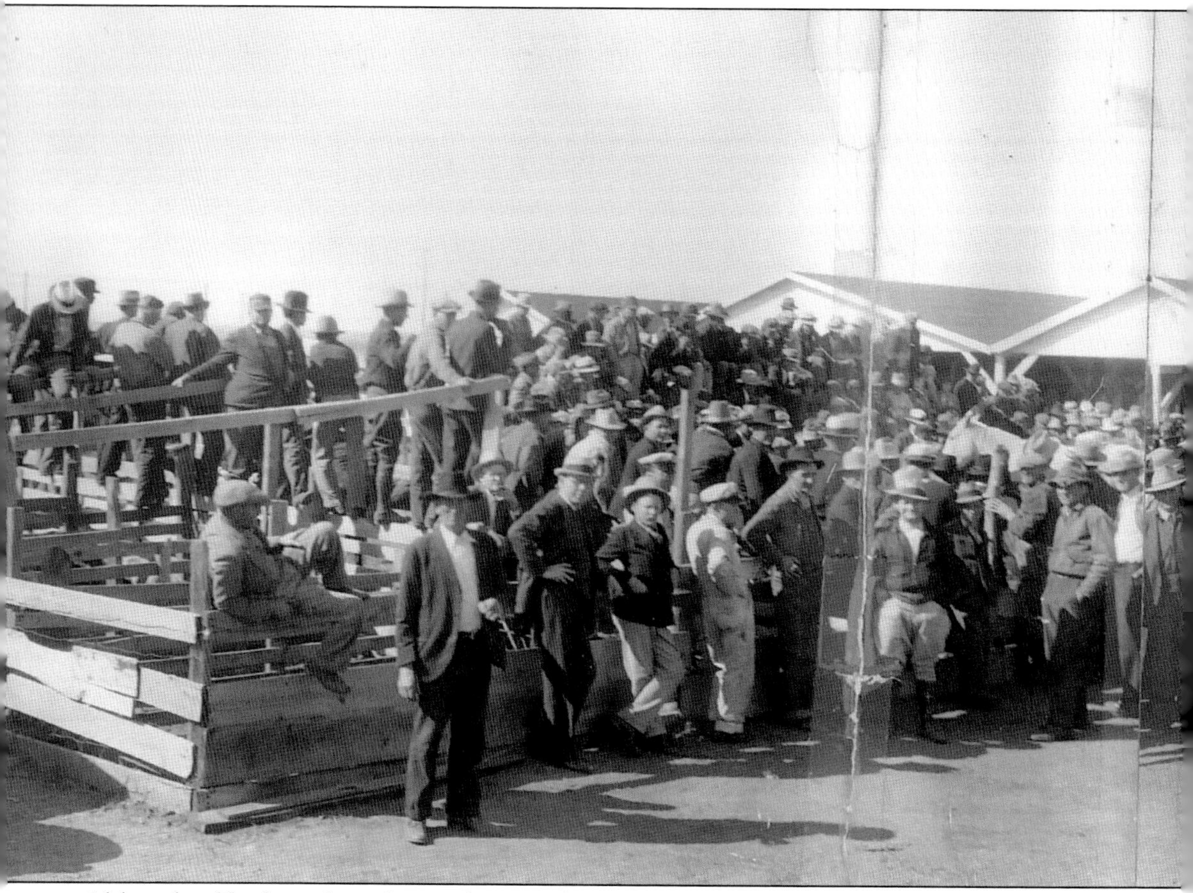

Although oil had supplanted agriculture in the 1920s as the county's highest income producer, the county was still supported by a broad, productive agricultural base. In the 1930s, with the

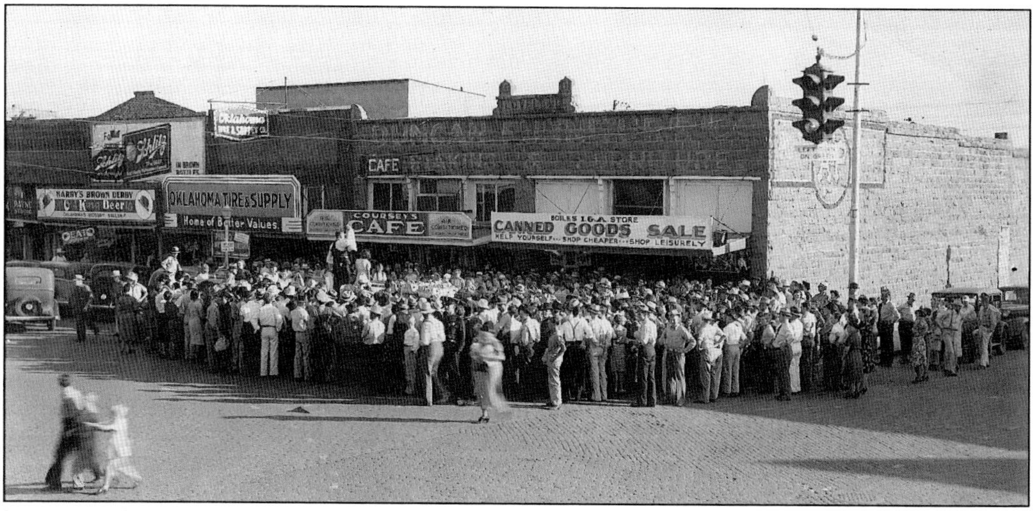

Drawings for food baskets and other goods were popular in the 1930s, as this one on Duncan's Main Street illustrates. The photo is looking southeast at the intersection of Ninth and Main Streets.

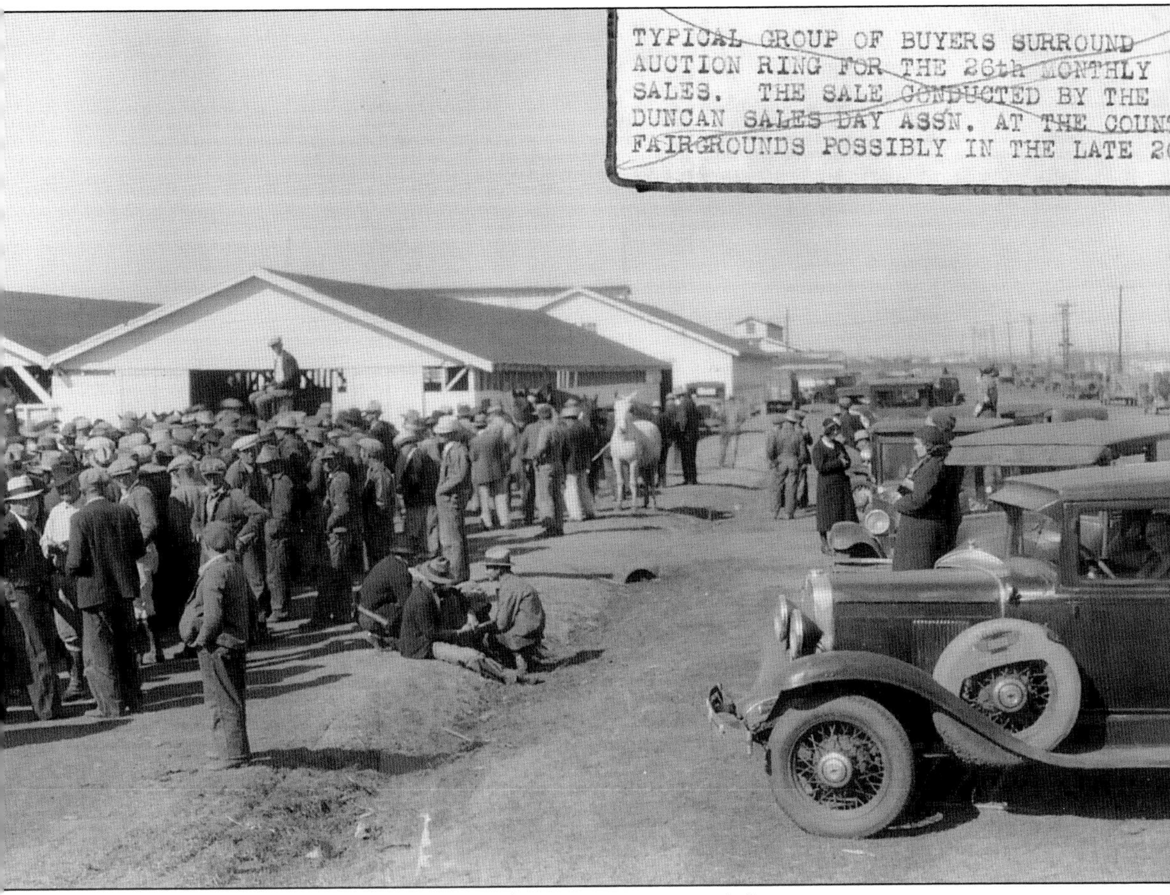

price of oil and production down, agriculture again sustained the economy.

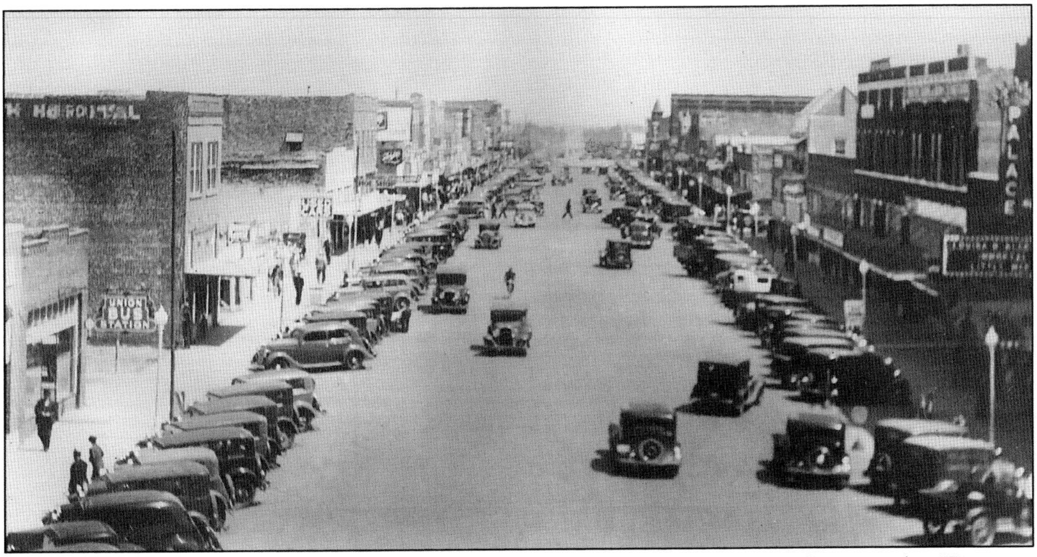

Duncan's Main Street still shows great activity, but not on the same scale as in the "Roaring Twenties." This view looks east, taken from the county courthouse.

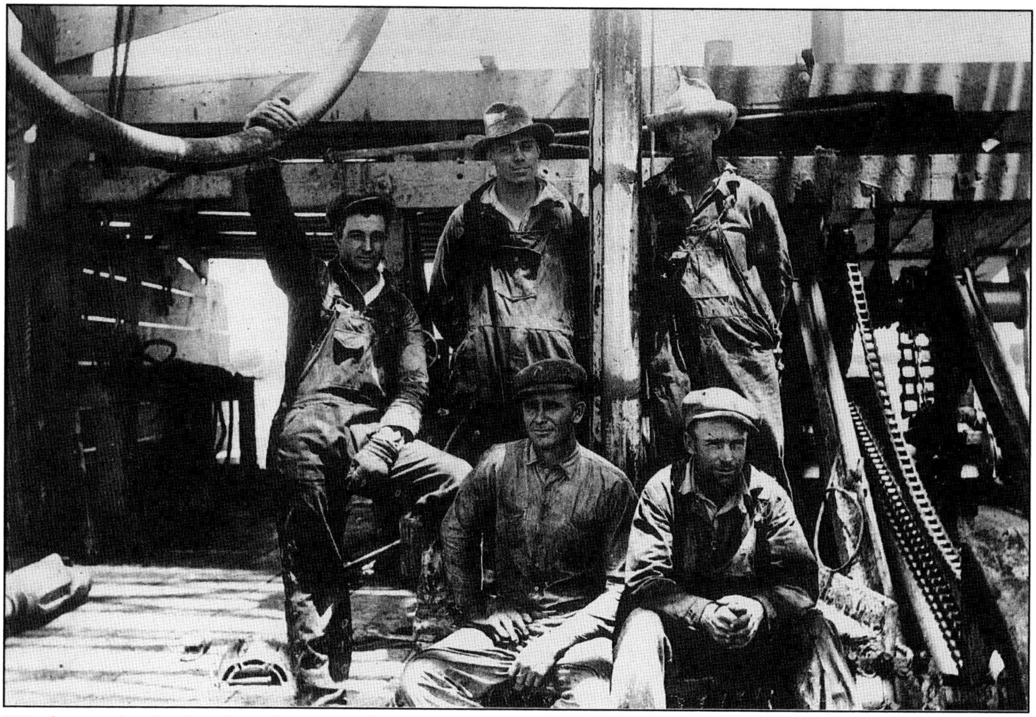

Work, or the lack of it, became the major issue of the Depression years. While the oil fields continued to provide some jobs, as above, communities were increasingly turning to public works. Duncan was no exception. Road building, below, both provided employment and improved rural roads.

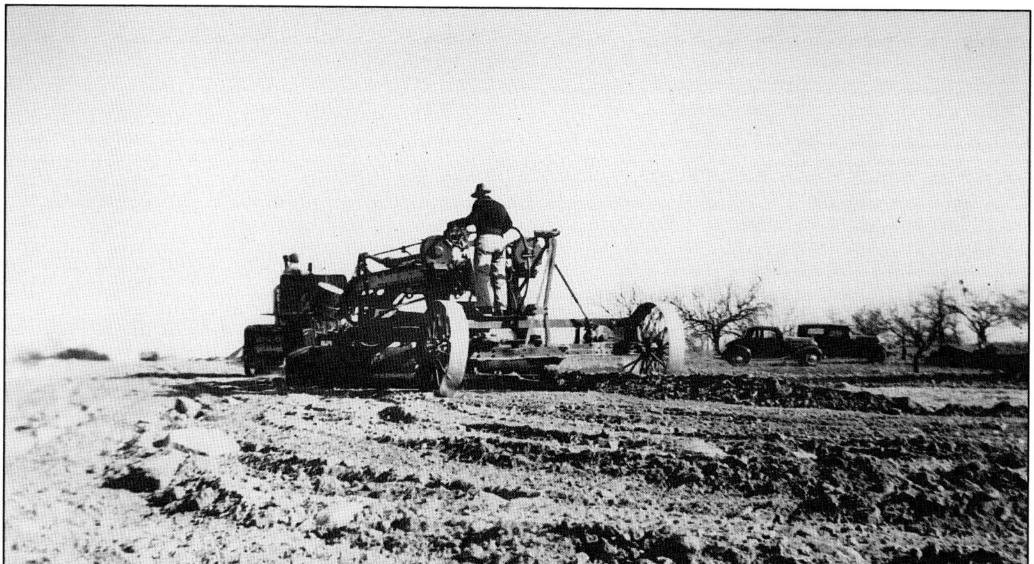

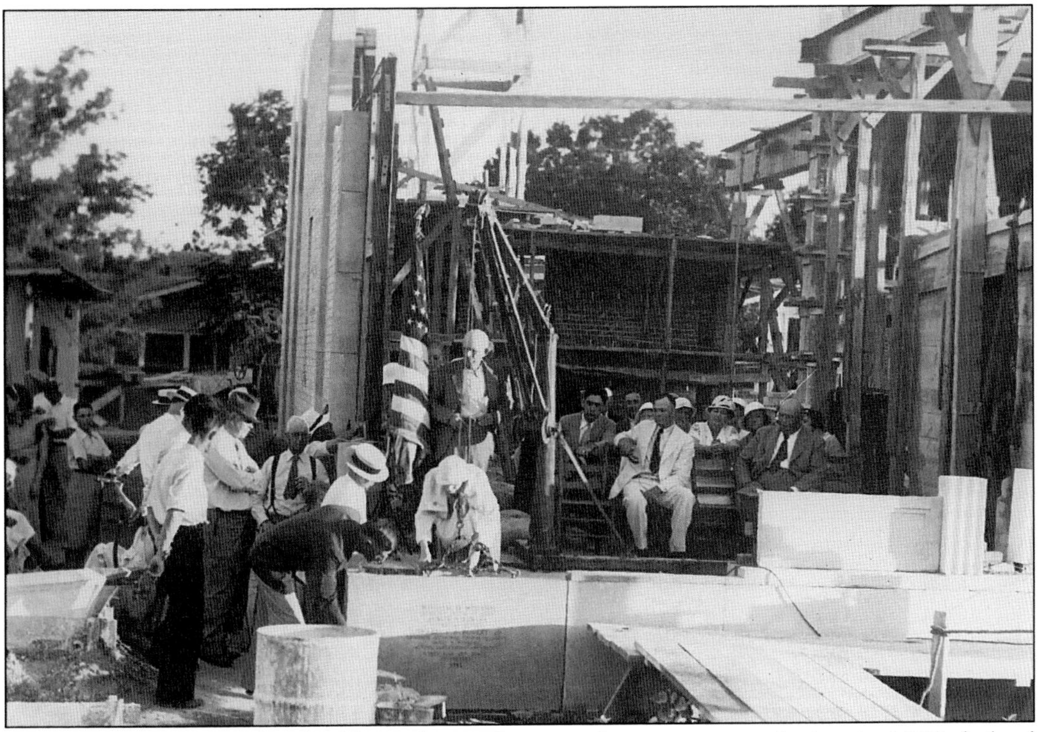

Duncan's new post office building, shown here at the cornerstone laying in 1933, helped local building trades.

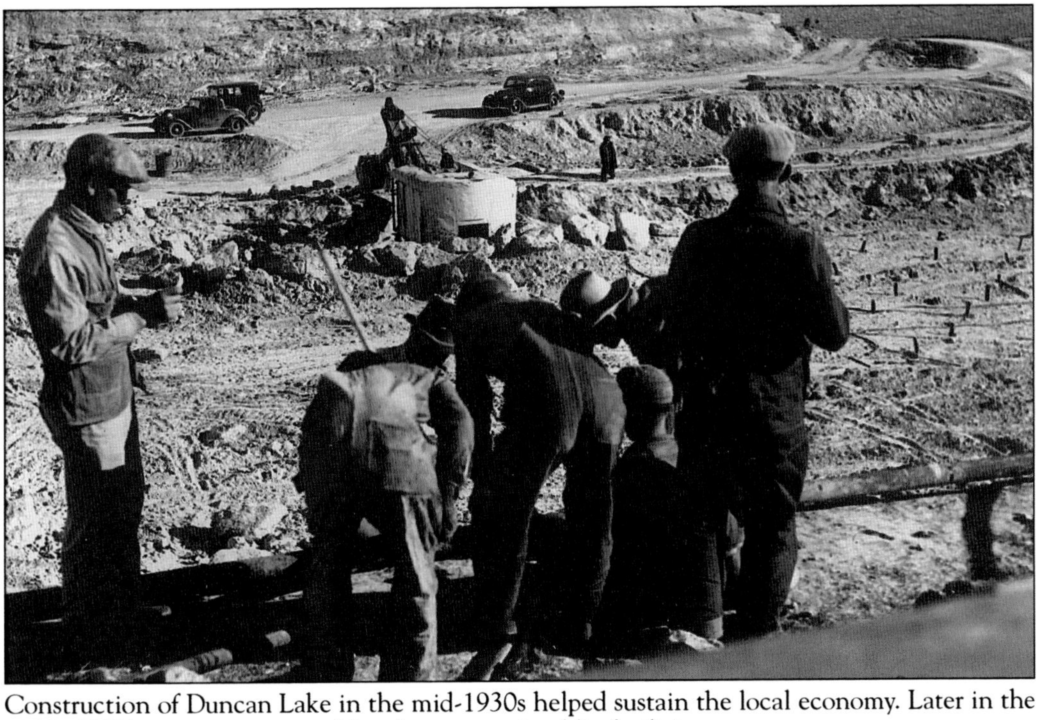

Construction of Duncan Lake in the mid-1930s helped sustain the local economy. Later in the 1930s, WPA projects improved local streets and public facilities.

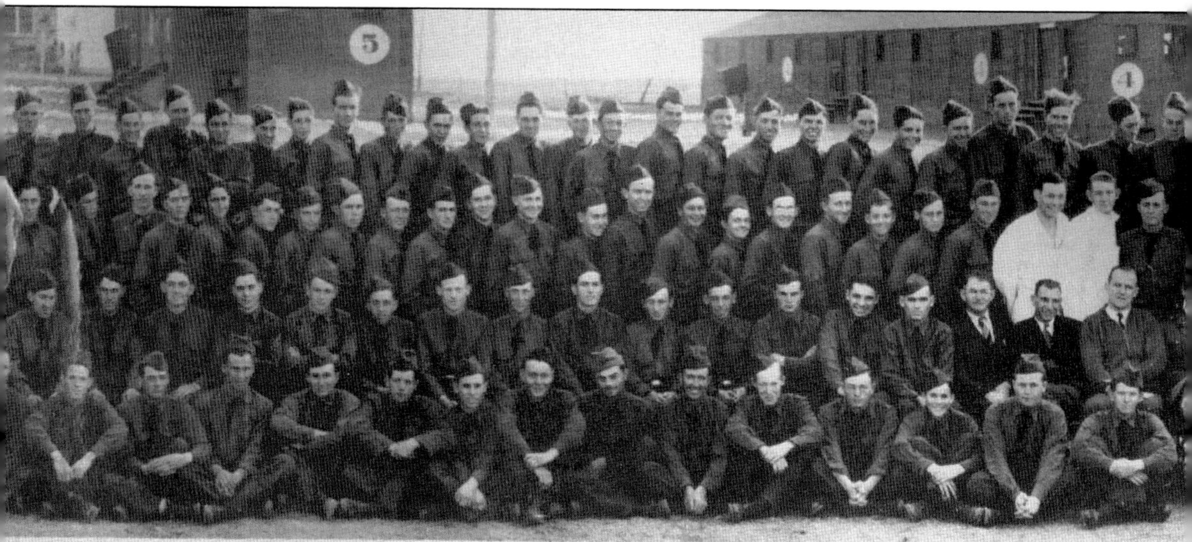

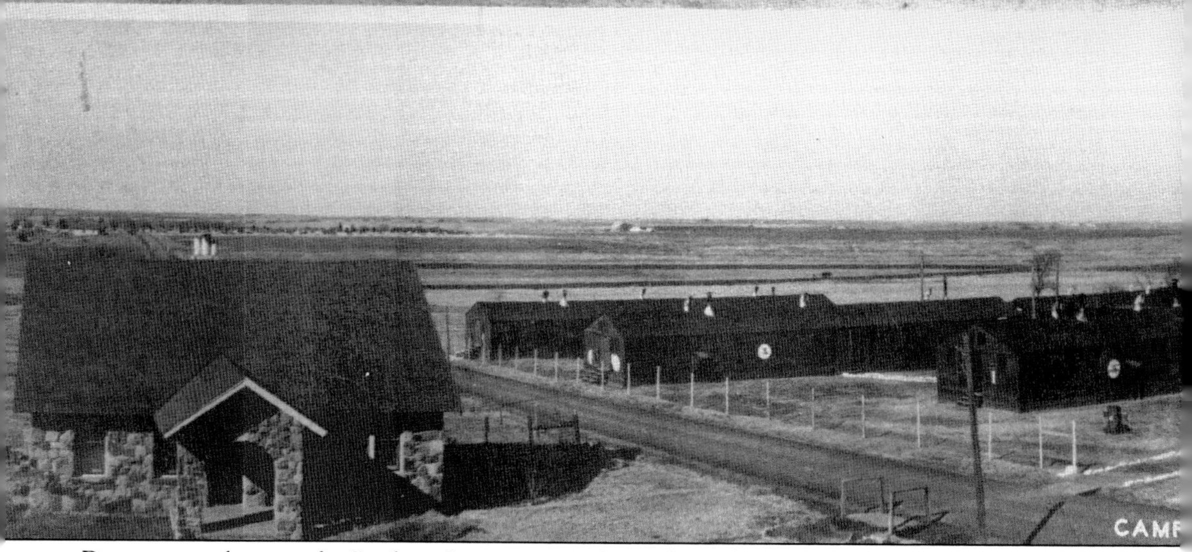

Duncan was the site of a Civilian Conservation Corps (CCC) camp during the latter part of the decade. A federal work program, it employed millions of young men in conservation projects across the country. In Stephens County, CCC workers contoured most of the county's fields to control erosion, and spent a good portion of their payroll in Duncan. Duncan's CCC camp

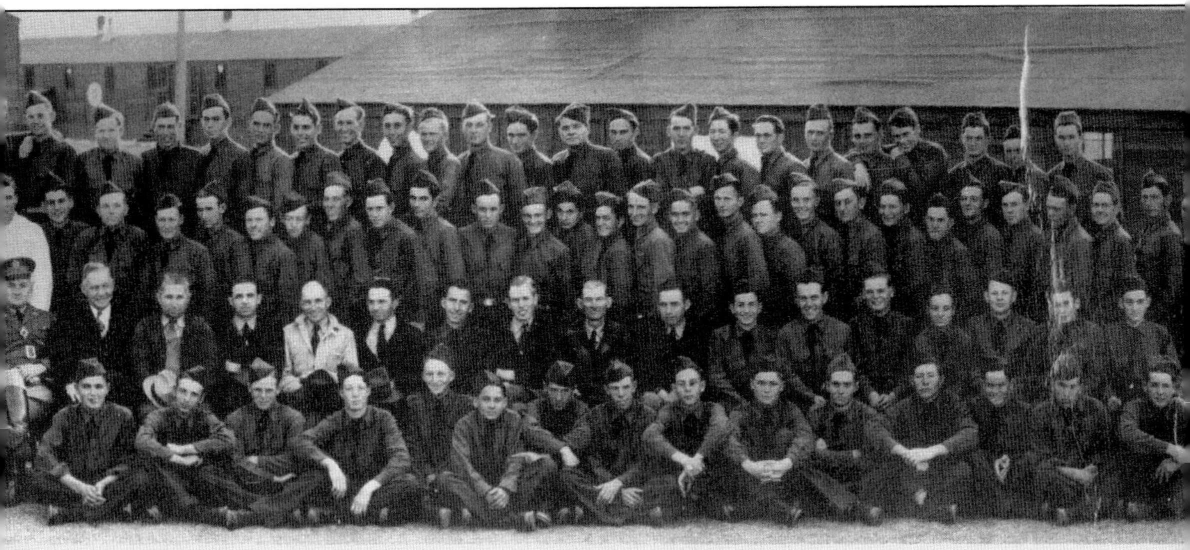

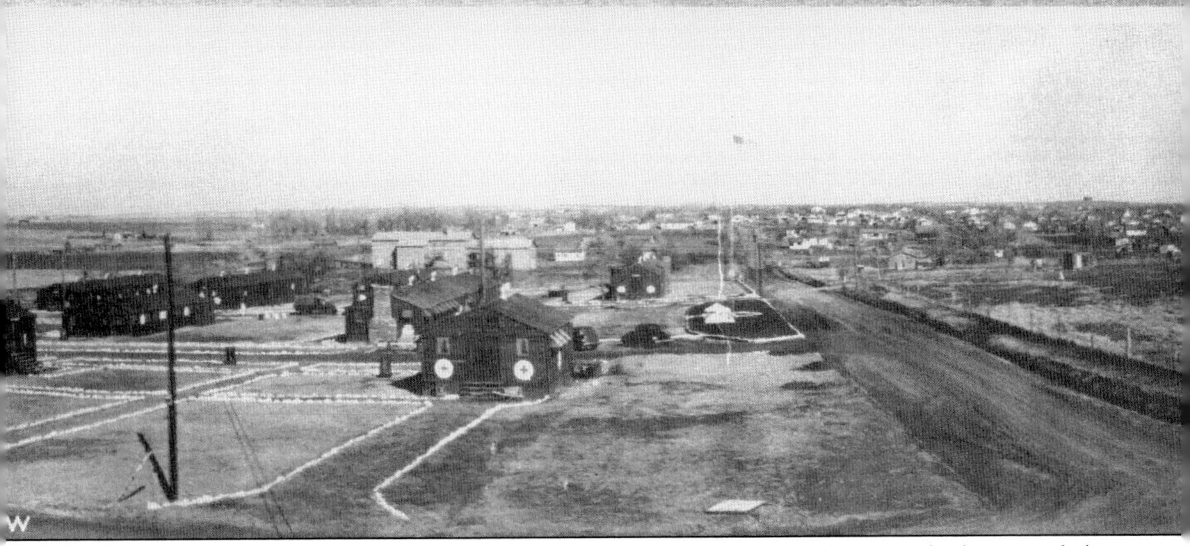

was located at the intersection of Cypress and Fifteenth Streets. This view looks toward the northwest and pictures a house, far left, that stands today. Many a Stephens County boy found himself in the CCC.

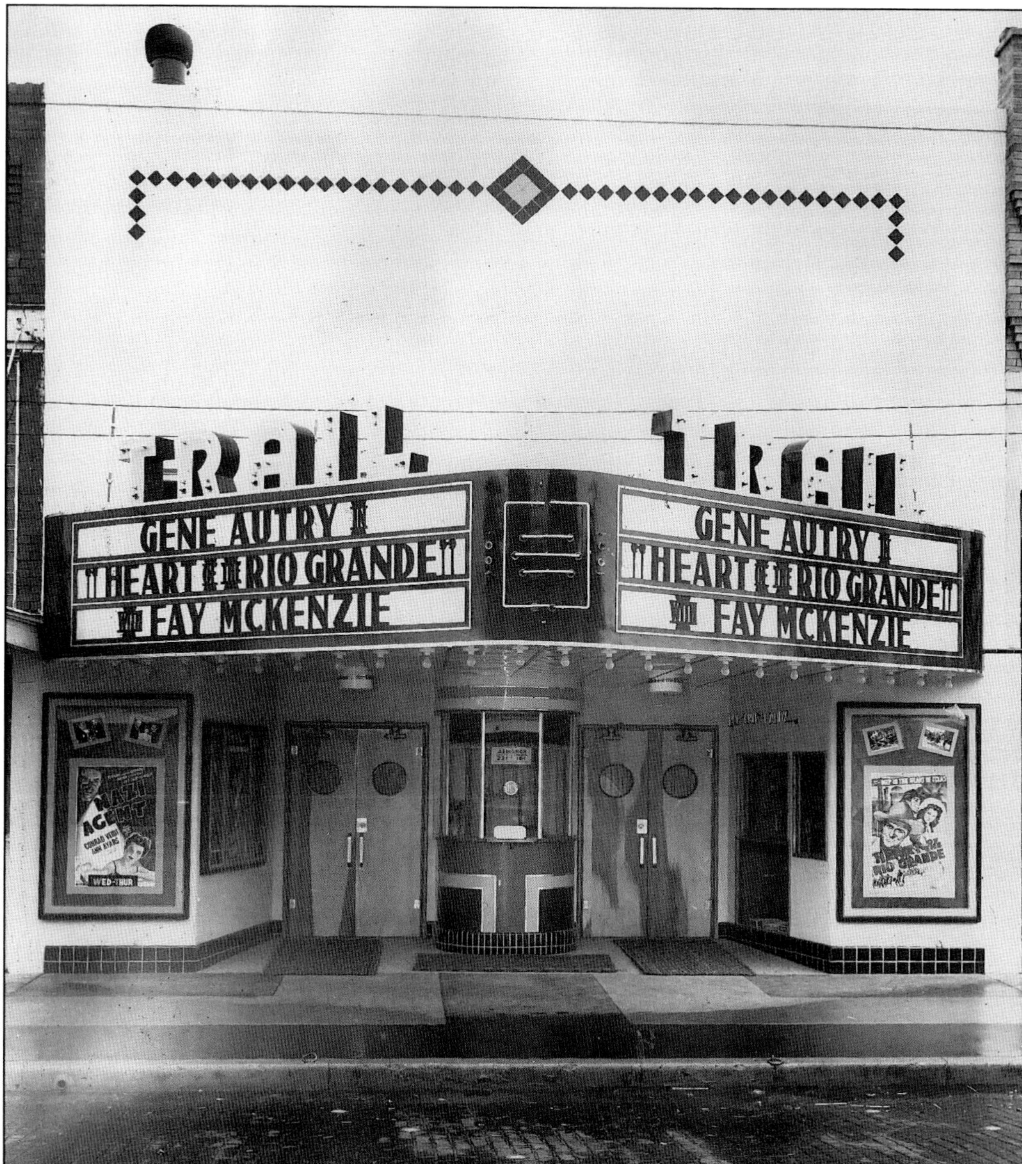

By the 1930s, movies had established themselves as the major form of low-cost entertainment in America. Duncan boasted five movie theaters: the Trail, pictured above, the Palace, the Ritz, the Moore, and the Folly. Marlow had the Alamo, and Comanche had the Quanah and the Ritz.

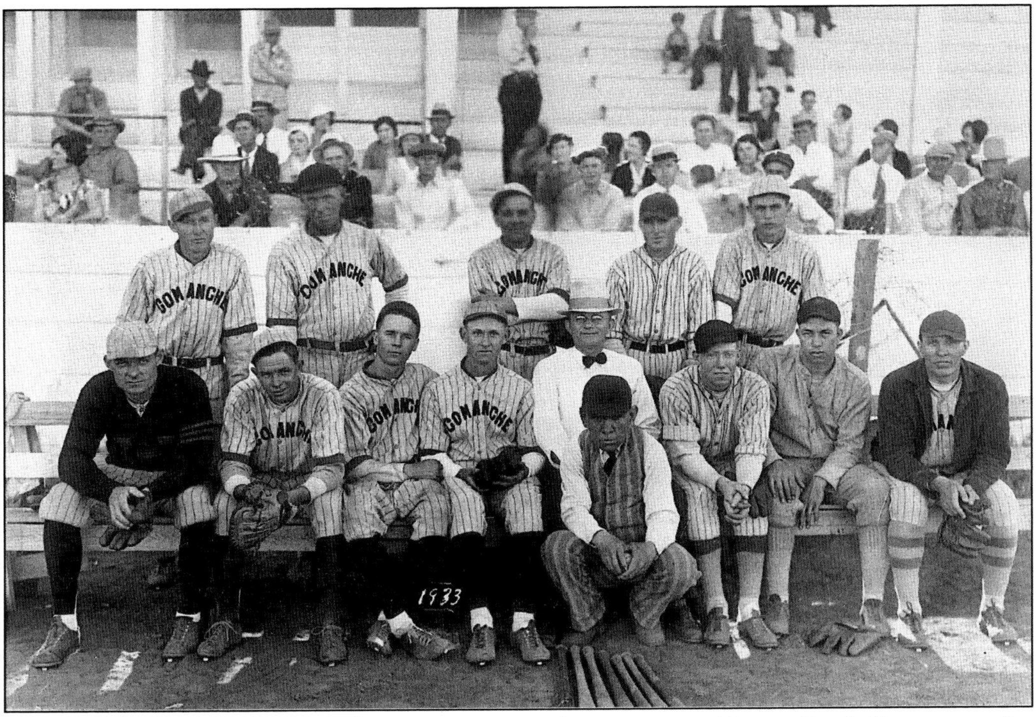

Movies did not furnish the only entertainment for county residents. Baseball was a major attraction, particularly Comanche's team pictured in 1933. Of course, rodeos have always been popular, even up to today. Below, Walter Cranin is pictured riding in a Duncan rodeo in 1936.

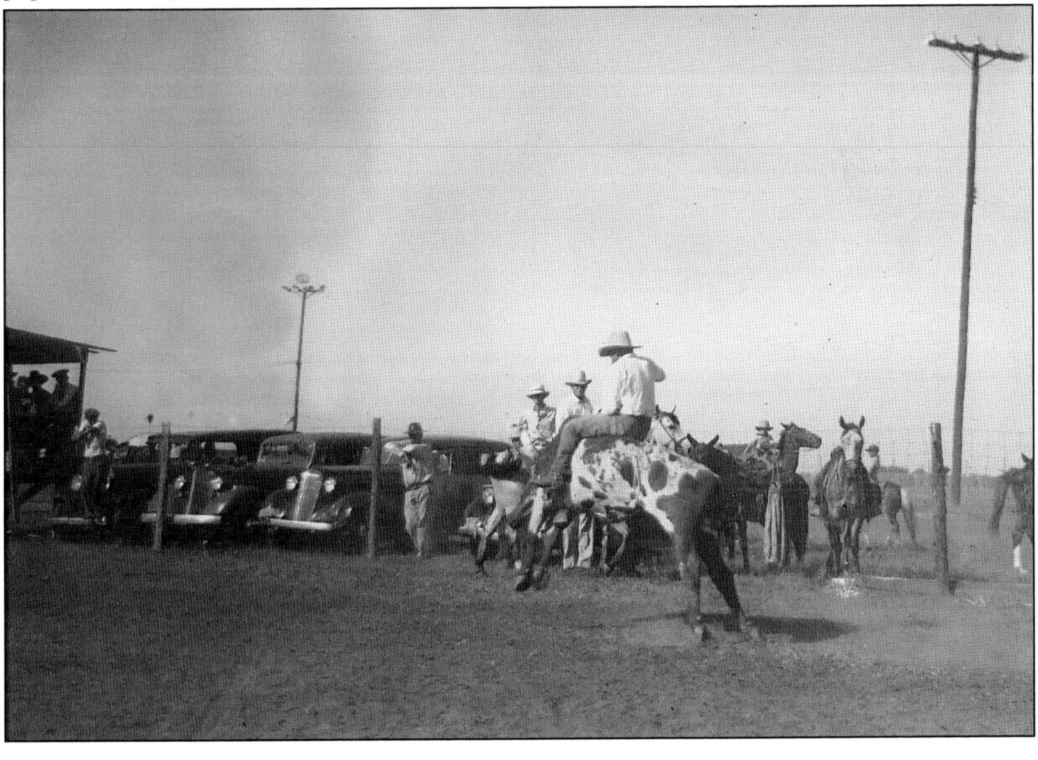

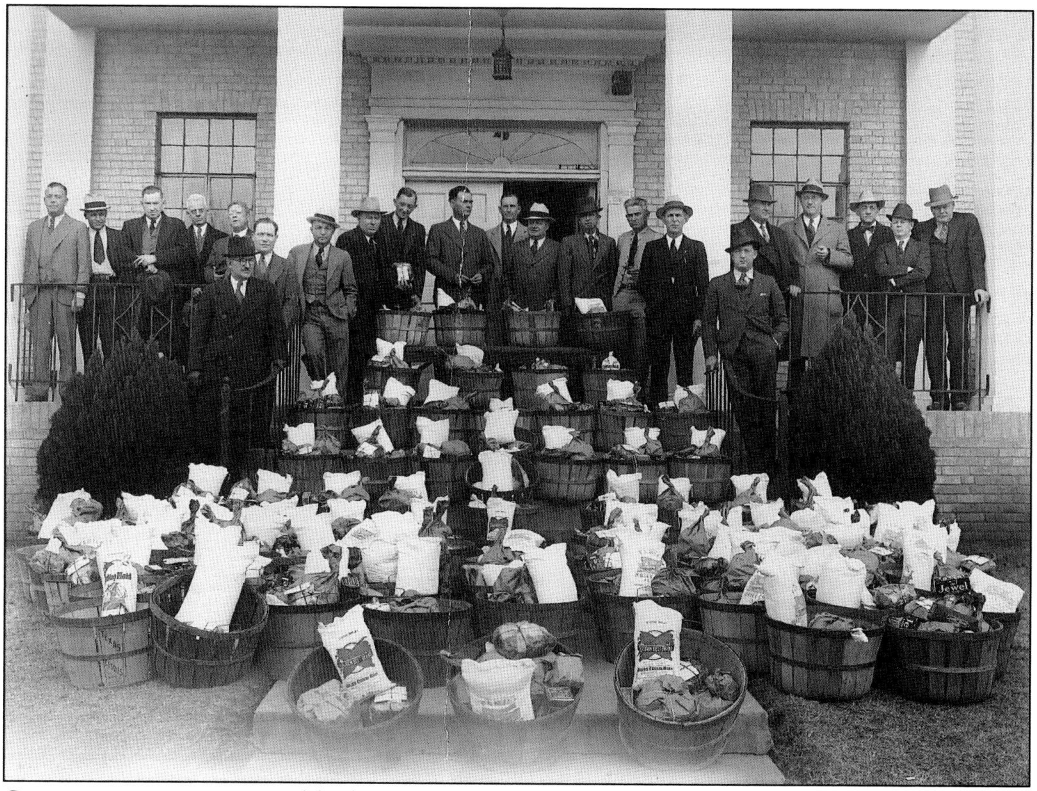

Community spirit remained high during the Great Depression, with civic groups performing many community activities. Above, Duncan's Elk Lodge prepares to distribute Christmas baskets in 1934. Pictured below is the men's group of the Methodist church.

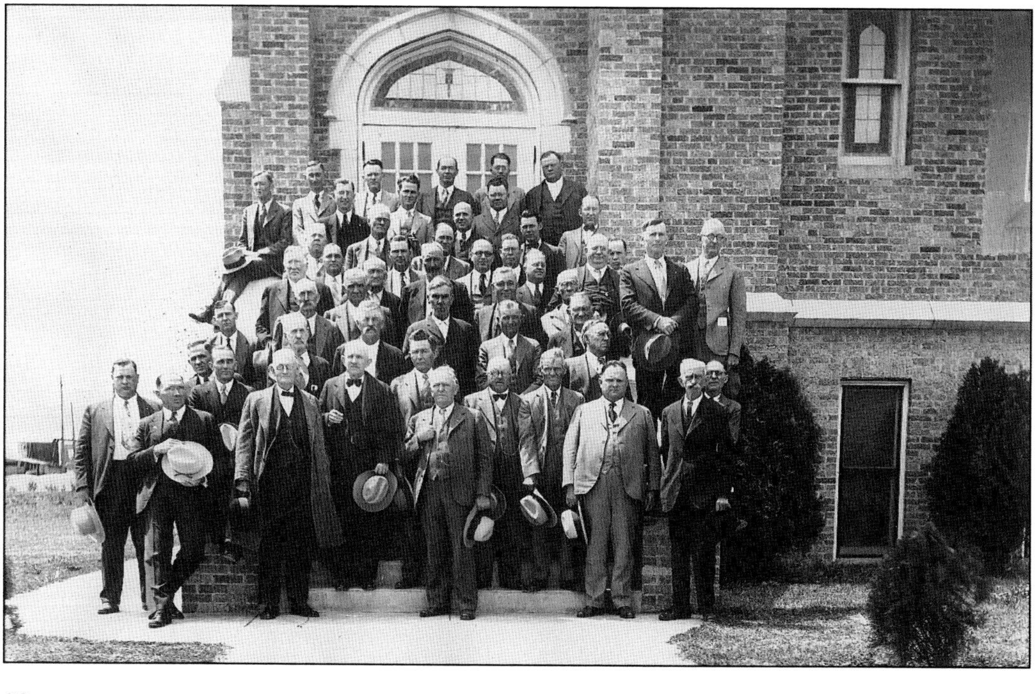

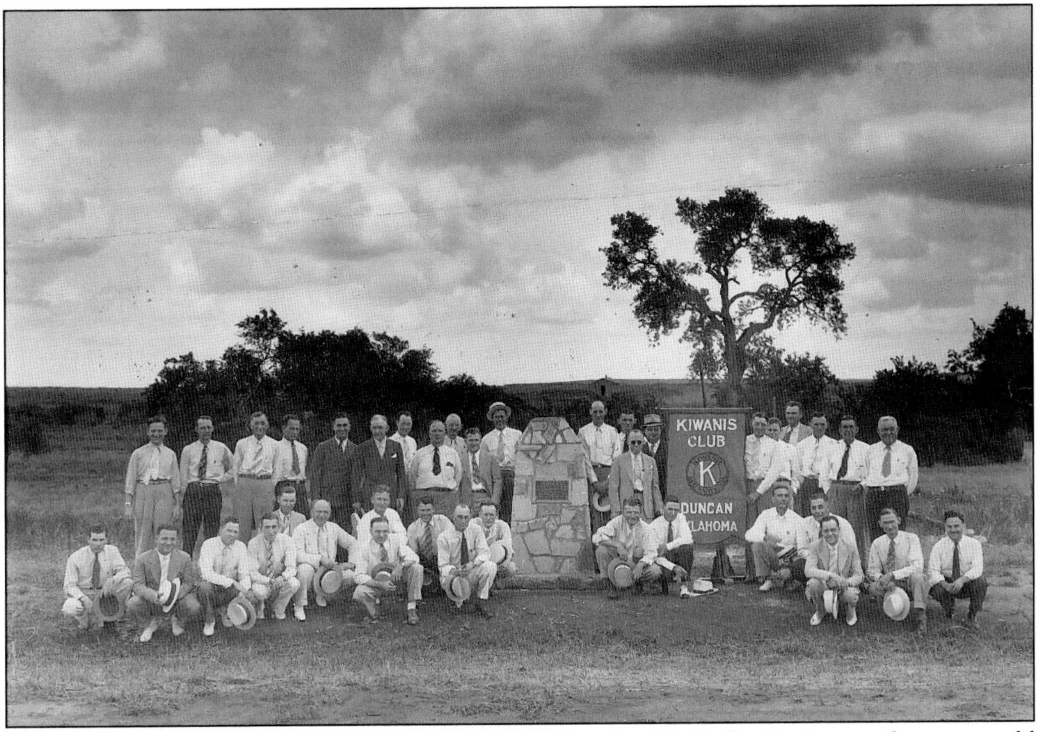

In 1937, the Kiwanis Club erected this monument to the Chisholm Trail east of town on old Highway 7. Below, Duncan High School's football team is pictured in training.

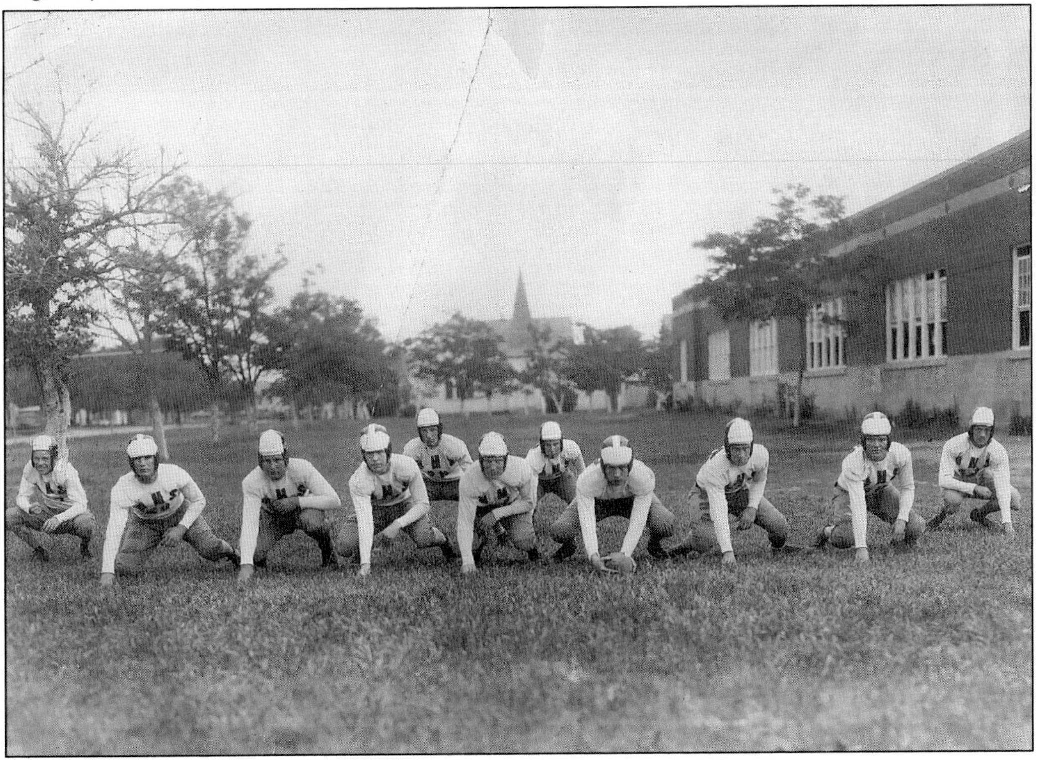

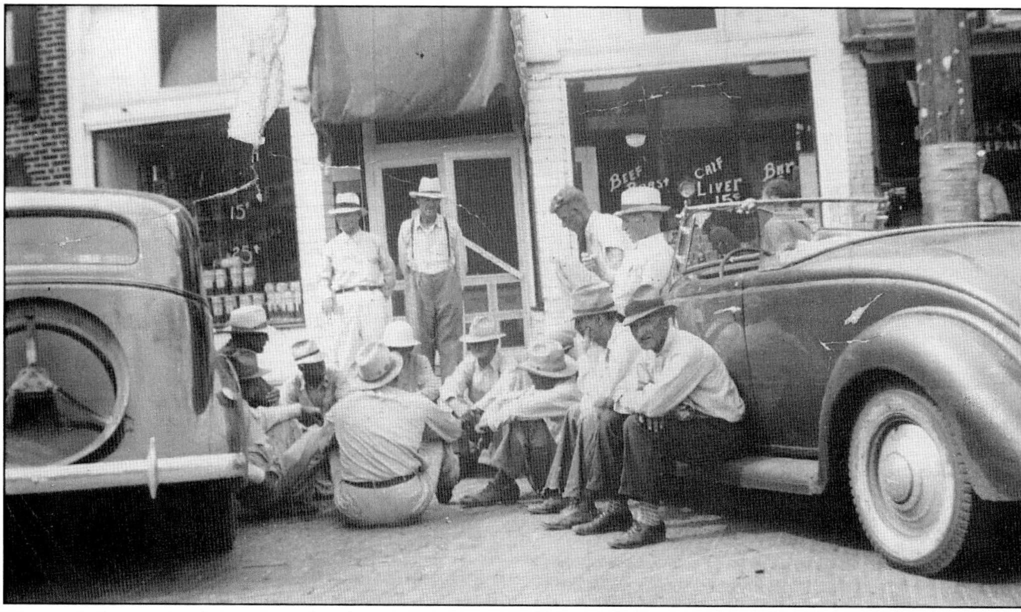

Toward the end of the decade, the debilitating effects of the Depression were moderating and increasing numbers of people were again working. But there was still time on a Saturday evening to gather and visit. A group of farmers assemble in front of Duncan's Speegle store in 1937.

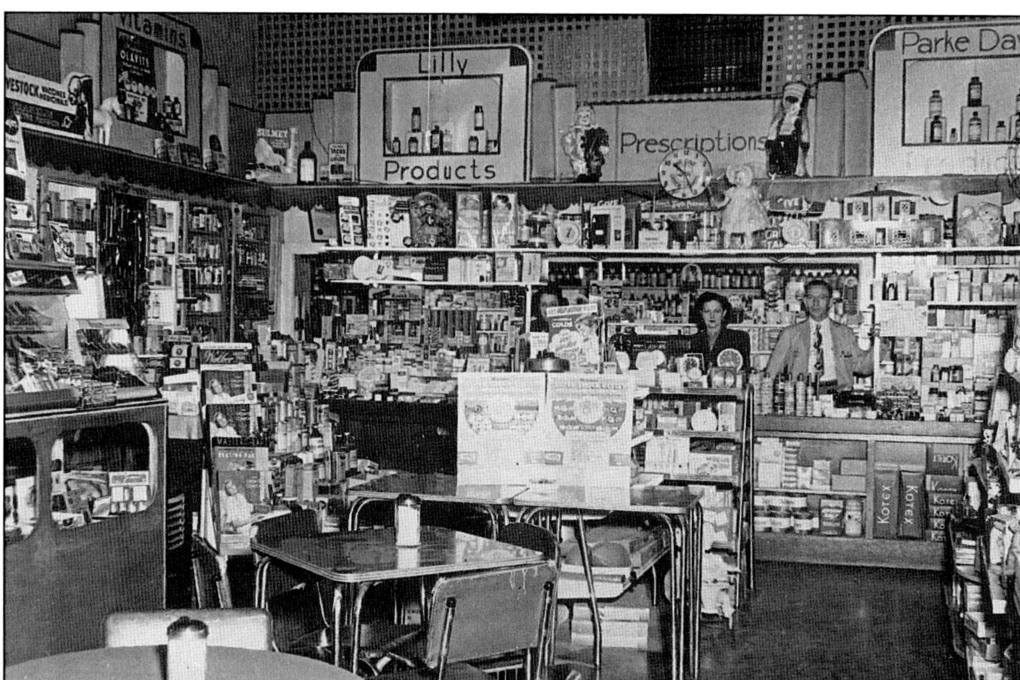

Bob Duncan's drugstore shows well-stocked shelves at the end of the decade.

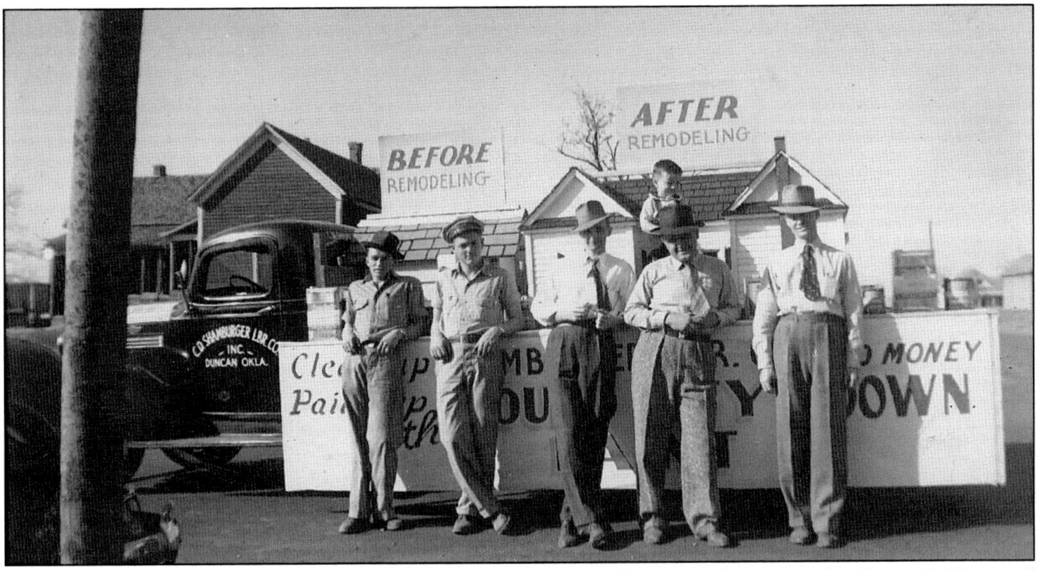

C.D. Shamburger Lumber Company advertises its building products in the late 1930s, and below, Millard O. Weaver, sponsored by local merchants, attempts to break the world's record endurance of 18 days.

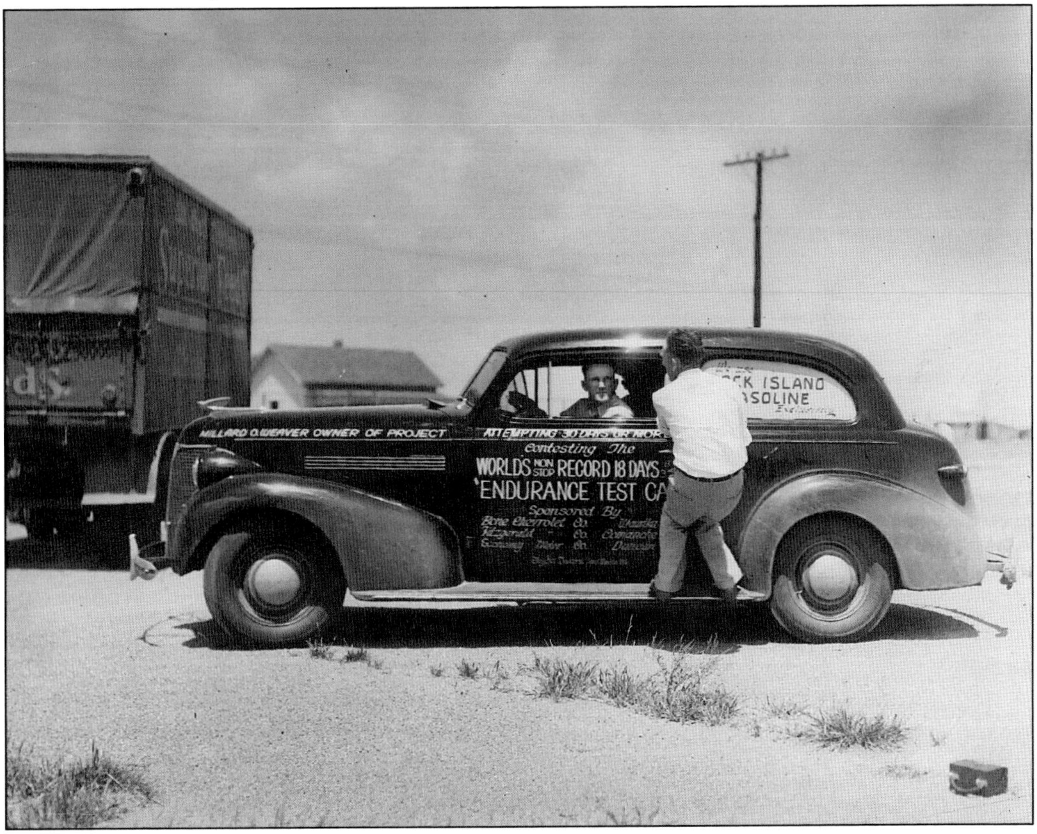

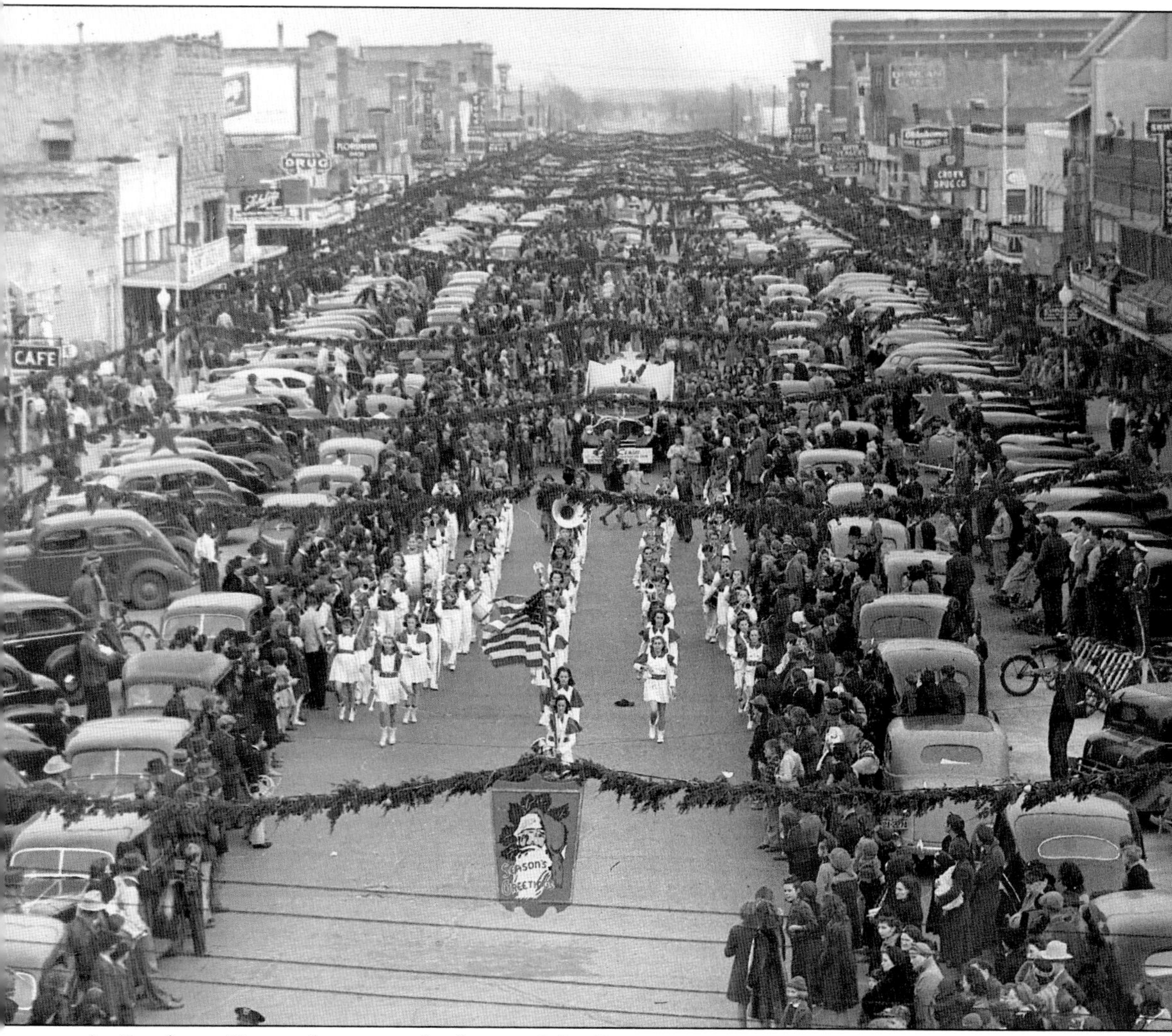

As Stephens County began to climb out of the Depression, community spirit soared. Duncan's annual Christmas Parade in 1940 suggests the community had a lot to celebrate. The view is to the east.

Six

The War Years and Renewed Growth
The 1940s

As great an impact that World War I had on Stephens County, when hundreds of county boys served, World War II had a decisive impact when thousands of its men and women went to war. Those on the homefront kept busy, doing their share, and when the boys returned, growth and prosperity were enjoyed by all.

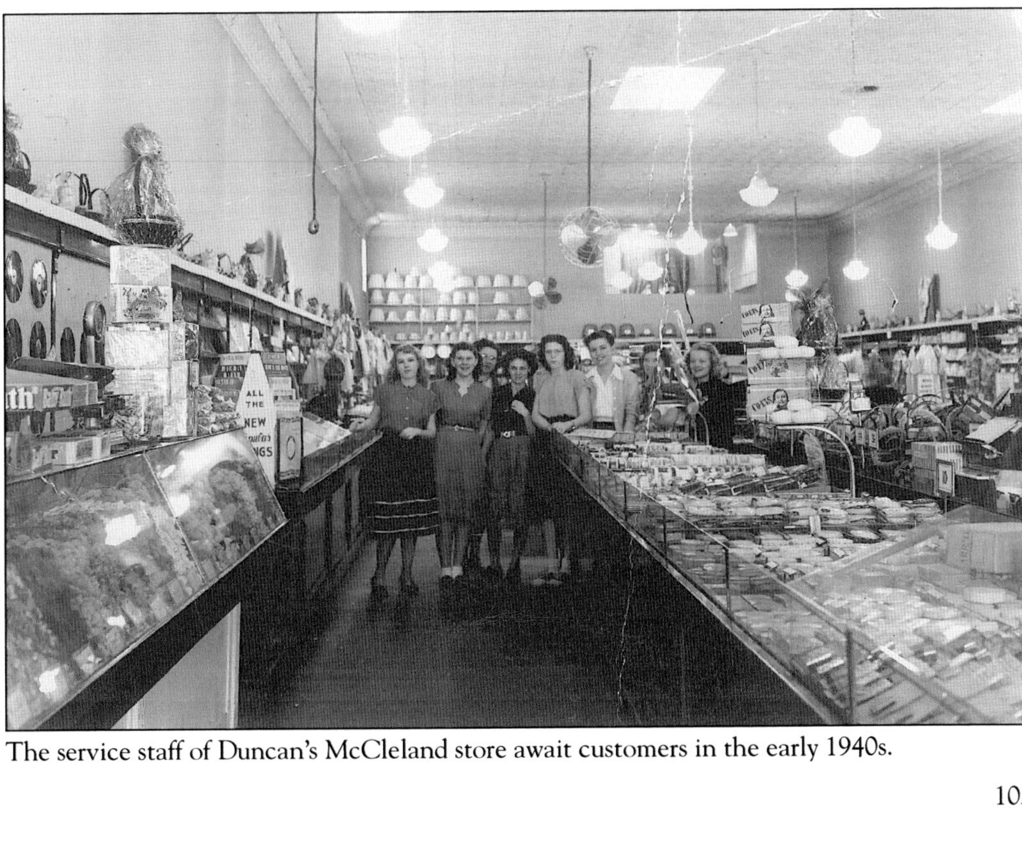

The service staff of Duncan's McCleland store await customers in the early 1940s.

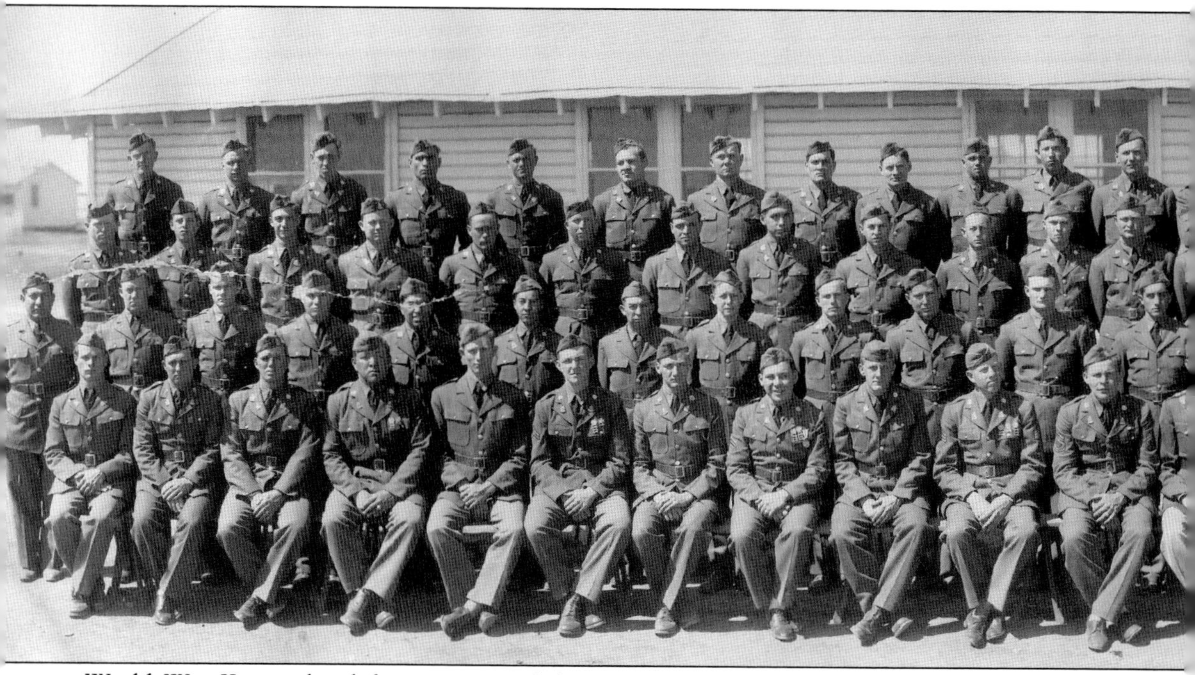

World War II was the defining event of the 1940s. In this rare photograph, Marlow's own Company L, 180th Infantry, Oklahoma National Guard, are pictured at Camp Barkeley, Texas,

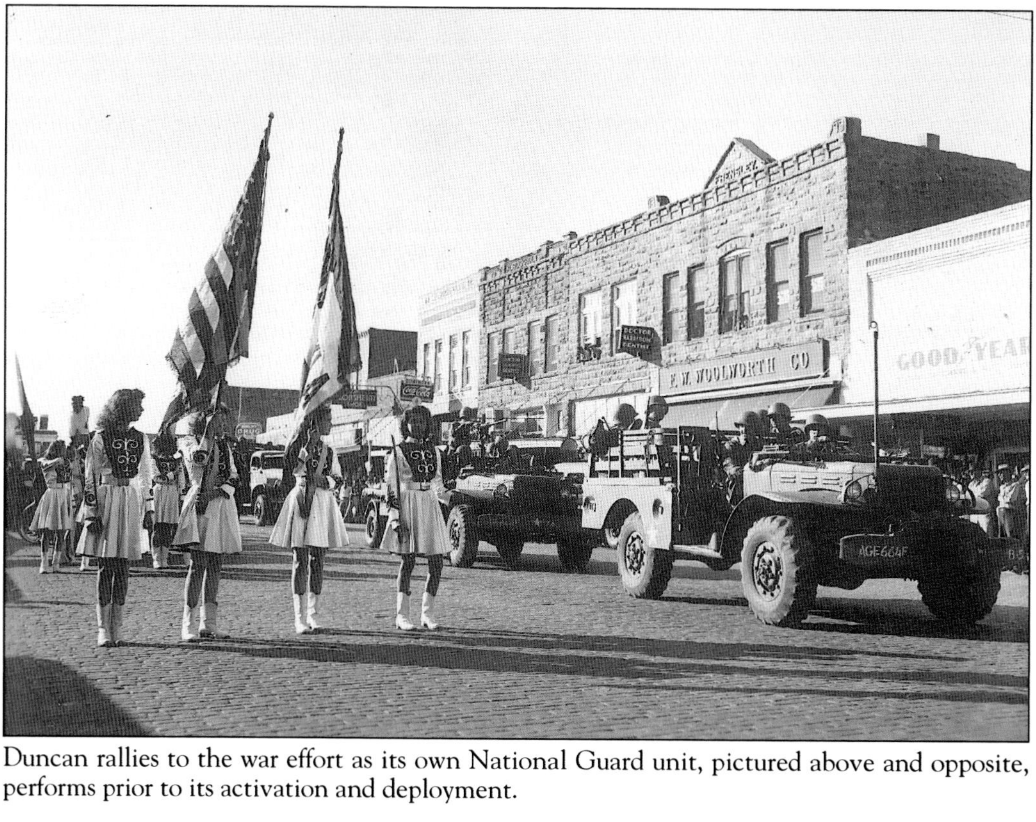

Duncan rallies to the war effort as its own National Guard unit, pictured above and opposite, performs prior to its activation and deployment.

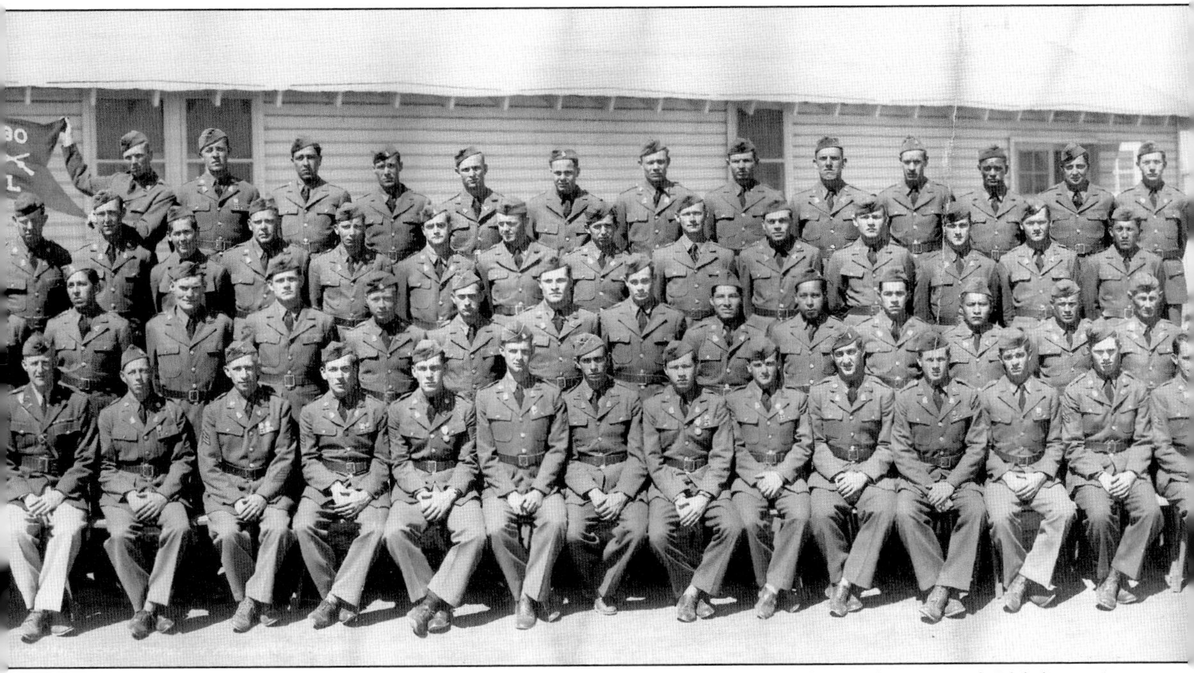

on April 7, 1941. When mobilized in less than a year, these men formed a unit of Oklahoma's famous 45th Infantry Division and saw extensive service during the war.

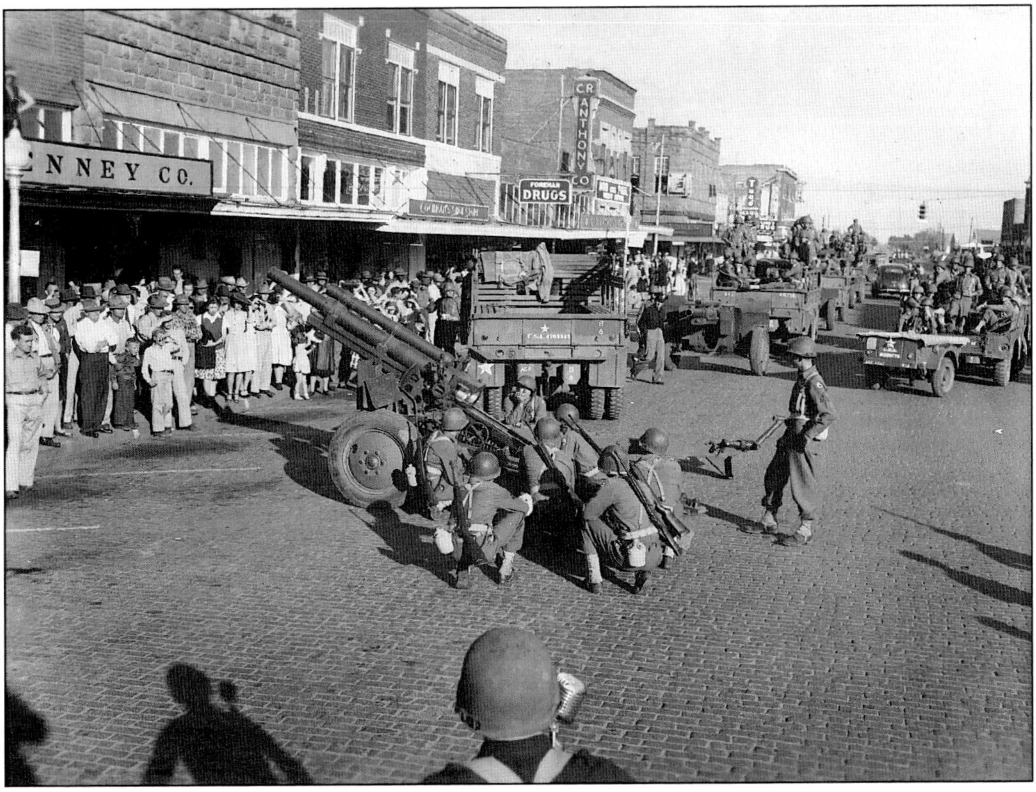

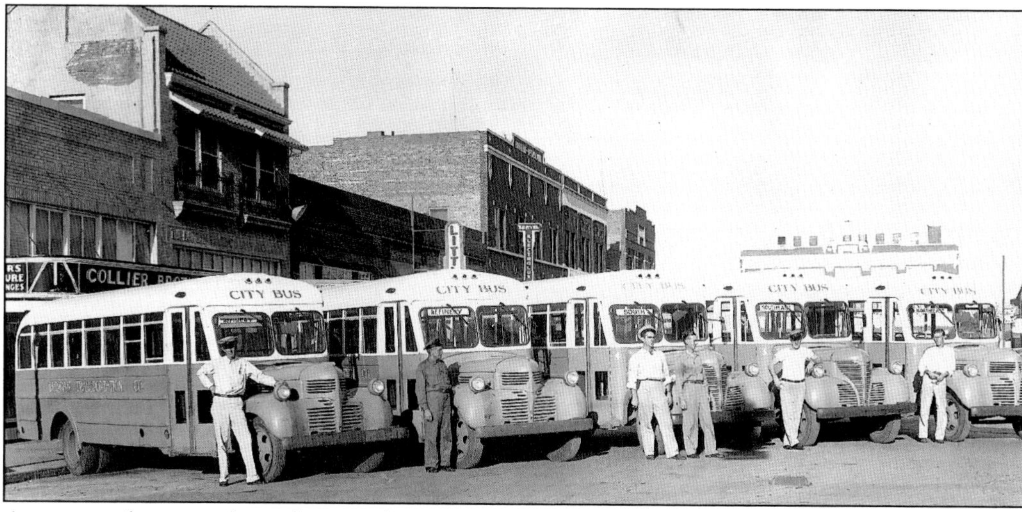

A wartime shortage of petroleum and spare auto parts led to extensive use of public transportation. Duncan's first city bus system is pictured above during the war years. Note the route posted in each windshield.

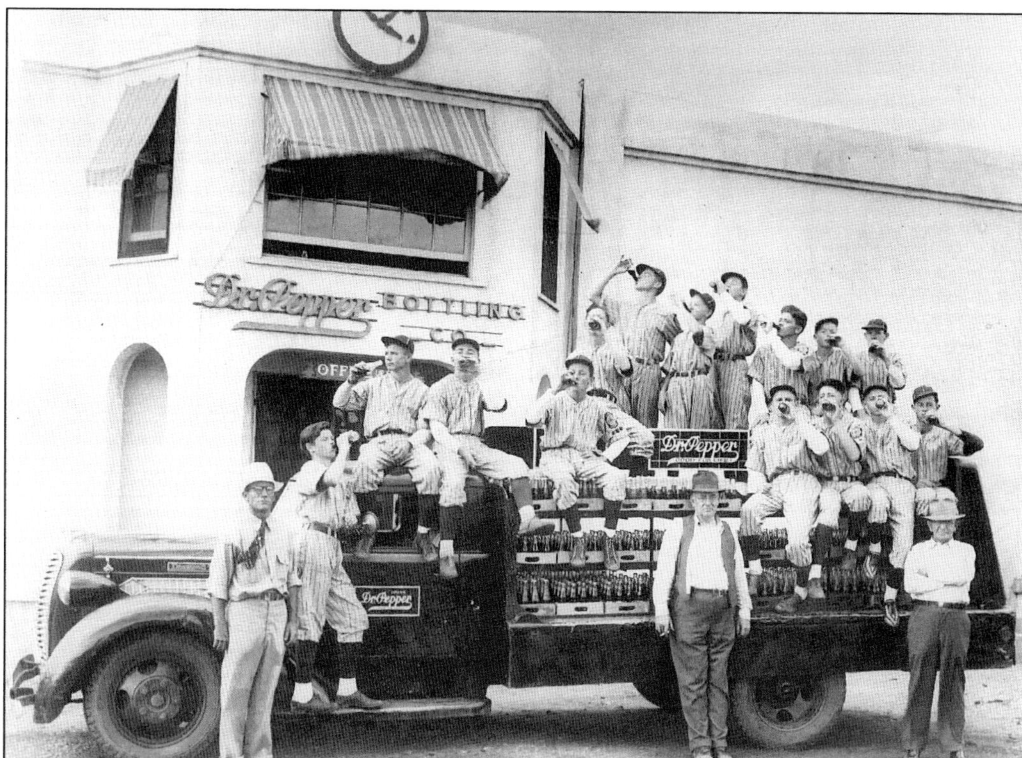

Comanche has the distinction of being the home to Oklahoma's first Dr. Pepper bottling plant, located there in 1929 because of the quality of the water. In this advertising photograph, the Stephens County American Legion Baseball Team is shown sampling the product. Note the "10-2-4" logo. It was implemented during the war years to remind workers to drink Dr. Pepper during their breaks at 10:00 a.m., 2:00 p.m., and 4:00 p.m. Dr. Pepper remains one of the county's favorite soft drinks, even today.

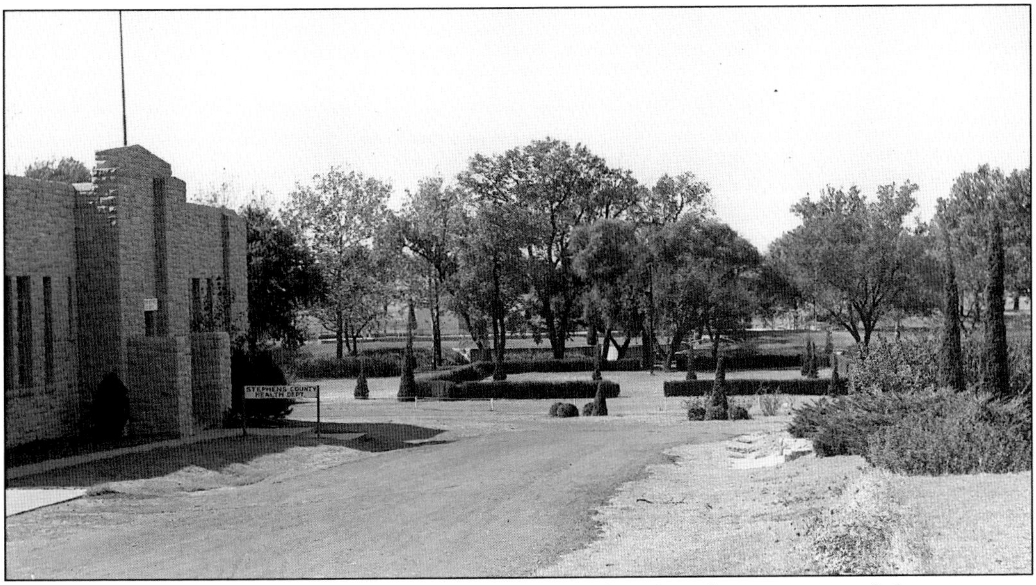

Duncan's National Guard Armory, unoccupied by the Guard since its mobilization, was occupied by the county health department until the war's end.

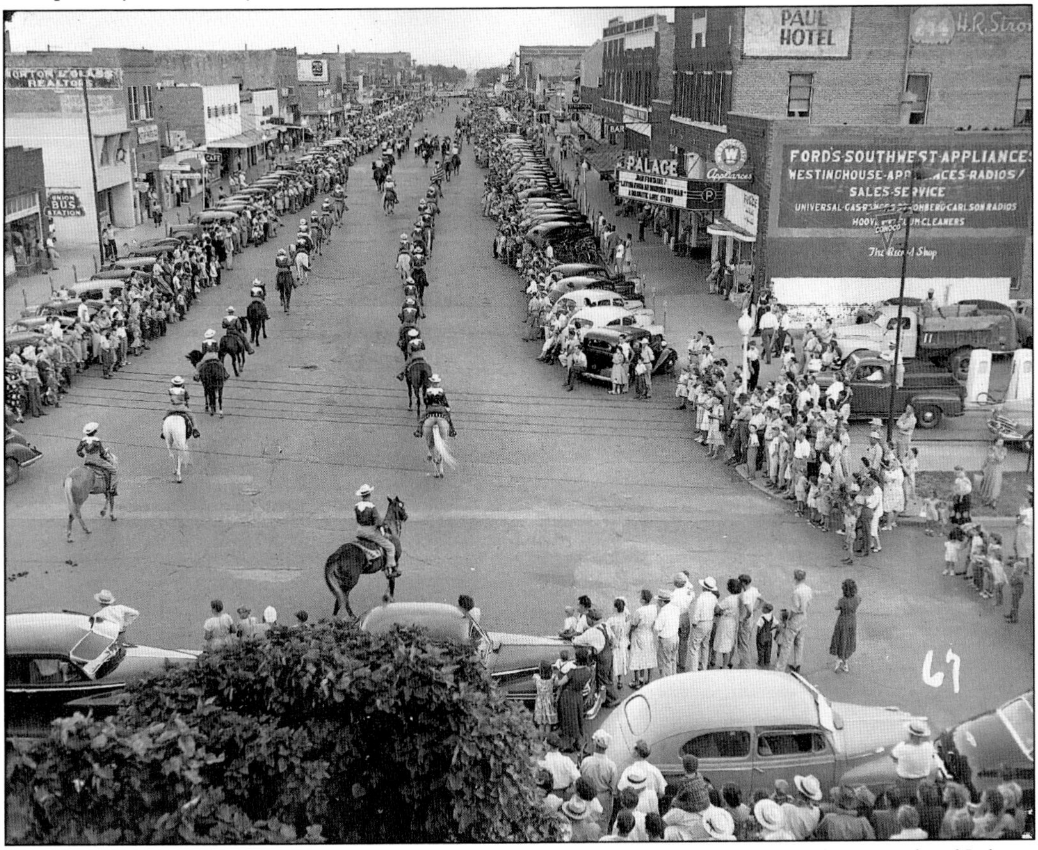

Parades remained popular during the war years. Here, Duncan celebrates the Fourth of July in the middle of the decade.

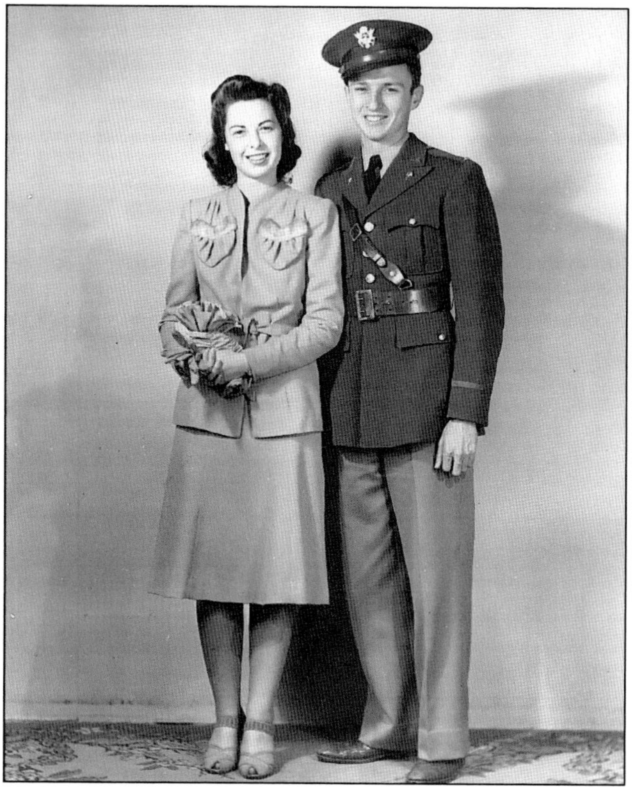

Thousands of Stephens County residents served in World War II. Representing the officer corps is Lt. Bob Diggs Brown, pictured with his new bride, Audrey, before shipping out for overseas. The enlisted ranks are represented by Earnest McDaniel of Comanche, pictured below with family members. (Brown's photo courtesy of Bob Diggs Brown.)

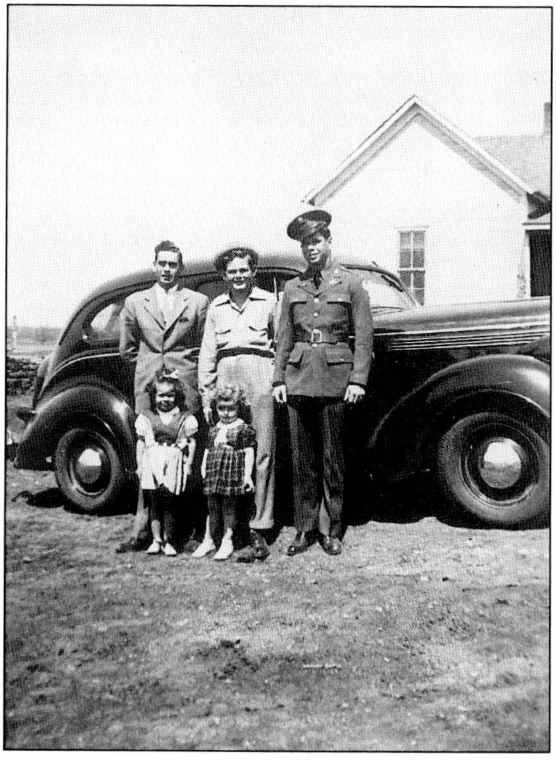

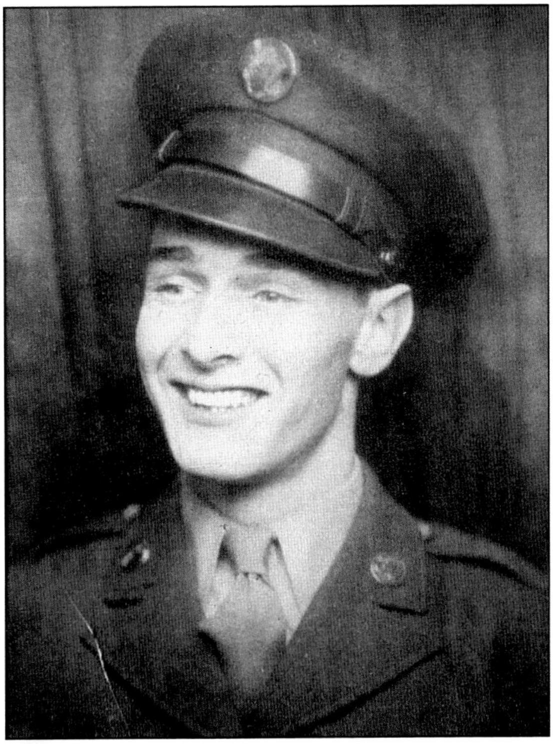

War's terrible toll is its dead. Almost 200 Stephens County servicemen were killed in World War II. Representing that tragedy is Jack Taliaferro, killed in action on November 29, 1944, during the Battle of Hurtgen Forest, in Germany. He is one of the thousands whose remains are in Europe, near where he fell. He is buried in the American Cemetery at Maastrich, Holland.

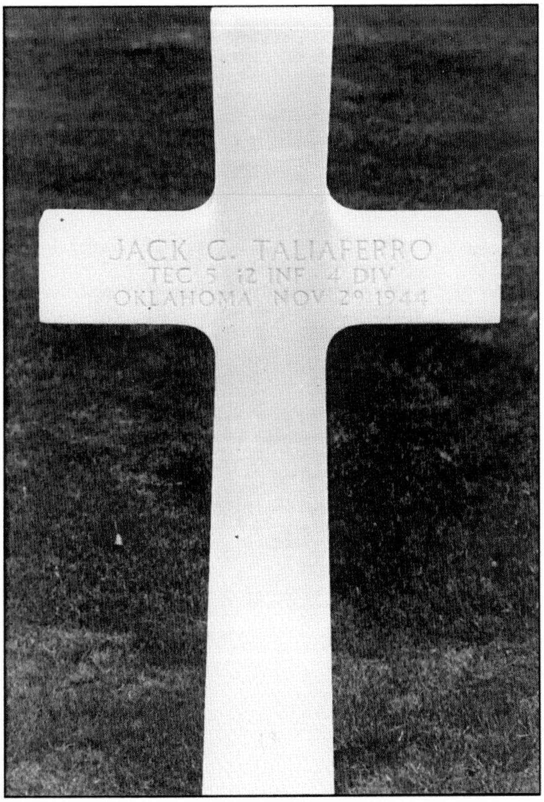

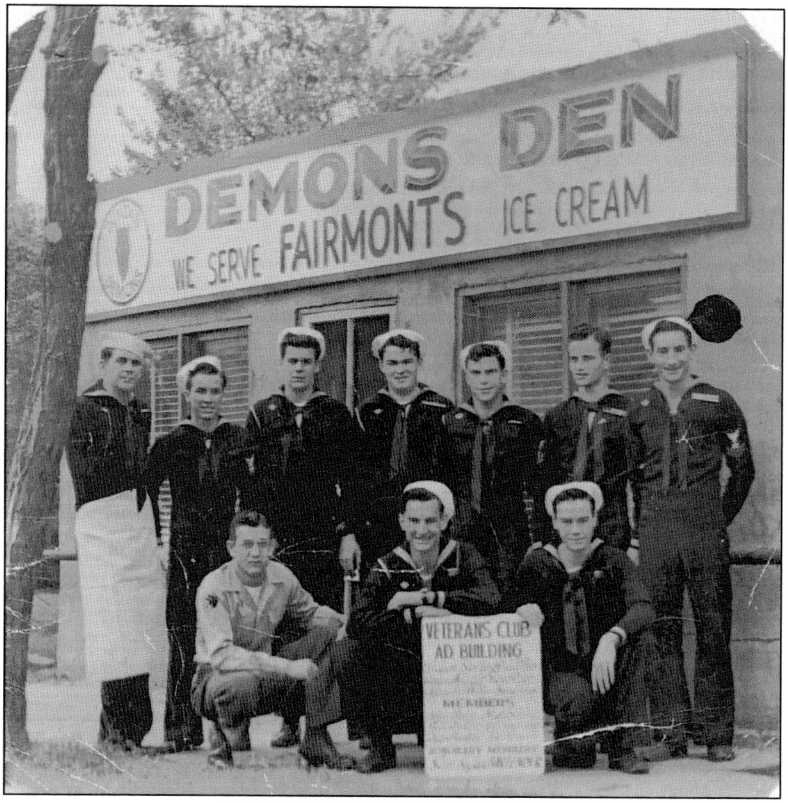

The end of the war brought home the servicemen, and a new post-war prosperity. Pictured at left, S.A. Boyles, standing at far left, opened the Demons Den, a confectionary and soda fountain, on September 23, 1946. Celebrating with him are members of the Veterans Club. Pictured below is the 1948 groundbreaking ceremony for the new Chisholm Trail Motel on North 81.

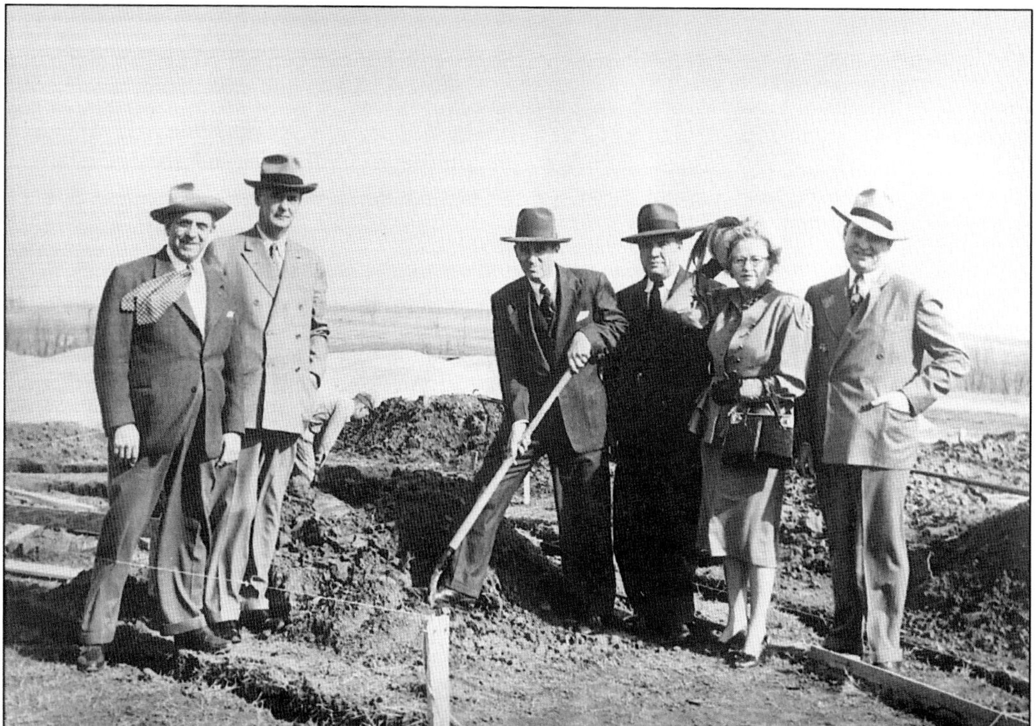

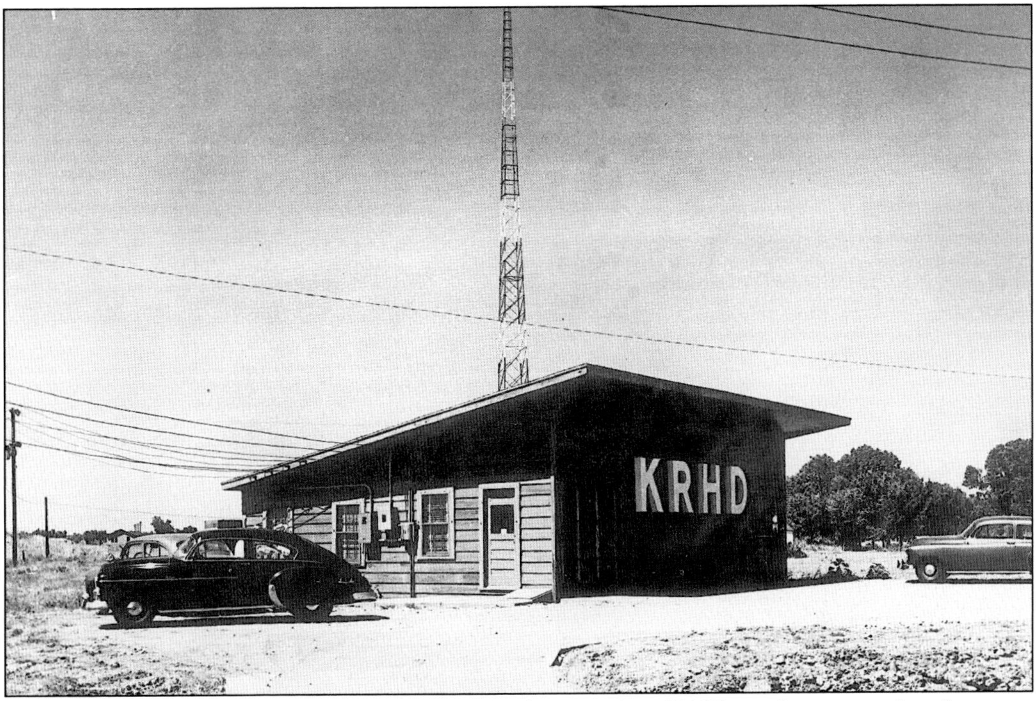

Duncan is home to a new radio station in the late 1940s, KRHD, and a new railroad station (seen below) completed in 1949. The station remained in use until passenger service was terminated in 1962. The station was torn down in 1990.

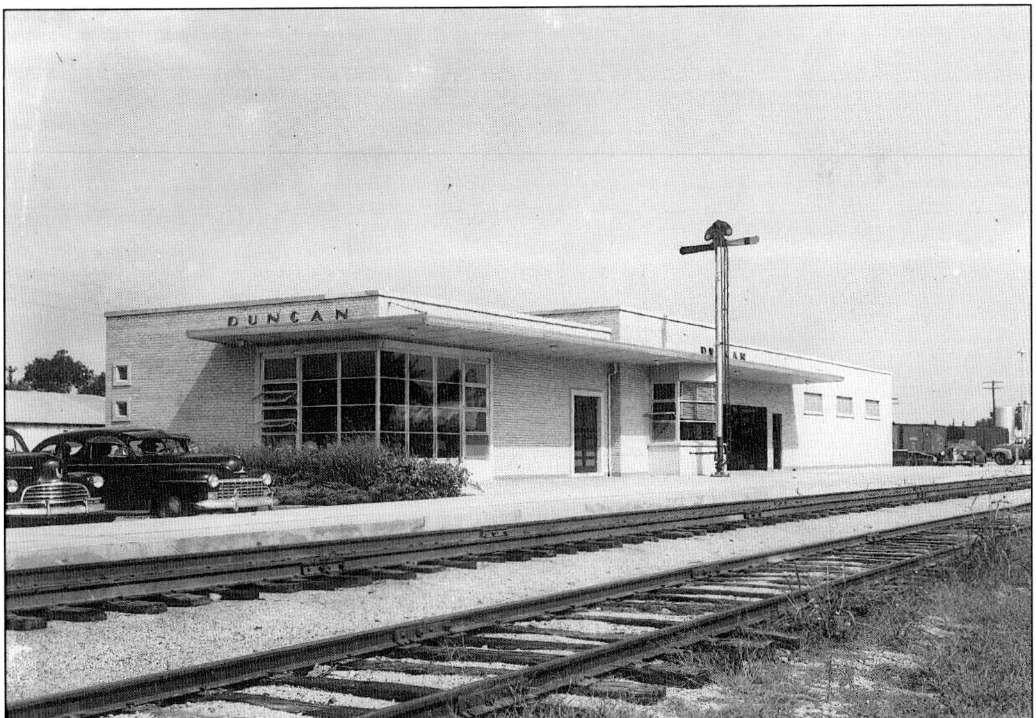

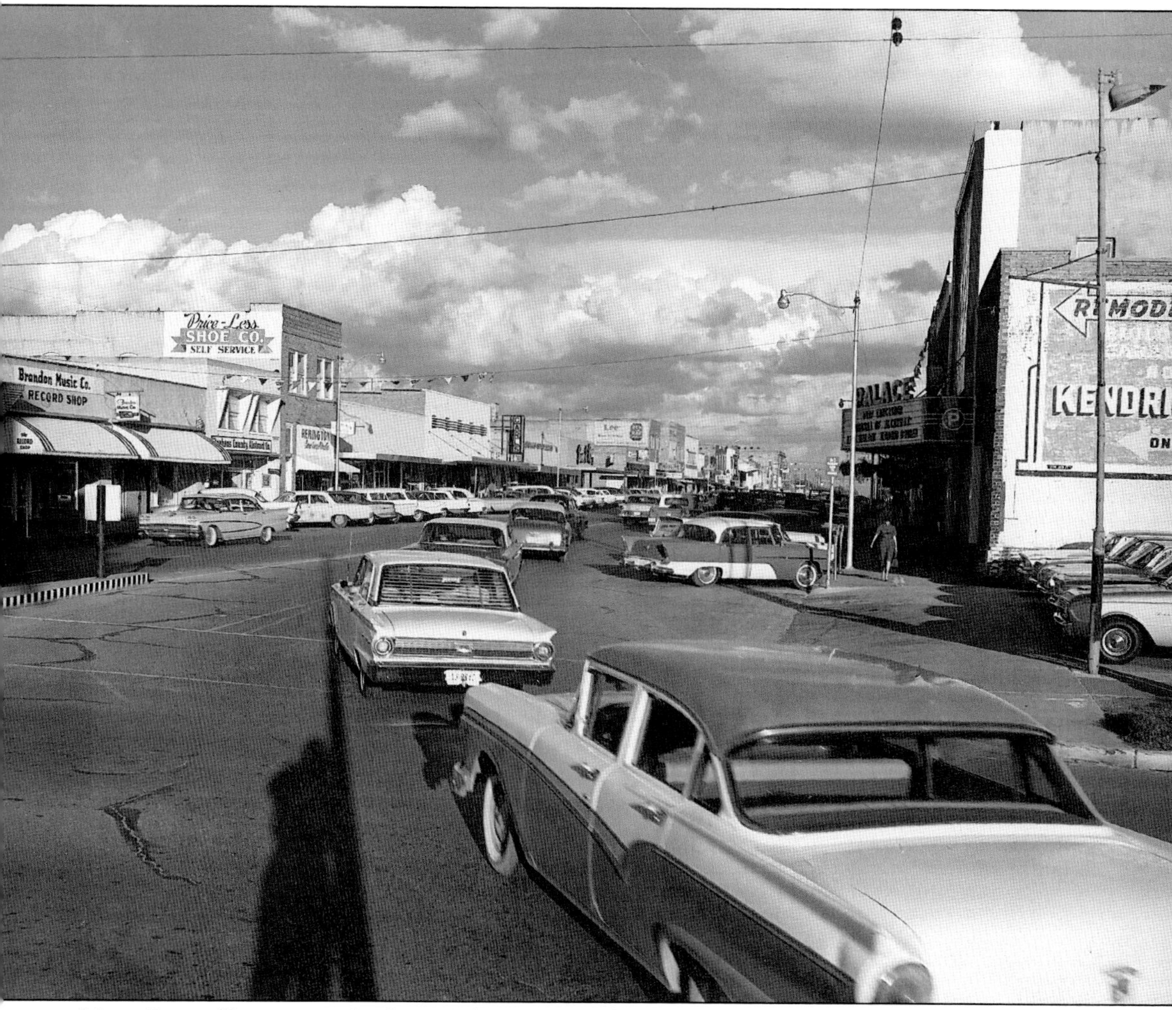

Main Street Duncan in the late 1950s suggests the stable, quiet, secure decade the 1950s has come to symbolize.

Seven

A Great Place to Raise Kids

The 1950s

The post-war boom continued to bring prosperity to the county, but with perhaps an unintended consequence: the sense of community so strong in the three towns began to fragment with more cars, suburban growth, and a slow decline of downtown areas. Still, the communities remained nice places to live.

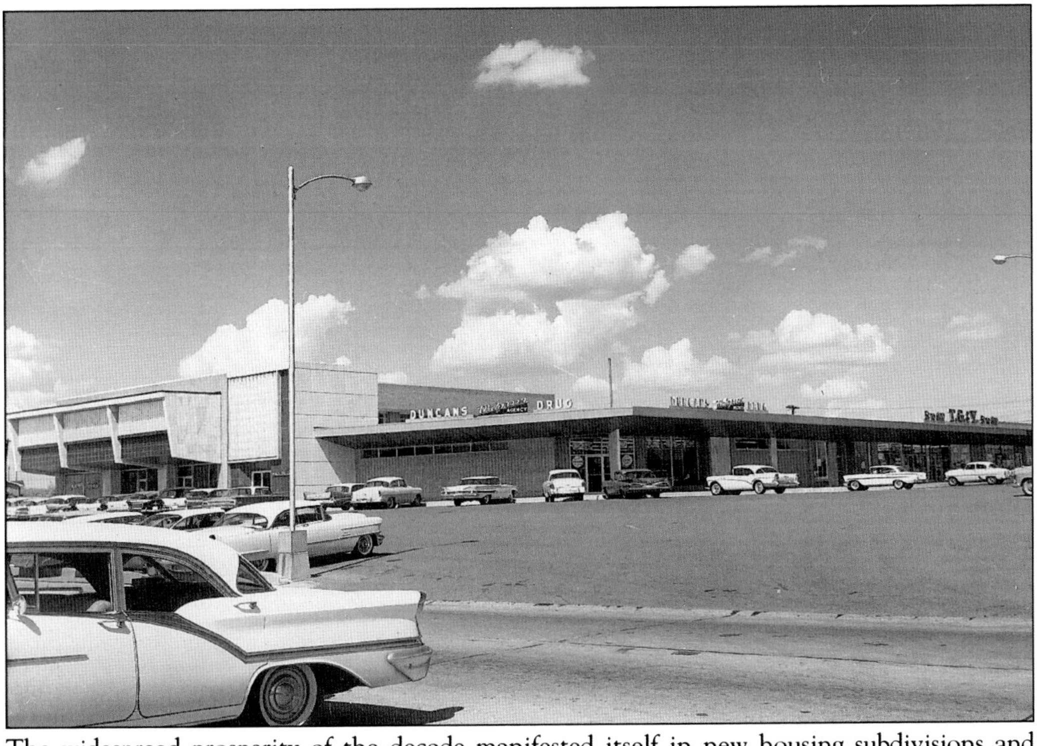

The widespread prosperity of the decade manifested itself in new housing subdivisions and shopping centers. The Mack Center was Duncan's first. While clearly popular, they foreshadowed a gradual decline of Main Streets across America, to include Duncan.

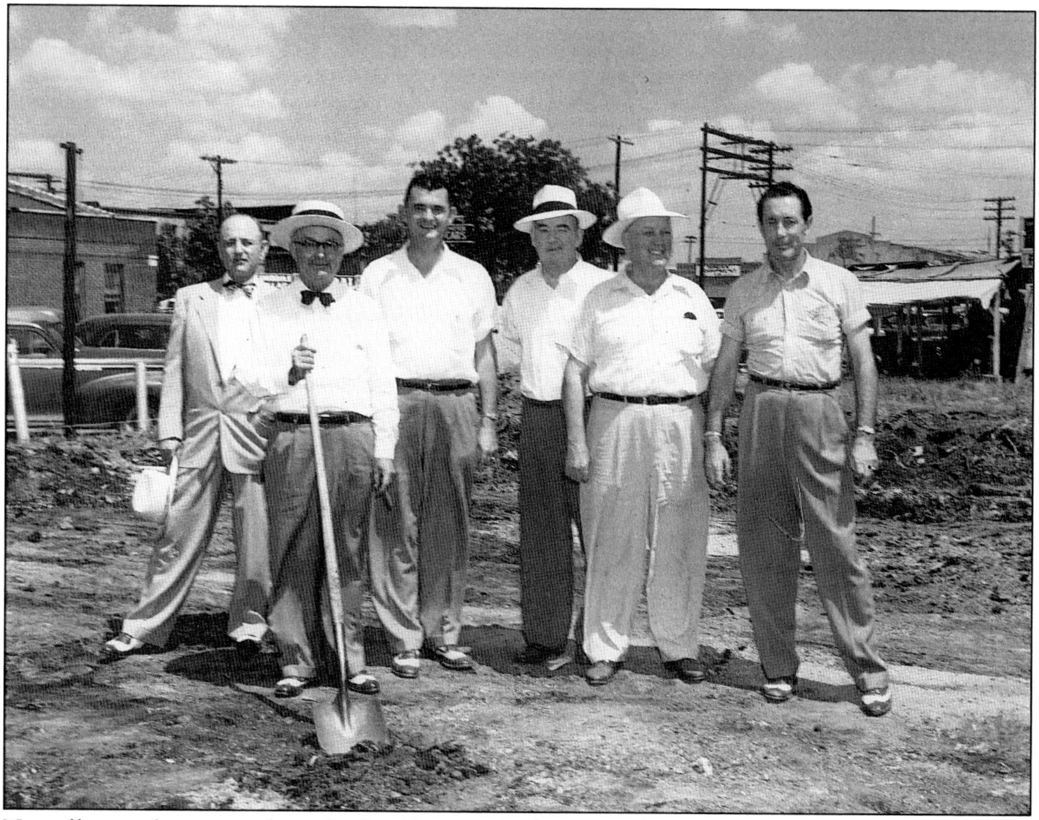

Not all growth was in the suburbs. Duncan broke ground for a new city hall a block south of Main Street in 1951. Pictured from left to right are the following: Jerome Sullivan Sr., Raymond Sharp, Leroy Tucker, Marvin Rasher, Mr. Gilbert, and Brice Wininger. The new city hall is pictured below. The old city hall, a classic Main Street landmark since 1909, was torn down in 1962.

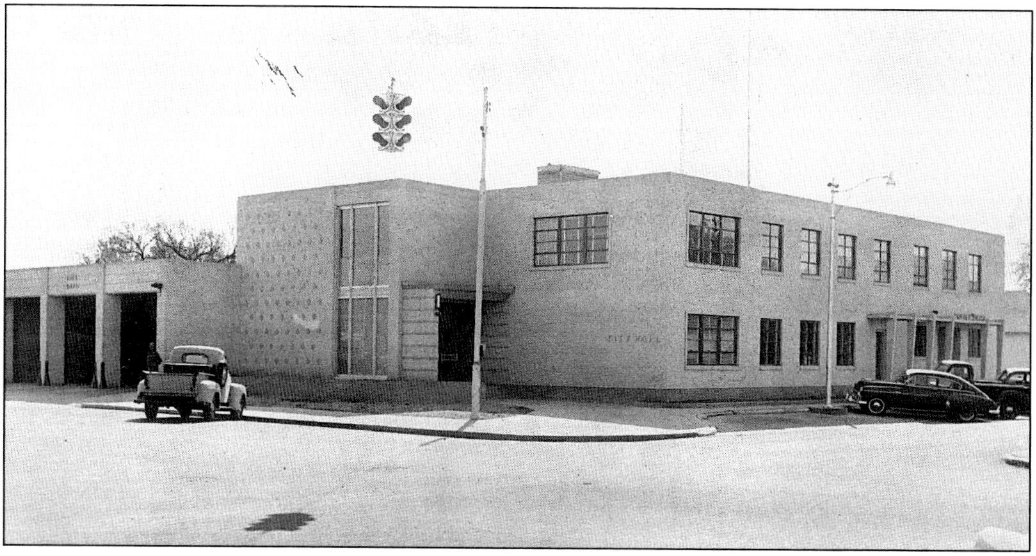

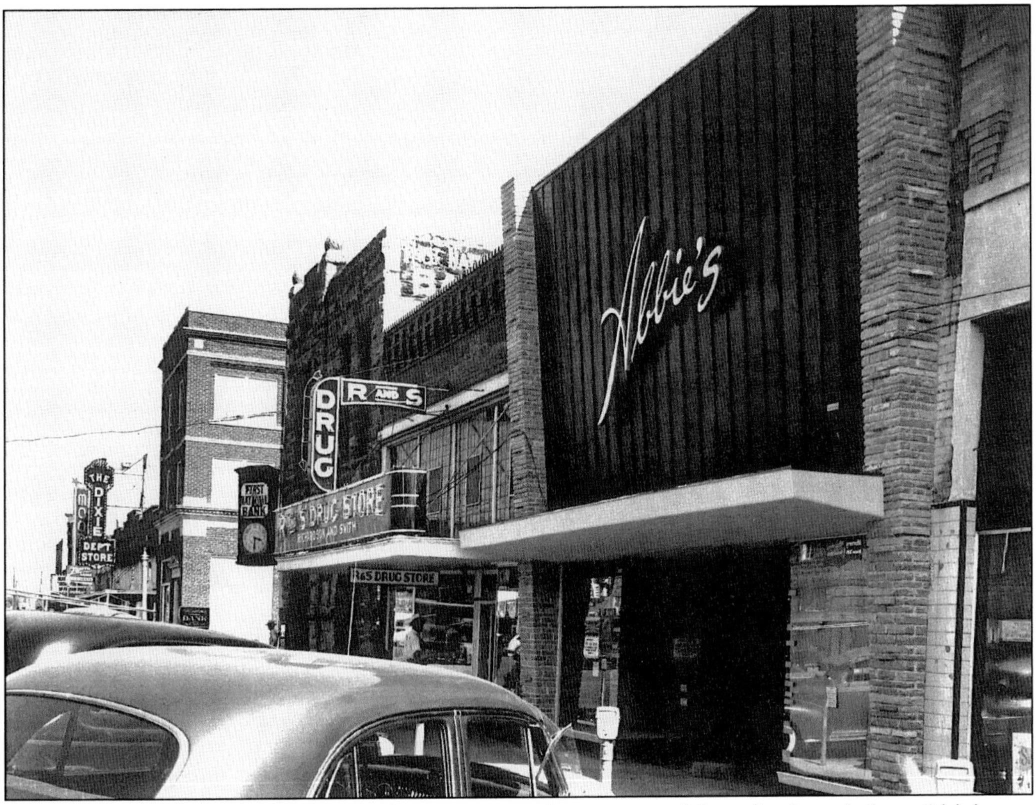

Main Street by the mid-1950s was beginning to show its age. Note the boarded-up Oklahoma National Bank building (mid-left), and the new facade for Abbie's. No longer the center of the community, Main Street experienced a decline that would intensify over the next several decades. Main Street Marlow, however, largely remained the center of its community. As shown below, Marlow's 1958 Main Street shows little of the modification typical of larger towns.

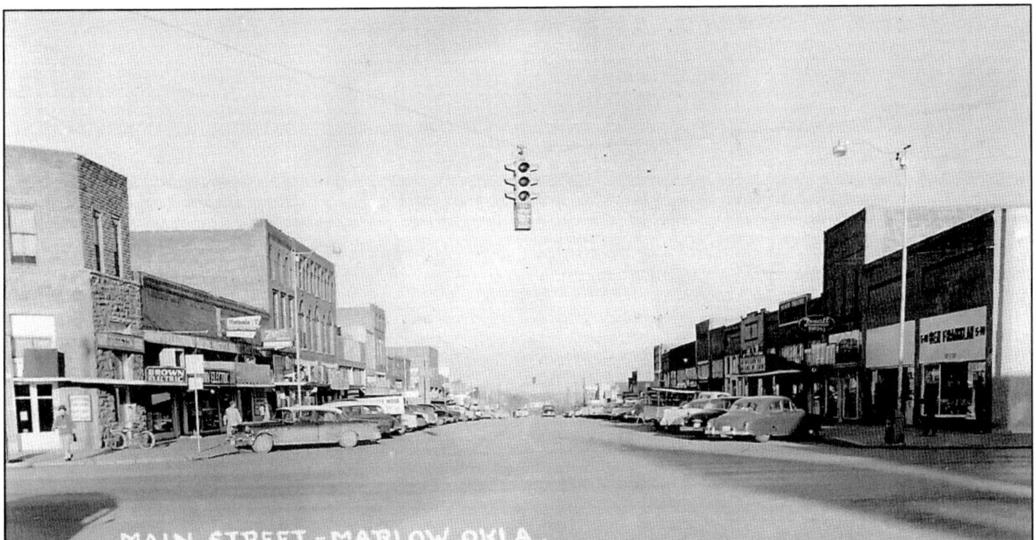

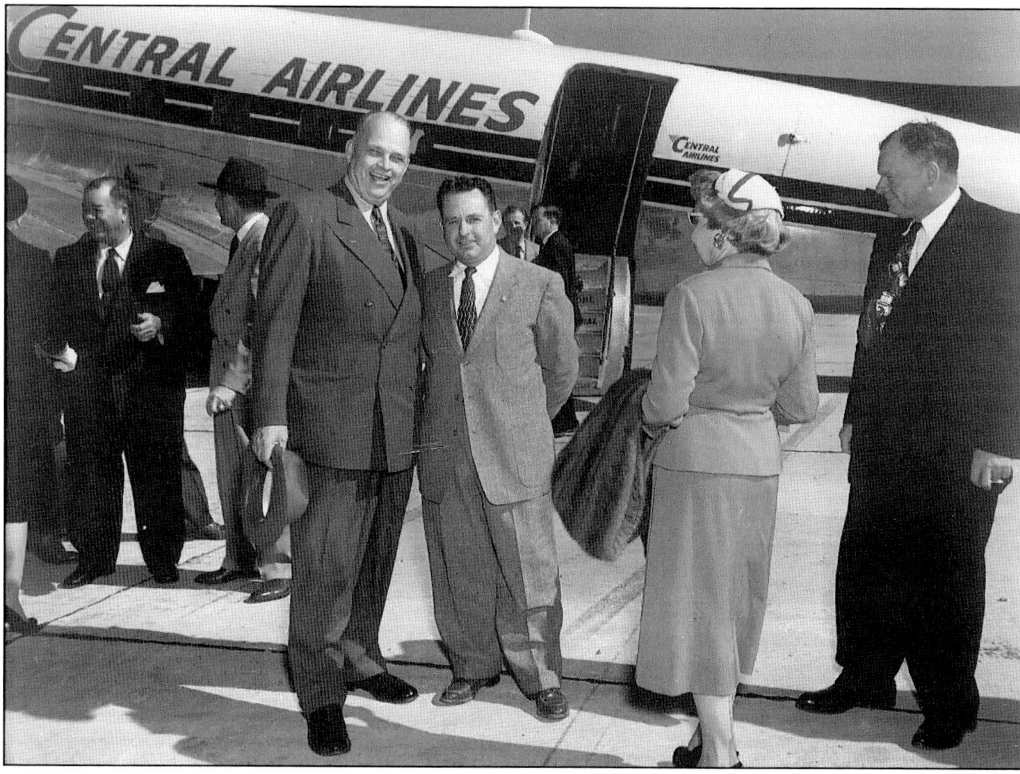

Stephens County was well connected to the outside world by the mid-1950s, offering scheduled airline service, train service, and bus service. The new Stephens County Airport dedication in 1954 was attended by Senator Robert Kerr, Mayor Wayne Holden, and Mr. and Mrs. Grover Kilgore, pictured above. The dedication also marked the inauguration of scheduled airline service to the county, the first since Halliburton's S.A.F.E. Airways ceased operations in 1930 (below).

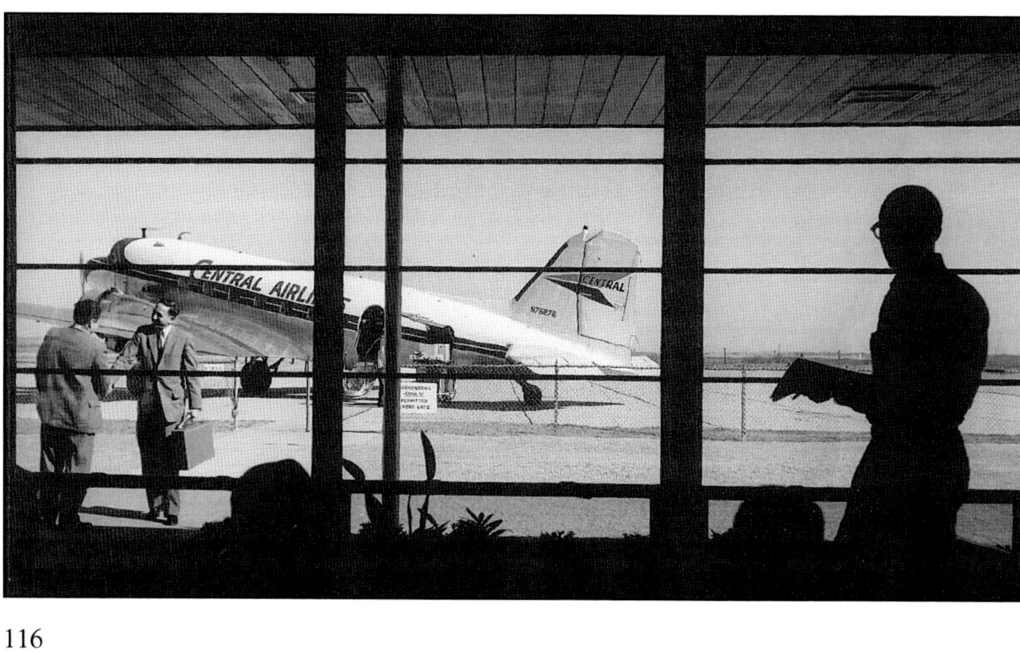

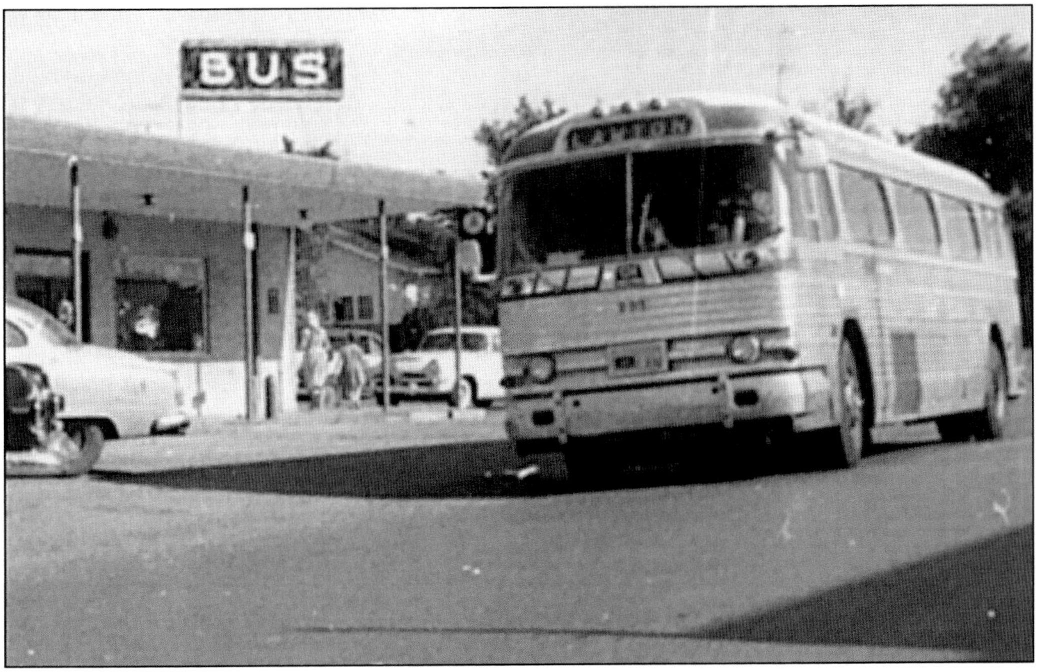

Duncan's bus terminal was an important, busy transportation hub in the 1950s. Train service began its decline in the 1950s, and was discontinued in 1962.

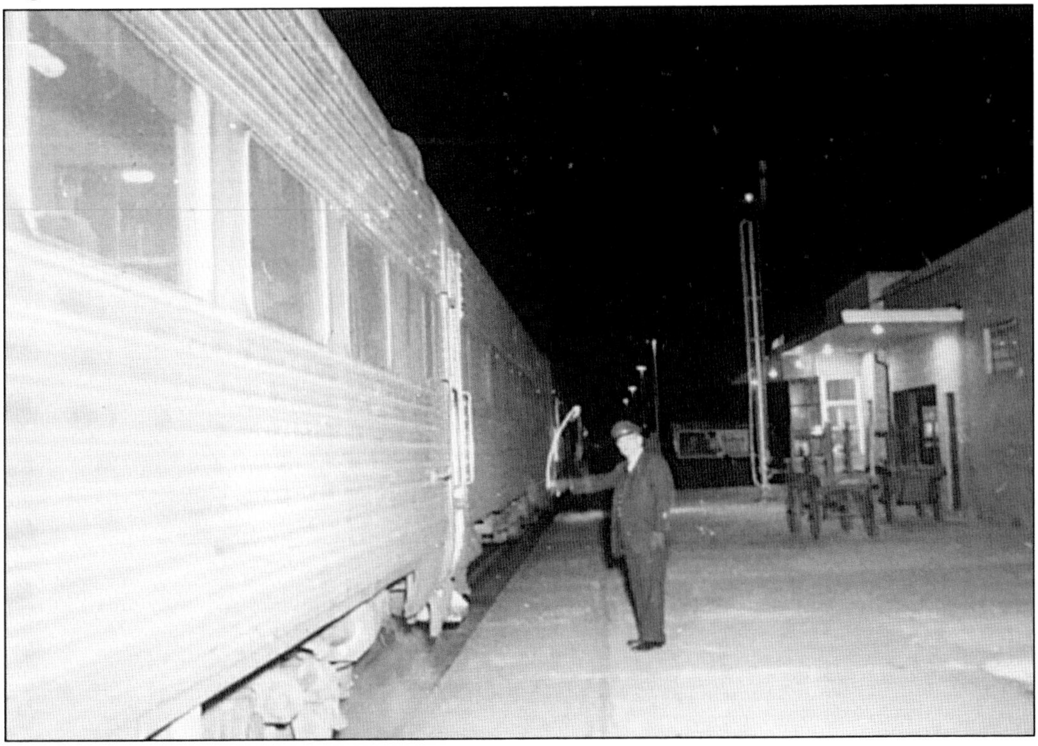

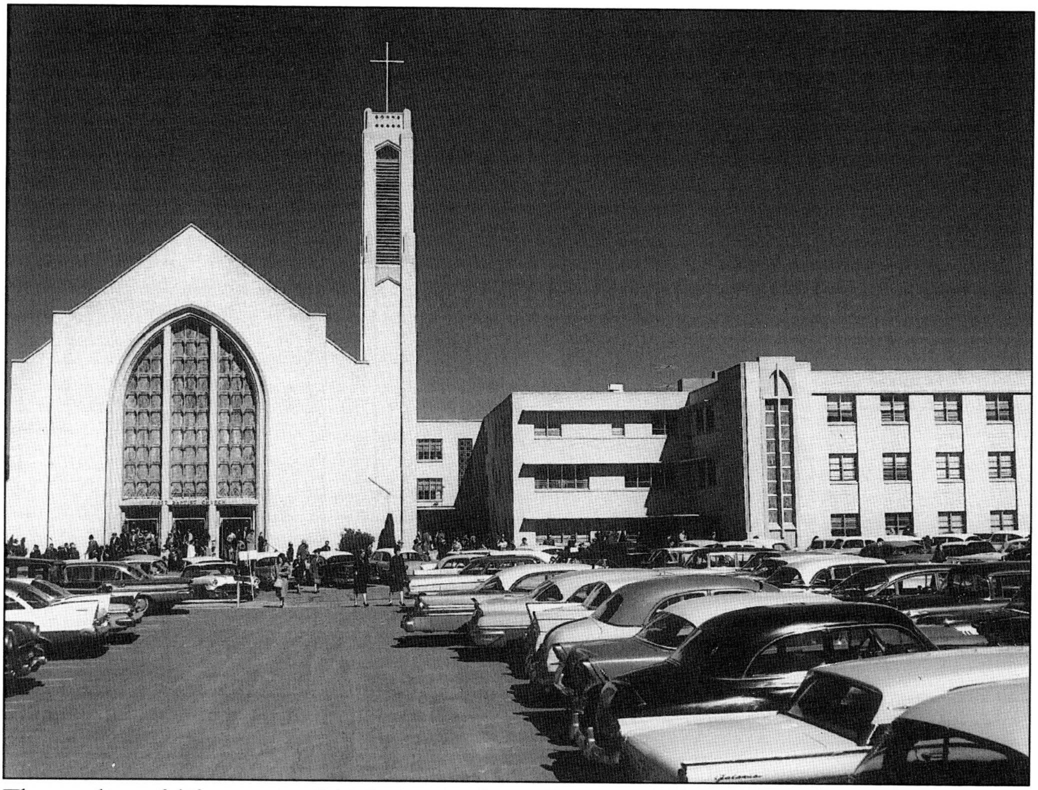

The quality of life remained high in Stephens County of the 1950s. Church membership swelled, and attendance rose. This view of Duncan's First Baptist Church at the end of the decade attests to the county's spiritual life in a scene repeated up to 70 times each Sunday.

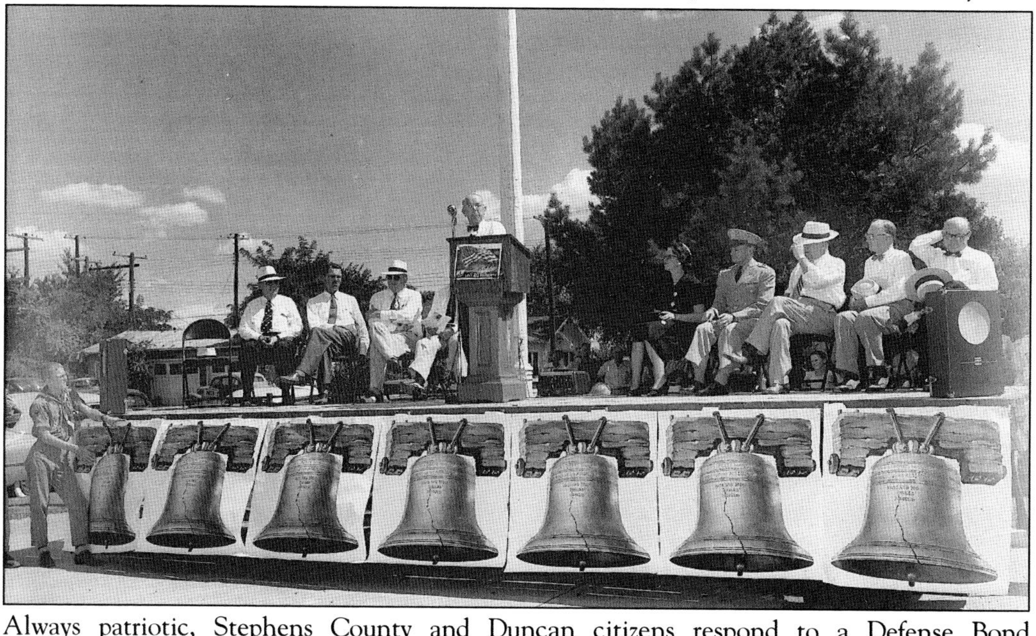

Always patriotic, Stephens County and Duncan citizens respond to a Defense Bond drive in 1951.

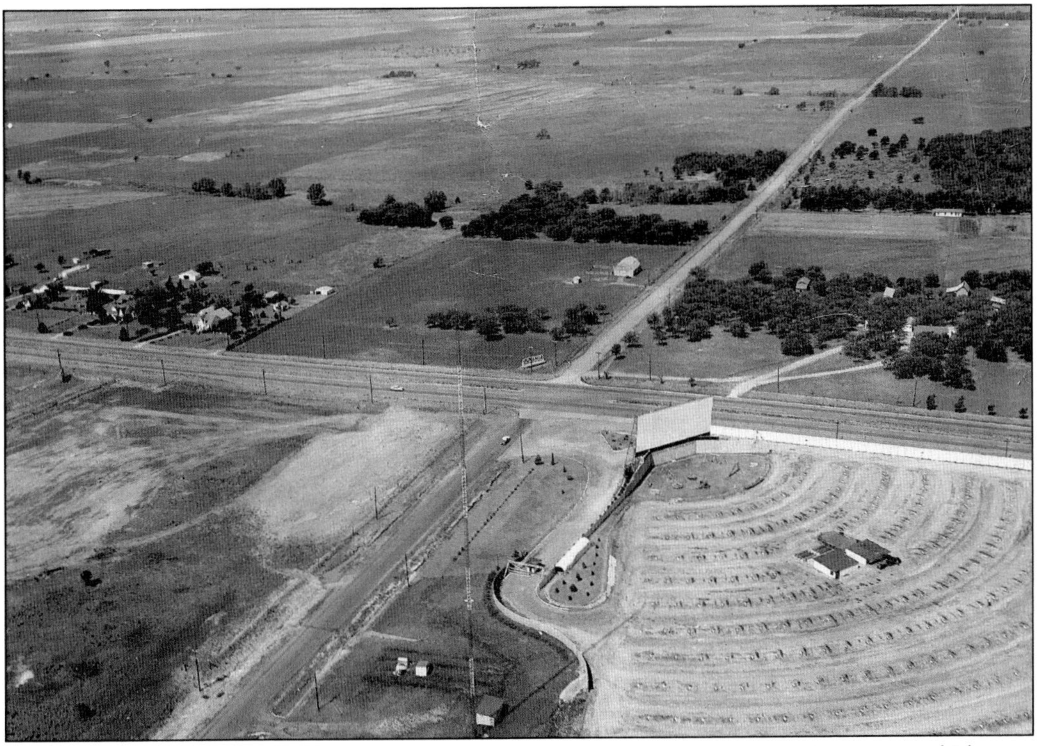

Many will remember the Duncan drive-in theater at the corner of U.S. Highway 81 and Plato—shown newly built in the mid-1950s—and will no doubt reflect on fond memories of Saturday nights gone by.

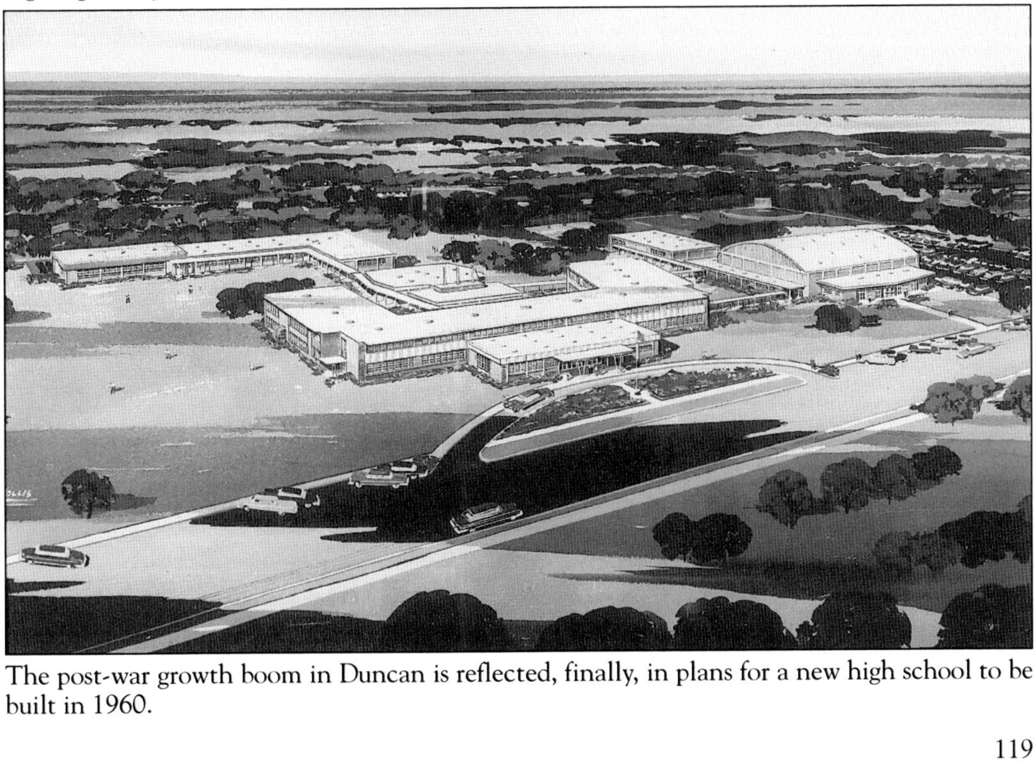

The post-war growth boom in Duncan is reflected, finally, in plans for a new high school to be built in 1960.

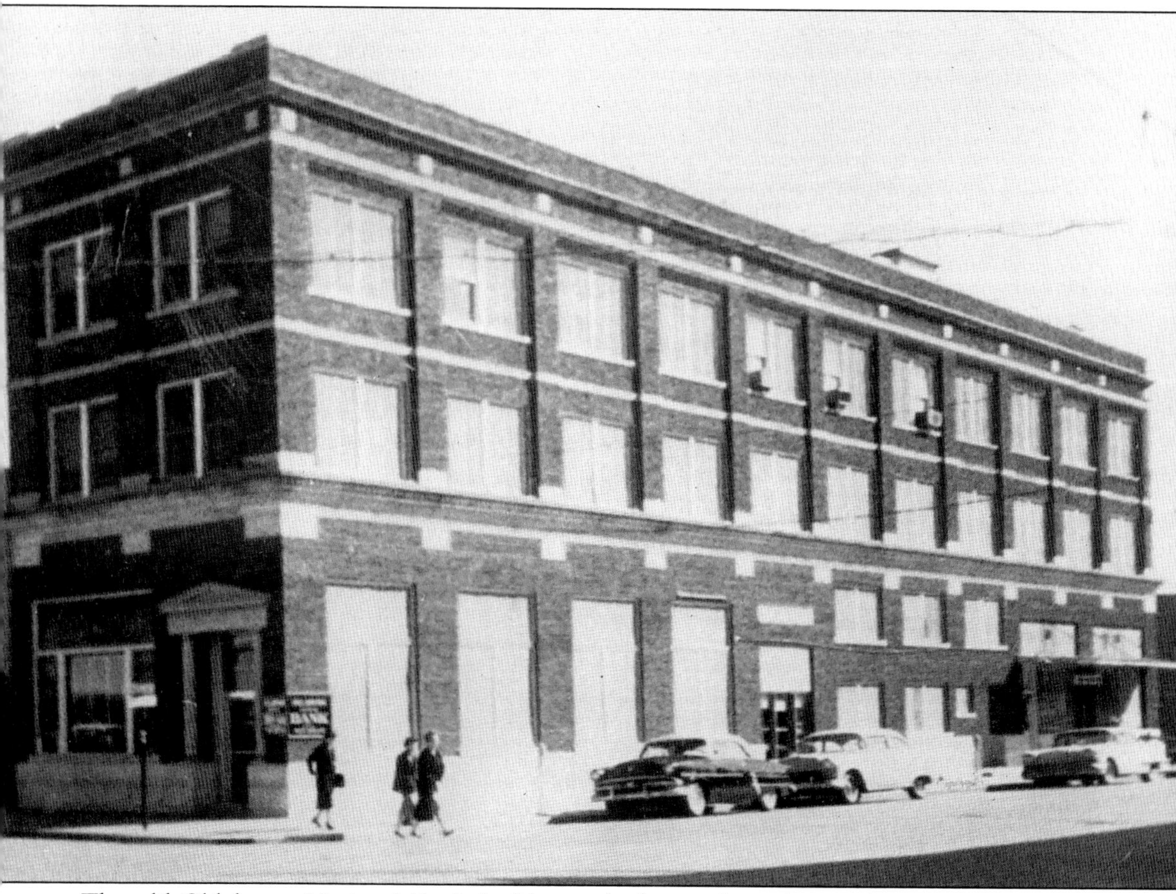

The old Oklahoma National Bank building, which stood on the southeast corner of Main and Eighth Streets, and their new bank constructed just across Main Street, shown opposite, summarize Main Street's fate through the 1960s and on to the 1980s. Although the old building's ground floor was saved, remodeling left it unrecognizable as the old bank.

Eight

STRUGGLING TO MAINTAIN COMMUNITY THE 1960S, 1970S, AND BEYOND

The sixties were a turbulent time for America, but the county saw little of it. Nevertheless, the patriotic county sent hundreds of its men and women to serve in Vietnam. Seventeen lost their lives there. However, the county shared with America a general decline of Main Street, the continued rise of shopping centers, and a struggle to maintain a sense of community. Still, prosperity remained strong until the oil crash of the 1980s. Paradoxically, it may have been the crash that reawakened the communities to the need to reassess and revitalize a community spirit.

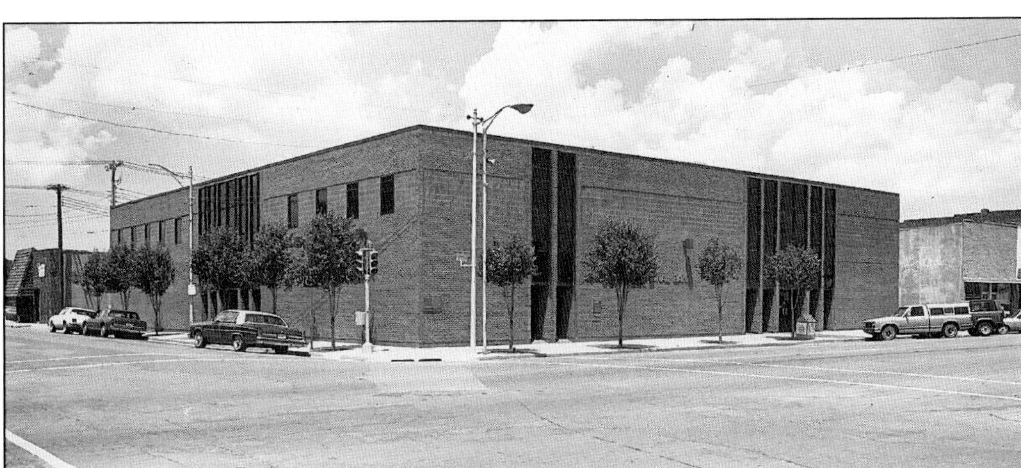

The new Oklahoma National Bank building is shown here.

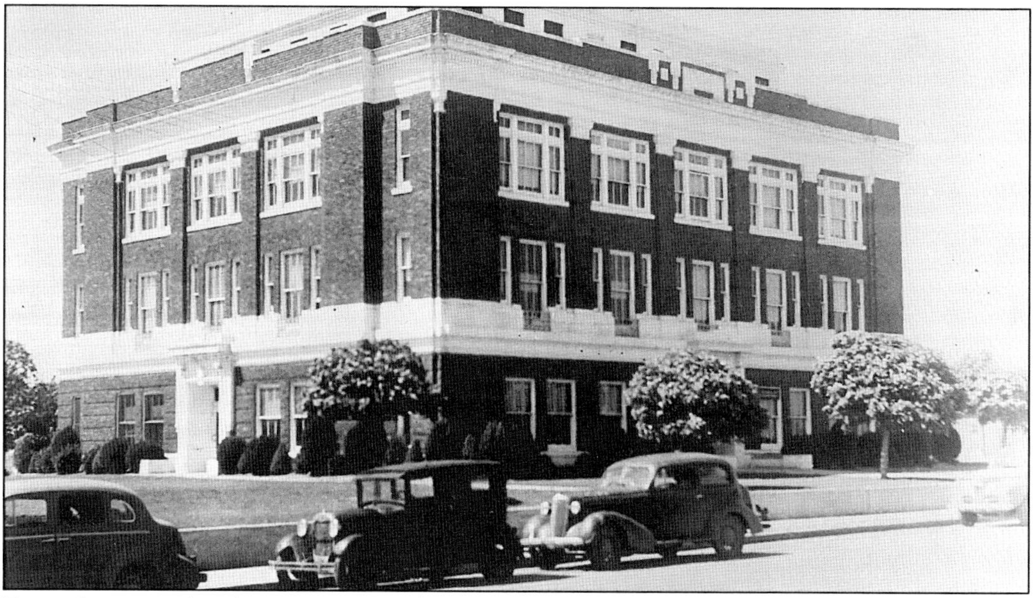

From the time the decision was made to demolish the old courthouse, pictured above in the 1930s, and the wrecking ball struck its first blow in 1968, many began to regret its loss. Although the county government had outgrown it, its destruction was controversial. Many Stephens County and Duncan residents felt an alternative use could have been found.

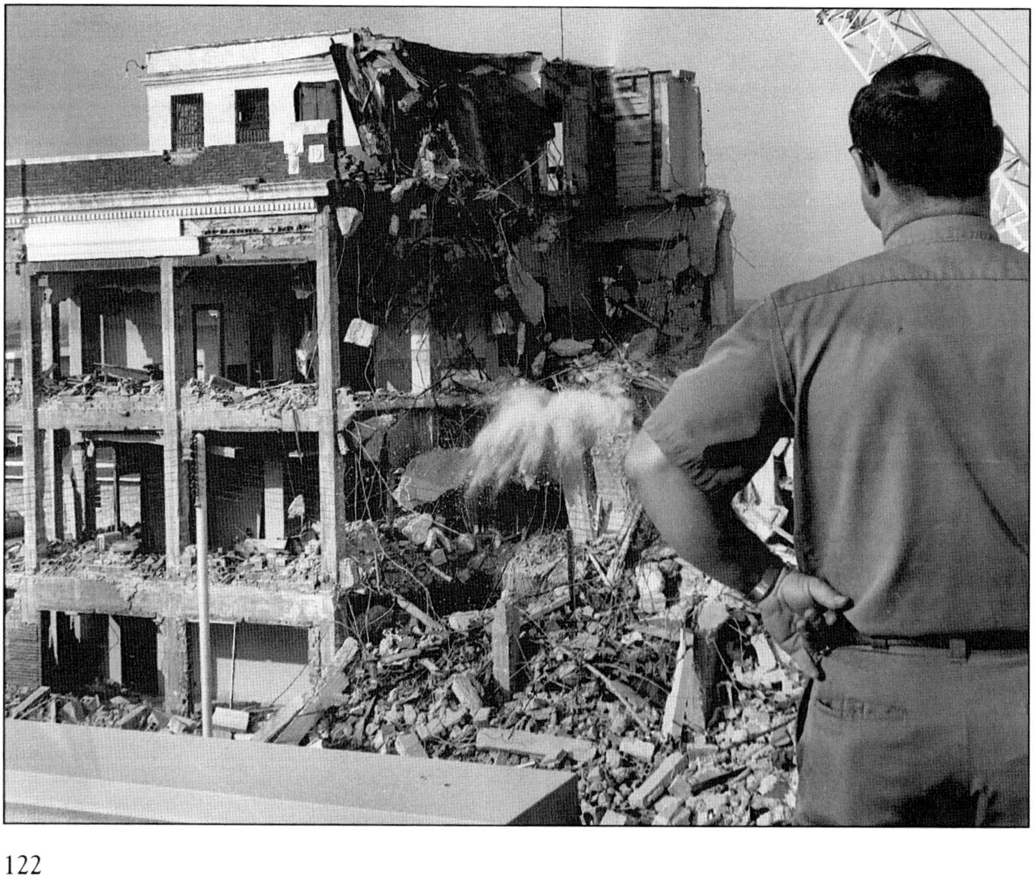

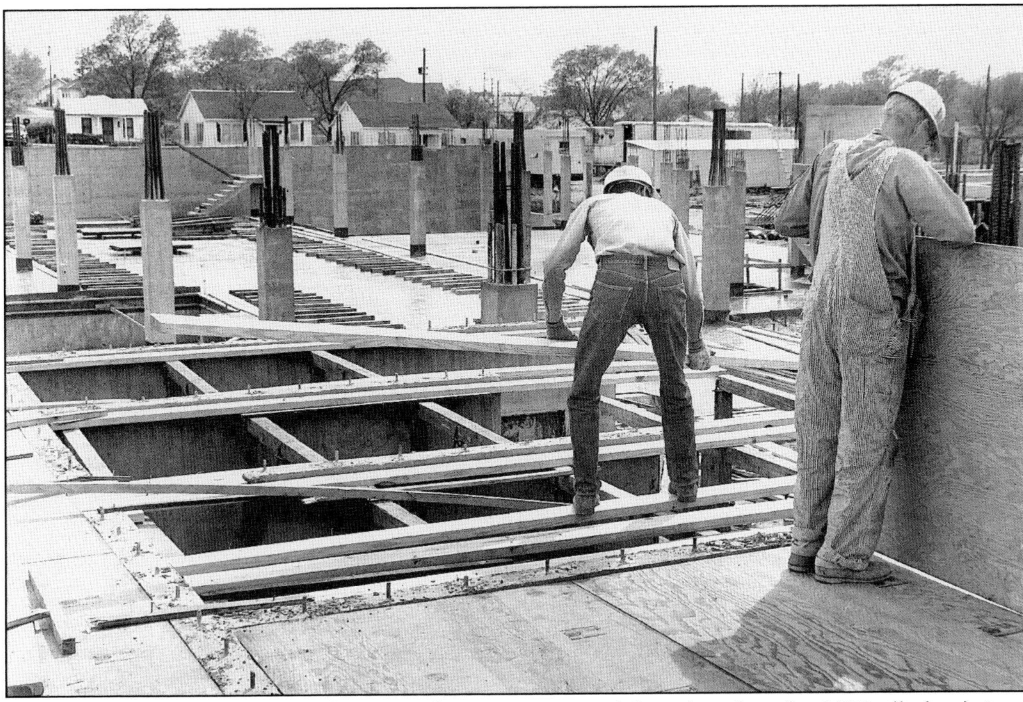

The new county courthouse, shown under construction (above) and in the 1980s (below), is no doubt a more functional building, but it lacks the classic charm of the old one.

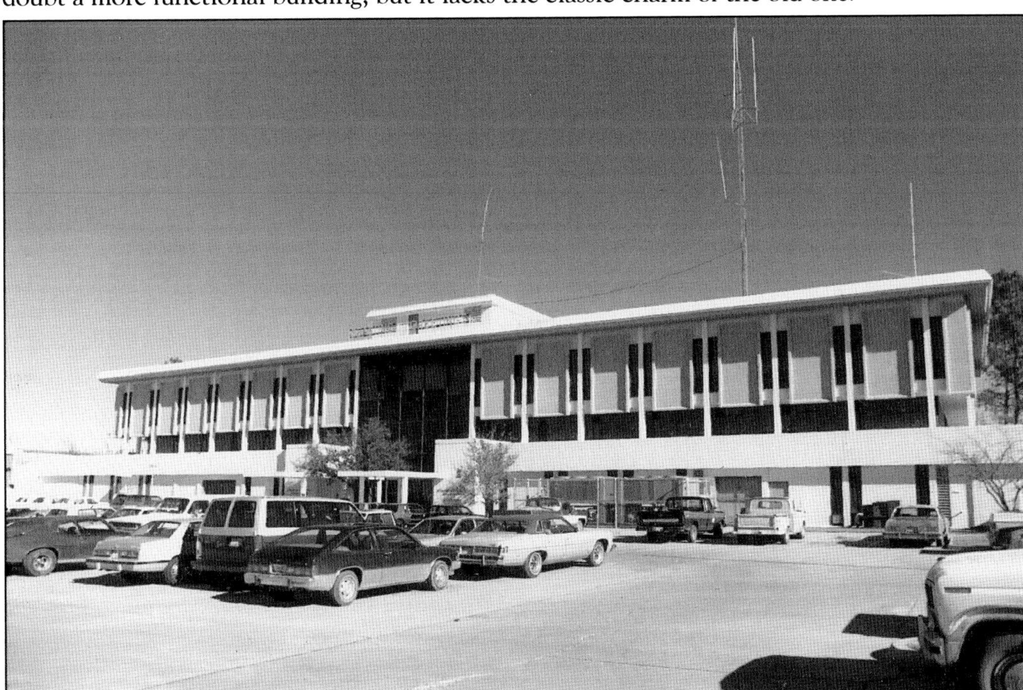

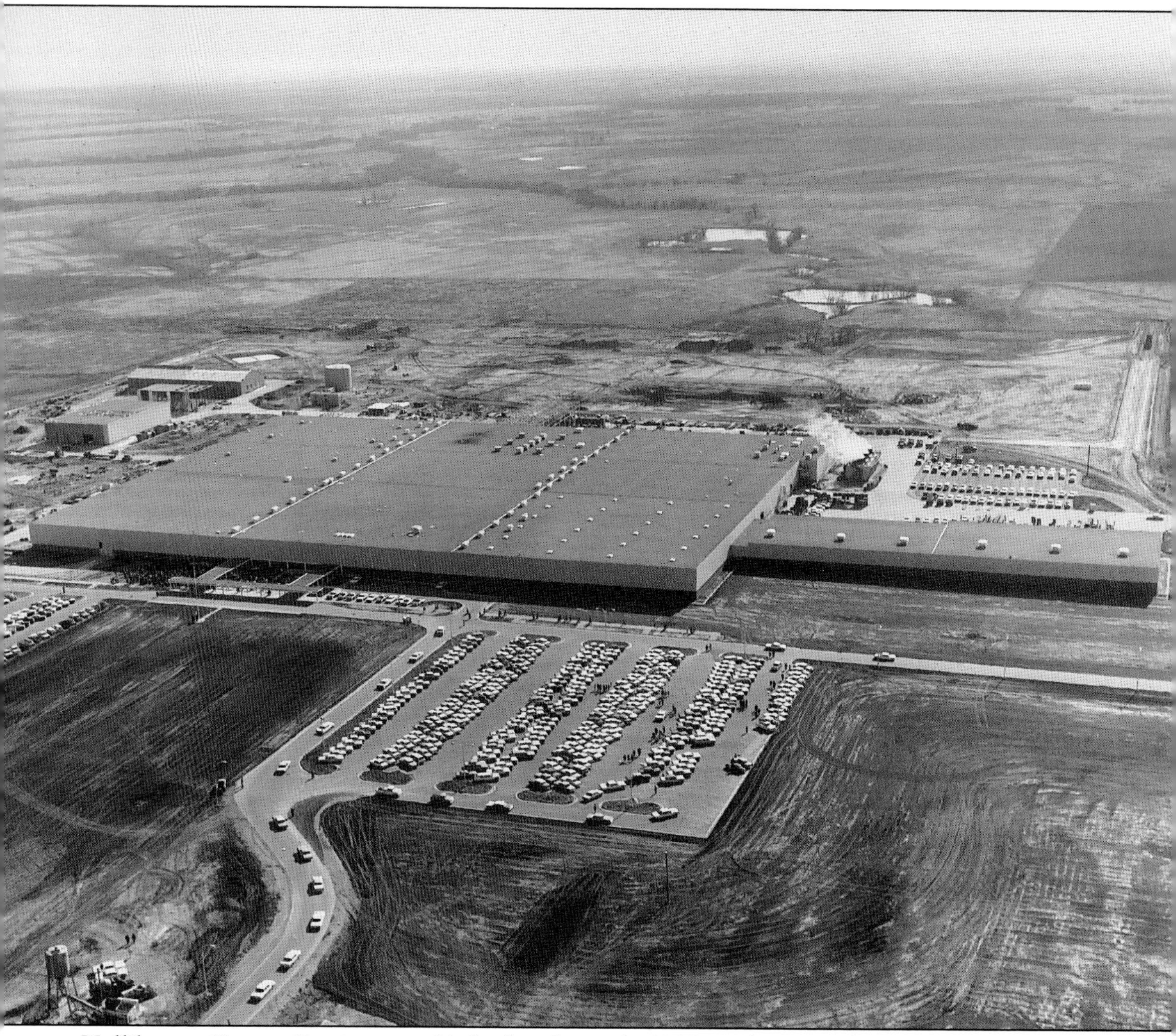

Halliburton Energy Services, established in the early 1920s and operated world-wide, continued to be the county's largest employer. For the county and its communities, this dependency has been both good and bad. The corporation has provided a standard of living well above similar rural communities elsewhere, but cycles in energy prices have made the county's economy vulnerable to fluctuations in the world economy. However, a deliberate and successful effort begun by the community in the 1980s to diversify the economy and attract other businesses has paid off. The county is slowly growing less dependent on the Halliburton. Moreover, Halliburton's retiree base in the county continues to grow through normal attrition and with each successive cut-back, acting as a damper on the fluctuations.

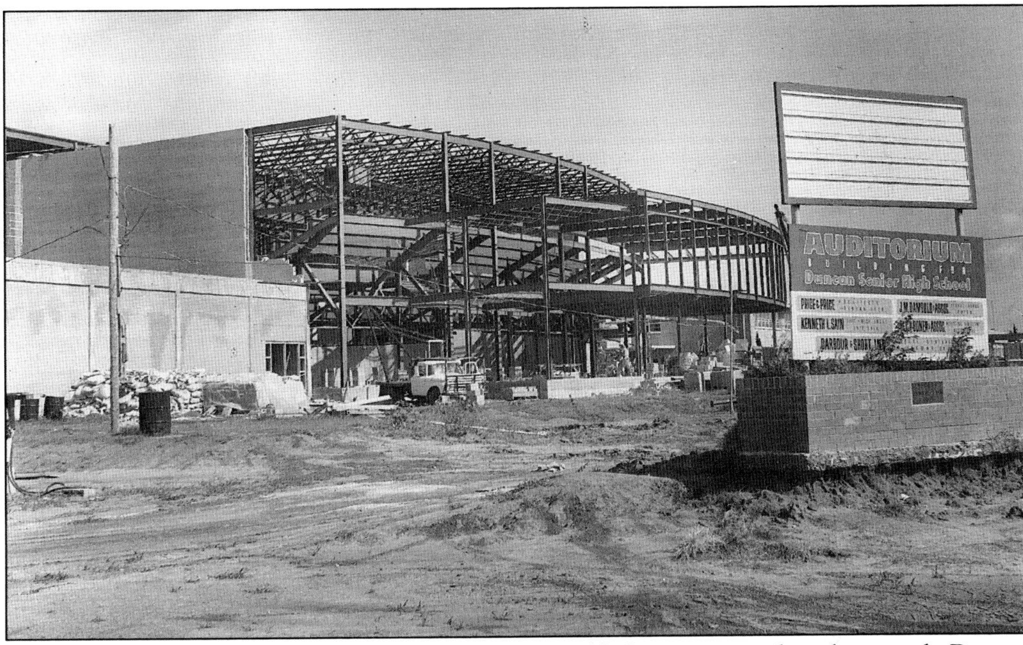

As the communities grew, community facilities were added to accommodate the growth. Duncan High School adds a new auditorium in 1967 (above), and the Duncan Regional Hospital was completed in 1982 (below).

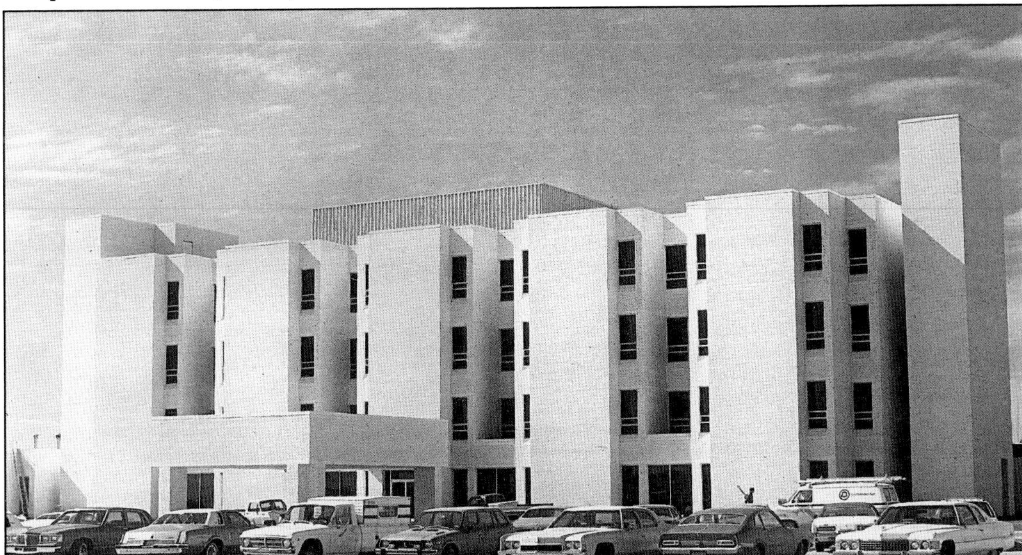

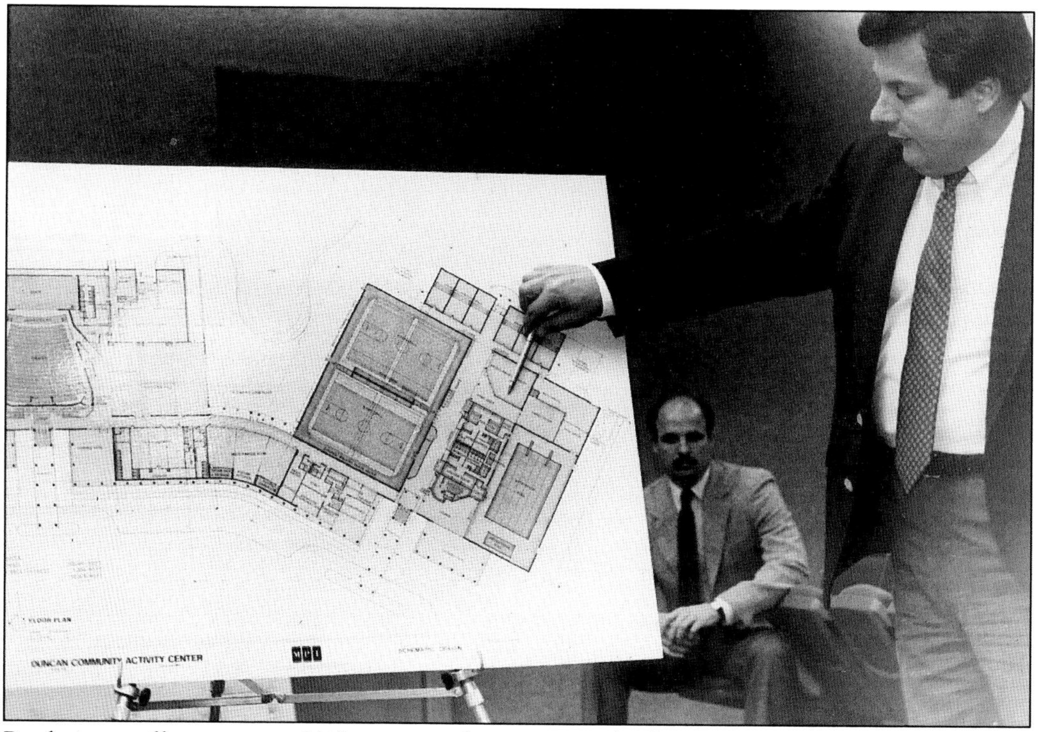

Partly in an effort to re-establish a sense of community, leading citizens proposed construction of a community activity center as early as the 1960s. Above, plans for the new center are presented in 1985. After groundbreaking in February 1987, construction ensued for the next four years, with the recreation facility completed in 1990.

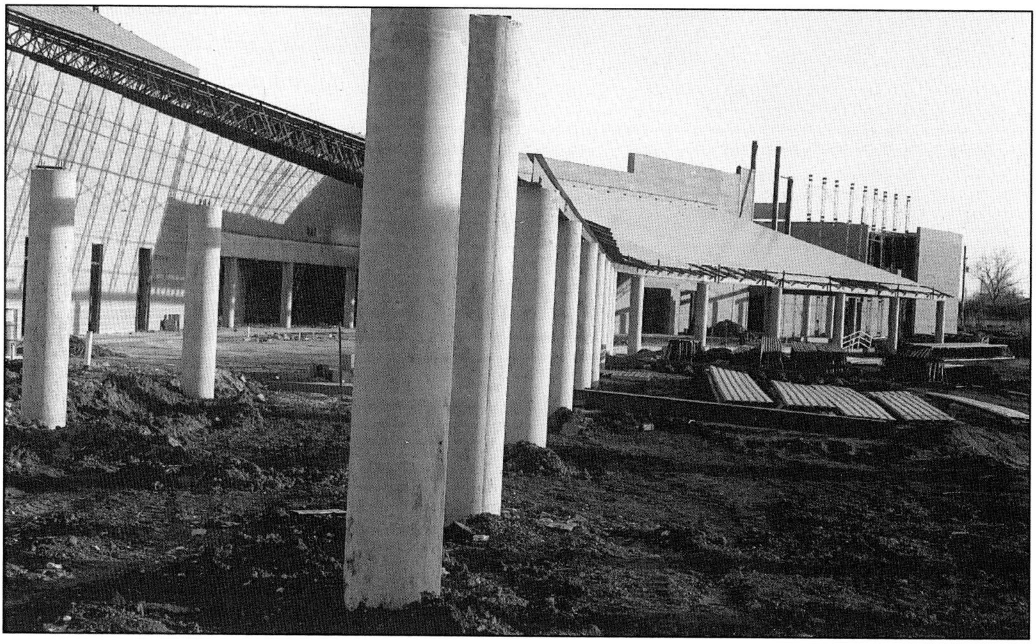

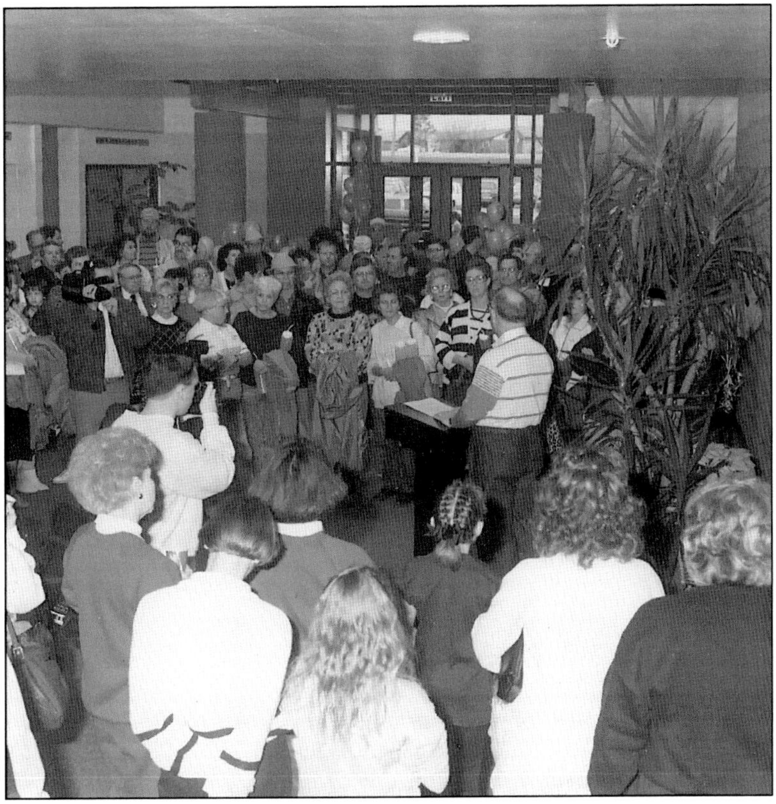

Dedicatory ceremonies were held in 1990. When initial plans were formulated, the city forecast a membership of about 600 members. Membership peaked at 3,300, five times the estimate.

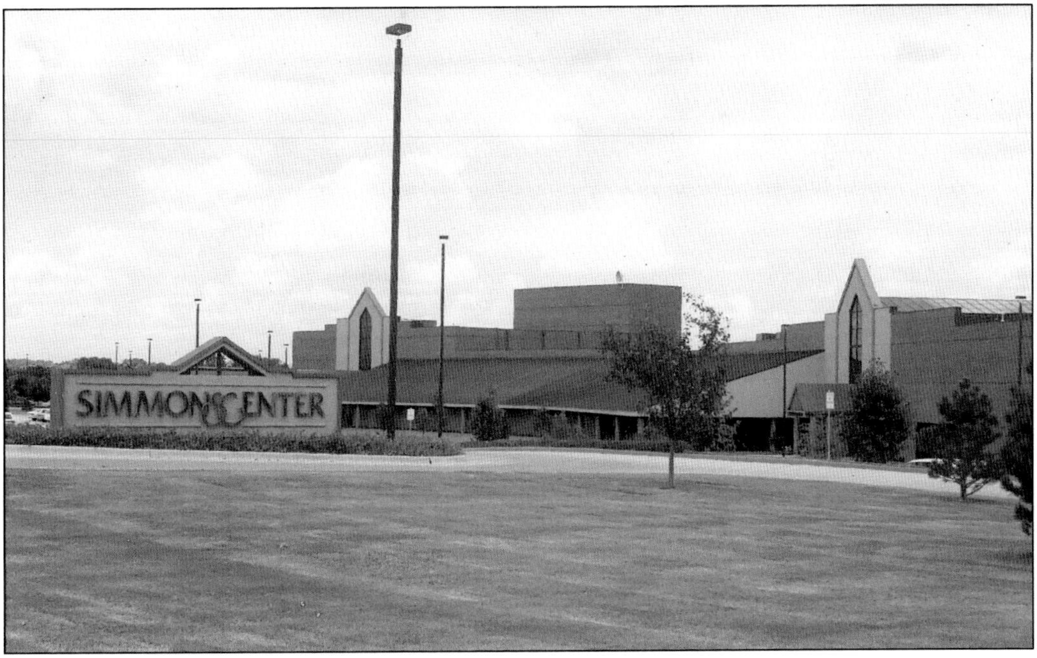

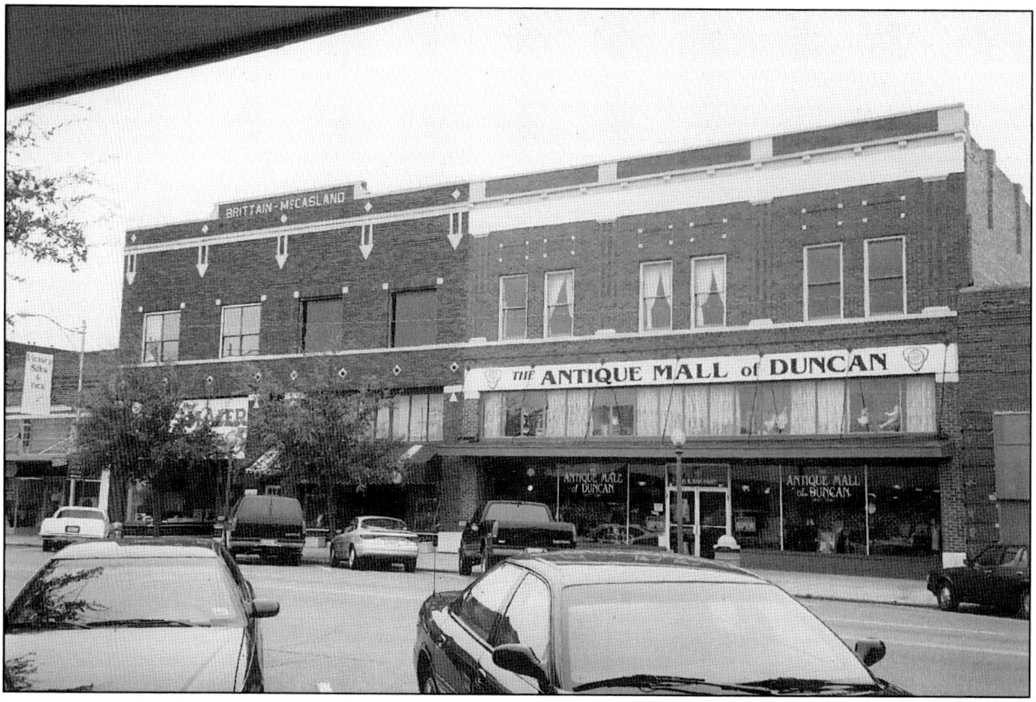

Lamenting the loss of many of Duncan's Main Street buildings and businesses, community leaders began efforts in 1986 to restore and revitalize Main Street. Taking advantage of federal, state, and local resources, Main Street Duncan has scored notable successes with the restoration of many old building facades and a growing resurgence of business. Its long-term goal is to once again make Main Street a center of the community.

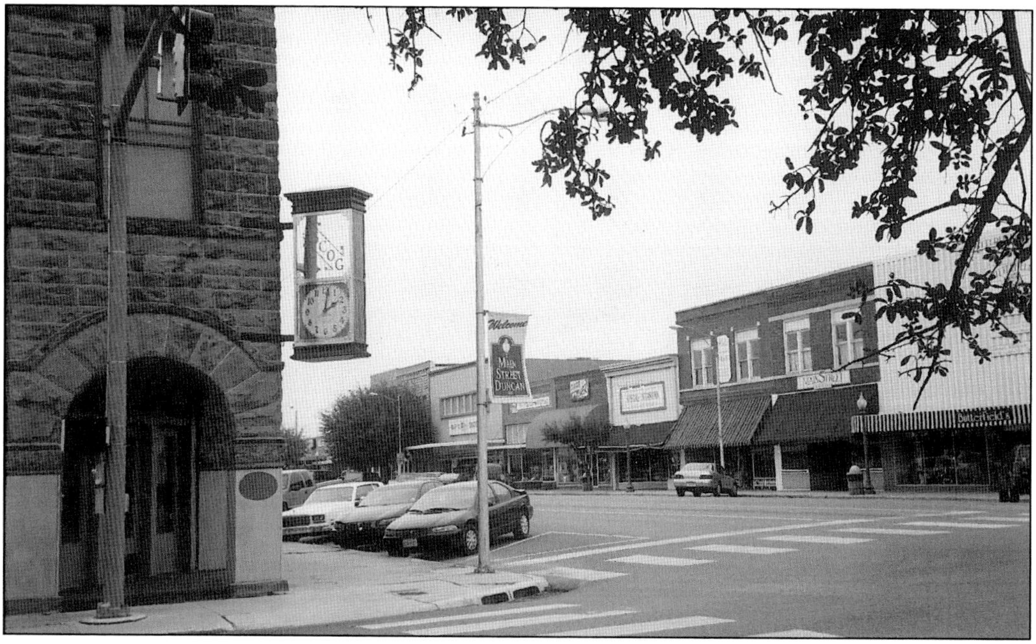